For Class and Country

The Patriotic Left and the First World War

STUDIES IN LABOUR HISTORY 9

Studies in Labour History

'...a series which will undoubtedly become an important force in re-invigorating the study of Labour History.' *English Historical Review*

Studies in Labour History provides reassessments of broad themes along with more detailed studies arising from the latest research in the field of labour and working-class history, both in Britain and throughout the world. Most books are single-authored but there are also volumes of essays focussed on key themes and issues, usually emerging from major conferences organized by the British Society for the Study of Labour History. The series includes studies of labour organizations, including international ones, where there is a need for new research or modern reassessment. It is also its objective to extend the breadth of labour history's gaze beyond conventionally organized workers, sometimes to workplace experiences in general, sometimes to industrial relations, but also to working-class lives beyond the immediate realm of work in households and communities.

For Class and Country

The Patriotic Left and the First World War

David Swift

LIVERPOOL UNIVERSITY PRESS

First published 2017 by
Liverpool University Press
4 Cambridge Street
Liverpool
L69 7ZU

British Library Cataloguing-in-Publication data
A British Library CIP record is available

ISBN 978-1-78694-002-5 cased

Typeset by Carnegie Book Production, Lancaster
Printed and bound in Poland by BooksFactory.co.uk

Table of Contents

Tables and Graphs

Illustrations

Abbreviations

ASE	Amalgamated Society of Engineers (Amalgamated Engineering Union after 1920)
ASLEF	Amalgamated Society of Locomotive Engineers and Firemen
BSP	British Socialist Party (Social Democratic Party before 1911)
BWL	British Workers' League
CWS	Co-operative Wholesale Society
The Fed	National Federation of Demobilised Soldiers and Sailors
GFTU	General Federation of Trade Unions
ILP	Independent Labour Party
NALRU	National Agricultural Labourers' and Rural Workers' Union
NDP	National Democratic Party
NEC	National Executive Committee (of the Labour Party)
NUR	National Union of Railwaymen
NUX	National Union of Ex-Servicemen
SDF	Social Democratic Federation (until 1908, then Social Democratic Party)
SDP	Social Democratic Party (until 1911, then British Socialist Party)
TUC	Trades Union Congress
UDC	Union of Democratic Control
WNC	War Emergency: Workers' National Committee
WSPU	Women's Suffrage and Political Union

Acknowledgements

This book was made possible by funding from the Arts and Humanities Research Council, and many people have contributed to this book in different ways. I would like to thank my doctoral supervisors, Nick Mansfield, David Stewart, and Craig Horner. In addition, all of the staff at the People's History Museum, in particular Darren Treadwell, Julie Parry, and Chris Burgess, and all the archive staff at the Working Class Movement Library in Salford, the Co-operative Archive in Manchester, and the Modern Records' Centre at the University of Warwick. I would also like to thank Keith Gildart, Andrew Thorpe, Steve Meredith, Julie Gottlieb, and Dan Todman, and the anonymous reviewers for their comments and suggestions. Finally, Alison Welsby and the staff at Liverpool University Press have been exceptionally patient and helpful. While I owe debts to a great many people, all errors and exaggerations are my own.

Introduction

The First World War has often suffered from comparison to the Second, in terms of both public interest and the significance ascribed to it by scholars in the shaping of modern Britain. This is especially so for the relationship between the Left and the two wars. For the Left, the Second World War can be seen as a time of triumph: a united stand against fascism followed by a landslide election win and a radical, reforming Labour government. The First World War is more complex. Given the gratuitous cost in lives, the failure of a 'fit country for heroes to live in' to materialise, the deep recessions and unemployment of the interwar years, and the botched peace settlements which served only to precipitate another war, the Left has tended to view the conflict as an unmitigated disaster and unpardonable waste. There is also the fact that Kaiser Wilhelm and imperial Germany were far less odious villains than Adolf Hitler and the Third Reich. This has led to a tendency on the Left to see the later conflict as the 'good' war, fought against an obvious evil, and the earlier conflict as an imperialist blunder, the result of backroom scheming, secret pacts, and a thirst for colonies. This ahistorical view fails to take into account the fact that the labour movement of 1914 lacked the paradigm of Nazi Germany as a reference point; the First World War was the great struggle of their day, 'the war to end all wars', a zero-sum conflict between British liberal democracy, however imperfect, and an authoritarian, autocratic regime commanding a highly industrialised economy and a vast military. Yet it was not necessarily the case that a belief that Germany had to be defeated translated into hatred of Germans, much less admiration for the British government. What then was the extent and nature of support for the war amongst the British labour movement, at both an elite and subaltern level? Was there a continuity between the patriotism of the war years and the decades before 1914, or did the war see a break with the traditions and attitudes of the past?

A great deal of work on left-wing attitudes towards the First World War has been undermined by one or two preconceptions. The first is a presumption that holding 'left-wing' views is inimical to patriotism. According to Geoffrey Field, 'patriotic loyalties for good reason have generally been viewed as a counterweight to class consciousness',[1] and for Paul Ward, 'ultimately, in 1914, the choice between socialism and patriotism had to be made'.[2] Yet most of the trade unionists, socialists, and Labour supporters who went to war, took up munitions production, or waved to their husbands and sons as they boarded the troop trains, did not agonise over whether their loyalties lay with their country or their politics.

This should not surprise us – during this period the pull of nationalism was powerful indeed. Historians such as David Silbey have sought to understand why men would leave their homes to fight in foreign fields with unpronounceable place names, but they themselves felt it was only natural.[3] Nations may well be artificial concepts, and countries such as 'England' and 'Britain' may well be imagined communities, but for their citizens – then and now – national identity is more than a vague, theoretical concept. For most Britons in the 1910s, their country was a very real, tangible community, delineated by biology as much as culture, and with genuine claims on their lives and labour. Chairman of the Parliamentary Labour Party Ramsay MacDonald concurred with this sentiment, believing that nations were not abstractions but real communities.[4] This patriotism need not be seen as anathema to 'class' solidarity and leftist politics; on the contrary, as Gerard DeGroot has argued, 'love for Britain and a willingness to defend her' was often 'a profound, but often discounted, *element of*, British working-class consciousness'.[5] Rather than limit class consciousness, national and local patriotism was often a real boon to the labour movement and, correspondingly, socialist convictions could bolster patriotic sentiment.

The second factor which has obscured left-wing attitudes to the war is the conflation of 'working-class', 'trade unionist', and 'Labour'. In 1914 the majority of the labour force was not unionised, and as the 'working-class', according to Duncan Tanner's figures, comprised seventy-five per cent of the Edwardian electorate, most of their votes must have gone to Liberal or

[1] G. Field, 'Social Patriotism and the British Working Class', *International Labour and Working Class History* 41 (1992): 21.

[2] P. Ward, *Red Flag and Union Jack: Englishness, Patriotism and the British Left, 1881–1924*, London: Boydell, 2011, 5.

[3] D. Silbey, *The British Working Class and Enthusiasm for War, 1914–1916*, London: Frank Cass, 2005.

[4] Ward, *Red Flag and Union Jack*, 9.

[5] G.J. DeGroot, *Blighty: British Society in the Era of the Great War*, London: Longman, 1996, 49. Emphasis added.

Conservative candidates. In much the same way as the Edwardian working class did not appreciate the contradiction between class awareness and patriotism which later historians would describe, most Labour leaders of the time – unlike some contemporary continental theorists and many later historians – did not assume that the votes and union subscriptions of the workers would inevitably flow towards them given enough time. They fought hard for every member and every vote, and where they fought successfully they used a language rooted in the local culture and coupled with pragmatic, practical, tangible aims and achievements. Discussing the 'labour patriots' of the war period, J.O. Stubbs argued that 'they were well to the right of the mainstream of political thought in the Labour world'.[6] This may well have been the case, but crucially, mainstream labour thought was well to the *left* of most working-class people at this time. It is a contention of this book that labour patriotism during the First World War had the effect of bringing the mass of the working classes towards the labour movement, but irrespective of the validity of this proposition, care must be taken to avoid the assumption that the Labour Party or the trade unions spoke for, or represented, the working class as a whole.

It is also important to avoid easy generalisations about the British working class during this period. Originally, due to the variety of factors and sources relating to class, politics, nationhood, and rhetoric in the home nations of Ireland, Scotland, and Wales, this study was intended to be restricted to the English experience. The source base, however, led to the broadening of the investigation to incorporate Britain, but not Ireland. Not only was there a tremendous amount of heterogeneity between – and within – the constituent nations of Britain, the same applied to the different counties and regions of England. For example, Jeremy Seabrook has noted how many Labour and workingmen's clubs in East Lancashire did not possess an alcohol license, as labourism was so closely intertwined with Methodism in that part of the county, while elsewhere in Lancashire it was essential for Labour to adapt to the pub-based popular culture.[7] The danger of applying generalisations to particular areas also applies to individuals. For example, even Robert Blatchford – former soldier and labour patriot, editor of *The Clarion*, and thoroughly grounded in working-class culture – became a teetotaller, vegetarian, and spiritualist. It would be a mistake, therefore, to see the Edwardian labour movement as polarised between hard-drinking, patriotic trade unionists and abstemious, Nonconformist, middle-class pacifists; the 'creeping Jesuses' of Orwell's derogatory phrase. Although there were many

[6] J.O. Stubbs, 'Lord Milner and Patriotic Labour', *The English Historical Review* 87 (1972): 729.

[7] J. Seabrook, *City Close-Up*, London: Penguin, 1973.

fissures in the labour movement during this period, patriotism was not a major fault line.

There has been fairly little scholarly attention paid to the Left and the First World War. Jay Winter's *Socialism and the Challenge of War* examined the impact of the war on the intellectual currents of the labour movement, and made some use of the War Emergency Workers National Committee files, but concentrated on the elites of the movement, and did not convey the experience of the war for ordinary men and women of the Left.[8] Similarly, John Horne's *Labour at War*, whilst offering a comparative perspective on the British and French labour movements, is focused on the elites of the Left.[9] In *Red Flag and Union Jack*, Paul Ward highlighted how pre-war Labour leaders had long utilised the language of nationalism to argue for parliamentarism. MacDonald, for instance, branded syndicalism 'foreign', and Keir Hardie argued that the earlier anti-parliamentarism of the movement had meant that 'Socialism, in those days, was treated as a plant of continental growth which could never find lodgement in Great Britain'. In this effort it seems that they were reasonably successful. For Ward, the post-war years saw radical, oppositional patriotism supplanted by social patriotism, and a general belief that reform would come through the state, not in opposition to it.[10]

Most of the literature concerned with the war and labour has focused on the anti-war movement. Andrew Rothstein's *The Soldiers' Strikes of 1919* and Gloden Dallas and David Gill's *The Unknown Army* both examine mutinies and soldiers' strikes in the final two years of the war and after demobilisation. A more recent contribution to the literature concentrating on anti-war agitation is Cyril Pearce's *Comrade of Conscience*.[11] Pearce argues that there was a significant pacifist movement in Huddersfield and that other towns and cities may well have experienced similar anti-war movements. Given that Pearce largely attributes the Huddersfield situation to specific socio-economic, religious, and cultural factors prevalent in that town, it is doubtful that pacifist inclinations were widespread across the whole country. Lesser-known radical contributions to the debate on labour patriotism include Julian Putkowski's *The Kinmel Park Camp Riots 1919*, Ken Weller's *'Don't be a Soldier!'*, and the journal *Gun Fire*, edited

---

[8] J.M. Winter, *Socialism and the Challenge of War: Ideas and Politics in Britain, 1912–1918*, London: Routledge Kegan Paul, 1974.

[9] J.N. Horne, *Labour at War: France and Britain 1914–1918*, Oxford: Oxford University Press, 1992.

[10] Ward, *Red Flag and Union Jack*, 197.

[11] Cyril Pearce, *Comrades in Conscience: The Story of an English Community's Opposition to the Great War*, London: Francis Boutle, 2001.

by A.J. Peacock.[12] Again, these studies tend to focus on specific localities and individuals, and it is difficult to argue that they are representative of working-class attitudes towards the war, given the continued support for the war effort, the pronounced anti-Germanism, and the general determination for a 'fight to the finish' prevalent until November 1918.

Martin Pugh has focused on the issue of Labour adapting to working-class conservatism, first in a 2002 article, 'The Rise of Labour and the Political Culture of Conservatism, 1890–1945', and as a major theme in his 2011 book, *Speak for Britain!*[13] In the latter he claimed that early disputes between J.H. Thomas and Philip Snowden 'signified the extent to which attitudes towards drink, religion and morality reflected the cultural divide within working-class communities – with which a Labour Party had somehow to come to terms'.[14] Pugh argues that the ideological links and overlaps between Labour and Conservatism, and the recruitment of politicians and voters from the Tories to the Left, has largely been neglected by historians.[15] He describes the patriotic, often culturally conservative views of men such as John Clynes and Thomas, and claims that they would 'scarcely have achieved lasting power in their unions and in the Labour Party had they not reflected rank-and-file sentiment'.[16] For Pugh, the success of Labour in the interwar years, culminating in the 1945 election victory, was down to 'the synthesis of Toryism and socialism', and the adaption to a 'conservative working class that, in certain circumstances, was prepared to vote Labour'.[17]

In terms of soldiers moving towards Labour, Nick Mansfield has described how the army served as a conduit leading people towards labour organisations such as the National Union of Agricultural Workers, the National Union of Railwaymen (NUR), and the Workers' Union, particularly in rural areas where the labour movement had been weak.[18] After the war, members of the National Federation of Discharged and Demobilised Soldiers and Sailors would physically break up right-wing meetings in Norfolk and South Wales.[19]

---

[12] J. Putkowski, *The Kinmel Park Riots 1919*, Harwarden: Flintshire Historical Society, 1989; K. Weller, *'Don't Be a Soldier!' The Radical Anti-War Movement in North London 1914–1918*, London: Journeyman Press, 1985.

[13] M. Pugh, 'The Rise of Labour and the Political Culture of Conservatism, 1890–1945', *History* 87 (2002): 514–37 and *Speak for Britain! A New History of the Labour Party*, London: Vintage, 2011.

[14] Pugh, *Speak for Britain!*, 19.

[15] Pugh, 'Rise of Labour', 516.

[16] Ibid., 520.

[17] Ibid., 536, 518.

[18] N. Mansfield, 'The National Federation of Discharged and Demobilised Soldiers and Sailors, 1917–1921: A View from the Marches', *Family and Community History* 7 (2004): 25.

[19] Ibid., 21.

At a local level, labour activists took a prominent role in the war effort: Mansfield draws attention to the schoolmaster socialist Tom Higdon, the central figure in the Burston school strike, who chaired recruiting meetings, to the surprise of those who expected him to be anti-war. Similarly, the Workers' Union journal, the *Record*, was full of war news from August 1914 onwards, and leading Workers' Union figures such as John Beard and Charles Duncan became prominent in the ultra-patriotic British Workers' League.[20] Mansfield argues that this military involvement made the unions seem more acceptable: 'In the absence of a lead from farmers, the farmworkers' unions, confident that their members had done their duty, assumed the mantle of patriotism, thereby legitimising their own activities, which had previously been regarded as unacceptable.'[21] Correspondingly, the war drew workers closer to the unions, by teaching them the value of organisation.[22]

Another contentious issue amongst the labour movement was state provision of welfare.[23] Unions were suspicious of any attempt to control labour supply, and felt that state welfare would undermine their status and leave them worse off financially, as claimed in Noelle Whiteside's article, 'Welfare Legislation and the Unions during the First World War'.[24] Although unions were willing to use state welfare as a means of guaranteeing recognition before the war, according to Whiteside, unions and employers would occasionally unite 'in opposition to the growth of state controls'.[25] While the war and its aftermath did see the extension of National Insurance coverage and unemployment relief, union hostility towards institutions of state control, such as labour exchanges, remained 'intense'.[26] The extent of labour patriotism's role in assuaging union suspicion of state welfare and intervention into the supply of labour remains an issue worthy of attention.

It has been claimed that the war undermined barriers between skilled and unskilled, as argued by Eric Hobsbawm and B.A. Waites, amongst others. According to Waites, 'the "one nation psychology" which was a pre-requisite of the national war effort had encouraged notions of classlessness', and

[20] N. Mansfield, *English Farmworkers and Local Patriotism, 1900–1930*, Aldershot: Ashgate, 2001, 107–08, 134.

[21] Ibid., 114.

[22] Ibid., 135.

[23] See P. Thane, 'The Working Class and State Welfare in Britain', *Historical Journal* 27 (1984): 877–900 and *Foundations of the Welfare State*, London: Longman, 1996.

[24] N. Whiteside, 'Welfare Legislation and the Unions during the First World War', *The Historical Journal* 23 (1980): 857–74.

[25] Ibid., 866.

[26] Ibid., 871.

blurred the distinctions between skilled and unskilled.[27] Furthermore, unions gained increased strength and significance during the war, and were brought into co-operation with the running of the state through recruitment, military tribunals, and pension administration. Indeed, whilst many trade union officials volunteered for the services, they were made exempt from conscription, a status reflecting their new-found importance. Waites's assertion that between 1910 and 1920, 'English society changed from a complex hierarchy in which stratification by status overlay the basic three-tier class structure to a more simple form' is an overstatement, yet overall the war did see increasing working-class (and national) homogeneity, an expansion in trade unionism, and new-found working-class confidence.[28] Alistair Reid has argued against the idea of increasing working-class homogenisation, claiming that while 'real changes did take place during the war, [this was] largely because organised labour was strong enough to demand them and, since this strength itself depended heavily on the peculiarities of wartime political and economic conditions, most of the changes were temporary'.[29] For Reid, the *experience* of the war itself was more significant than changes in socio-economic conditions:

> There was a general tendency for organised labour to drop its pre-war separation of 'economic' and 'political' issues. Thus the unions most centrally involved in the war effort began very rapidly to raise non-industrial issues when they made demands on the government (perhaps most marked in the case of house rents), there was a slowly growing acceptance among all trade unionists that the election of Members of Parliament could have a direct effect on industrial conditions, and there was a marked increase in trade union support for the permanent nationalisation of key industries, above all coal mining and railways.[30]

This book makes frequent use of terms which are somewhat contentious. For example, 'nationalism' here is taken to mean simply the belief that nations are real, tangible concepts and that there are differences between people of different nationalities. It does not necessarily have any chauvinistic connotations in this context. 'Patriotism' will be used here in a more active sense, to denote *pride* – not necessarily in nation – but in community, city, or country. There were, of course, many different kinds of 'patriotism': from supporting the war effort whilst refusing to condemn the German

[27] B.A. Waites, 'The Effect of the First World War on Class and Status in England, 1910–20', *Journal of Contemporary History* 11 (1976): 34–35.

[28] Ibid., 45.

[29] A. Reid, 'The Impact of the First World War on British Workers', in R. Wall and J. Winter (eds.), *The Upheaval of War*, Cambridge: Cambridge University Press, 1988, 222.

[30] Ibid., 228.

people, through supporting the British people while condemning the British government, through to a jingoistic 'my country right or wrong' which eventually translated into a chauvinistic anti-Germanism. 'Militarism' will be used to signify the lauding of military values and the desirability of military conquest. 'Socialism', when it is used, is used in a vague sense to mean socio-economic 'Leftism': perhaps historians of this period have paid too much attention to whether or not labour leaders or the labour movement generally were 'socialist'. It is doubtful that the ordinary men and women of the labour movement cared much as to whether they were 'socialists', 'labourists', or just trade unionists. John Holford has said of the Edinburgh labour movement at the end of the war: 'The apparent unimportance of Clause 4 in discussion of the new constitution is remarkable. There is no record of its having even been mentioned, let alone discussed, in Labour's Edinburgh branch meetings in late 1917 and early 1918. The ILP [Independent Labour Party] did not consider it; neither did the Trades Council'.[31] It could well be that the division between 'socialism' and 'labourism' was not as defined, and far less important, than historians have assumed. 'Labour', when capitalised, refers to the Labour Party; 'labour' and 'labour movement' are used as terms to encompass the whole of the British Left.

The first chapter of this book surveys the relationship between the Left and patriotism in the decades prior to the First World War, in order to provide context for the developments of the war years. Chapter 2 is concerned with patriotic labour in the years 1914–18, and focuses on support for the war effort across the British Left. While this book concentrates on labour patriotism, it would be insufficient for a treatment of the Left in this period to exclude strikes, opposition to conscription, and the anti-war movement. Chapter 3 addresses these issues, to ascertain the extent to which anti-war agitation was characteristic of the labour movement as a whole.

Chapter 4 examines the implications of Labour's support for and involvement with the war on the electoral prospects of the party after 1918 via two questions: Did Labour's record secure its patriotic credentials and help to win broader working-class support? Was there a 'reconciliation' – if one was needed – between the Left and patriotic, working-class values? This chapter discusses specifically the impact of the war on support for Labour, in terms of both former Liberal and Conservative recruits, ex-servicemen and their families, and working-class individuals hitherto unsympathetic to the Left. Chapter 5 explores the relationship between labour and the state. To what extent did the scope and apparatus of the state extend in wartime, and how much of this receded after 1918? How far was Labour drawn

[31] J. Holford, *Reshaping Labour: Organisation, Work and Politics – Edinburgh in the Great War and After*, London: Croom Helm, 1988, 172.

into the British state during the war, and what did Labour do to protect working-class interests? If the pre-war labour movement had an ambiguous relationship with the state, how did the war affect this? What were the implications of labour's experiences with the wartime state on the type of Labour Party which emerged in 1918? This last question is the focus of Chapter 5, which analyses the growth of the wartime state, the role of labour outside of government in protecting the interests of the most vulnerable, and the importance of wartime experiences in engendering a statist labour movement after 1918. Chapter 6 addresses the troublesome issue of labour cohesion during this period: why, if the war fatally split the Liberals, and European labour movements suffered schisms and the emergence of competitors, was British labour – and the British Labour Party in particular – able not merely to survive the war intact, but to emerge stronger and with a greater sense of purpose?

This book hopes to move away from a concentration on machinations at the elite levels of the labour movement, events inside Parliament, and the intellectual developments of men such as Sidney Webb and G.D.H. Cole. This is reflected in the methodology and source base: whilst official documents such as Labour Party Annual Reports and Trades Union Congress Annual Reports have been examined, there is a focus on less well-visited material. For example, extensive use has been made of the Labour History Archive and Study Centre (LHASC) at the People's History Museum, Manchester. In particular, the papers of the War Emergency Workers' National Committee, numbering some sixteen thousand documents, have been thoroughly utilised. This resource, although used sparingly by Jay Winter and Royden Harrison, amongst others, has been used systematically here, resulting in the uncovering of previously unknown material. Significantly, these papers are full of very local complaints and tensions, and give an important understanding of grassroots concerns. This provides a counterbalance to the relative rarity of local Labour Party and trade union records from the war period. Also at the LHASC are the personal papers of several important trade union and Labour Party figures of this period, such as Ben Tillett and John Ward, and First World War combatants who were to become significant figures on the Left, such as Douglas Houghton. The published reminiscences of key figures from this period, such as George Edwards of the farmworkers' union and Clement Attlee, have provided further qualitative evidence. Similarly, the labour publications chosen represent the broad range of the movement, from co-operators, *Clarion* readers, ILP members, to orthodox Marxists.

The Modern Records Centre at the University of Warwick contains the papers of several diverse trade unions, ranging from broad-based professional groups such as the National Union of Teachers, to more specific unions such as the Amalgamated Society of Papermakers and the Amalgamated Society of Watermen, Lightermen and Bargemen of the River Thames. Similarly, the Working Class Movement Library in Salford has provided the monthly journal and reports of the Amalgamated Society of Engineers; the monthly reports of the Boilermakers' Union; the minutes of the Miners' Federation of Great Britain; and the minutes of the Shipconstructers' and Shipwrights' Union. Furthermore, newspapers of trade unions such as the NUR, the Fawcett Association (postal sorters), the National Union of Clerks, and the South London Gasworkers have all been utilised for this volume. This has provided a great deal of interesting qualitative evidence – the correspondence columns of these journals are particularly revealing of rank-and-file views – and, crucially, reflect the positions of different types of trade union: craft and unskilled, local and national, those generally supportive and those more sceptical of the war.

Aside from union journals, various types of newspaper have been used: the strongly patriotic *Justice* and *The Clarion*; those sceptical of the war such as *Plebs*, the *Bradford Pioneer* and the Glasgow *Forward*; *The Co-operative News* and two magazines attached to the Co-operative movement, *Wheatsheaf* and the *Millgate Monthly*. One may question why a treatment of the British labour movement does not make substantial use of the *Daily Herald* and the *Labour Leader*. In this case, these publications have not been put to systematic and extensive use given the attempt to move away from a London-centric, elite-focused analysis, and the focus on labour patriotism. The newspapers and trade union journals have also furnished the book with many photographs and cartoons, which will be analysed within. Finally, the Imperial War Museum has an audio archive of interviews conducted with ex-servicemen from the First World War. Several of these were also labour or trade union activists, and the recordings of their interviews have provided further valuable insights into the minds of individuals alive at the time.

The idea of an ideological 'choice' between patriotism and socialism is a major theme of Paul Ward's book, but to claim as he does that 'ultimately', such a choice 'had to be made' in 1914 advances a false dichotomy.[32] In fact, major figures on the Left – MacDonald, Snowden, and Hardie as much as the labour patriots – had been expounding the very British nature of their socialism for decades, as Ward himself notes. Indeed, Ward later argues that labour patriotism during 1914–18 was not an aberration, but rather a logical conclusion of pre-war views.[33] It seems, then, that the First World War did not force the labour movement to make a choice between 'patriotism' and 'socialism', for Labour leaders stressed the intertwined nature of the two concepts. Perhaps the real significance of the war was that it managed to

---

[32] Ward, *Red Flag and Union Jack*, 5.
[33] Ibid., 108.

convince the electorate of this. This account is not a general vista of the Left and patriotism over a long period, but rather concentrates specifically on the war years and the early 1920s.

This book argues that the Left in 1914 had two types of concerns to overcome in order to broaden its appeal. The first were economic, material questions: Were the socio-economic claims of labour valid? Could British society and the economy be organised more effectively for the betterment of all? Was there room for greater state interference and regulation, or would this strangle the free enterprise culture upon which Britain's success had been built? The objections of the second type were cultural and symbolic: Was the 'socialism' posited by Labour after 1918 a continental import, tainted by French, German, and Jewish influences, or was it fundamentally British, built upon centuries of mutualism and co-operation? Was it a creed for those who abstained from the bottle, who spent their meagre disposable incomes on books and self-improvement, who agitated for temperance reform, Home Rule, and votes for women? Or was it a movement buttressed by, rather than contrary to, a culture built around the family, the pub, football, and patriotism? It will be argued here that the war allowed Labour to successfully overcome both of these types of objection. To be sure, a great deal of work remained to be done, and the Labour Party of the early 1920s – much less that of the early 1930s – was never merely one election away from a convincing majority. However the critical early objections – that their political economy was fundamentally mistaken and their principles alien to British values – had been successfully overcome.

Another, less significant dilemma was also overcome by the war. The labour movement before 1914 had a slightly paradoxical relationship with industrialisation, urbanisation, and modernity. Karl Marx was very much the modernist, not only in his belief in communism as the ultimate stage of development, but also in terms of cultural chauvinism: he regarded colonial conquest by the West as desirable and despised peasant life.[34] While Marxist thought did inform a strand of Edwardian socialism – notably the Social Democratic Federation and the Plebs' League – the mainstream of labour thought owed more to either the 'advanced Liberalism' of the early ILP and Fabian Society, or the more nostalgic, anti-industrial, and ultimately vague socialism of William Morris. Popularised by Morris's *News from Nowhere* and Robert Blatchford's *Merrie England*, a reactionary, culturally sensitive socialism was appealing to many thousands of ordinary men and women, but had little influence upon the elites of the labour movement. A year before his death, Morris remarked to the leading Fabian Sidney Webb in

---

[34] A. Bonnett, *Left in the Past: Radicalism and the Politics of Nostalgia*, London: Continuum, 2010, 25.

1896: 'the world is going your way, Webb, but it is not the right way in the end'. Blatchford was more of a modernist, and certainly more of a populist; he deplored the effects of industrialisation on the lives of British workers, yet wanted them to seize control of their country and share the benefits of the modern world more efficiently and effectively.[35] He also understood that there were many aspects of modern life that the working classes rather enjoyed, and he and his newspaper, *The Clarion*, were strident advocates of sport and leisure pursuits. Blatchford's encouragement of sport and music hall culture sat ill with the more austere socialism proffered by Hardie, who, Alastair Bonnett believed, 'surely had the Clarion movement in mind when he noted, in 1903, that "For a time in England, the fibre of the Socialist movement was almost destroyed by a spirit of irresponsible levity"'.[36] This tension between modernism and nostalgia was resolved by the war, and this book argues that the war ultimately brought about the triumph of a very particular kind of leftism in Britain: reformist, statist, patriotic, thoroughly modern, and comfortable with the Britain which emerged after 1918.

[35] Ibid., 73.
[36] Ibid., 77.

1

'If this is to be a jingo, then I am a jingo'
– Labour Patriotism before 1914

'Socialism, in those days, was treated as a plant of continental growth which could never find lodgement in Great Britain.'

—Keir Hardie, 1909[1]

This chapter is intended as a brief discussion of the ideological and practical relationship between nationalism, patriotism, and the labour movement before 1914. It introduces some of the principal concepts and personalities that would dominate the Left during the years of the First World War, surveys the debate surrounding the Boer War, examines the history of 'radical patriotism' on the British Left, and notes the theoretical and actual commitments of the British Left to internationalism and pacifism. Outside of the British labour movement, reference is made to the contemporary pacifism of the period and one of its most noted advocates, Norman Angell.[2] The chapter aims to contribute to our understanding of the extent and nature of labour patriotism during the war by examining the continuity or lack thereof in the decades immediately preceding 1914. The argument outlined here is twofold. Firstly, across the labour movement as a whole there was an ambiguous attitude towards nationalism and patriotism. Uncertainty and contradiction resulted from abstract commitments to peace and camaraderie coupled with the realities of the European situation, popular nationalism, and broader British culture. Nonetheless, for many across the labour movement, commitment to internationalism and pacifism

[1] Ward, *Red Flag and Union Jack*, 87.
[2] A pacifist known for his 1909 pamphlet *The Great Illusion*, Angell was a founding member of the anti-war Union of Democratic Control and would later sit as Labour MP for Bradford North from 1929 to 1931. He won the Nobel Peace Prize in 1933, a year before wartime Labour leader Arthur Henderson.

was superficial at best. Very often their left-wing views were based around an idea of community and nationhood that belied any internationalism. The fight for national survival against imperial Germany allowed the façade of internationalism to slip, and confirmed the compatibility of left-wing and nationalist sentiment.

In terms of both his own personality and the principles and approach to politics he represented, Robert Blatchford was a profound influence on many working-class socialists in this period. Born in Maidstone in 1851, the son of a comedian and an actress, Blatchford began performing on stage himself from a young age; it is probably no coincidence that both he and Ben Tillett, two men who had such an acute understanding of the mind of working-class Britain, came from the music hall background that dominated mass culture at the time. An avid reader of the Bible and John Bunyan's *Pilgrim's Progress* as a young man, he joined the army and eventually rose to become a sergeant major, before leaving to take up work as an office clerk and aspiring journalist. He was soon able to secure articles with provincial newspapers, and struck up a friendship with Alex M. Thompson, later to become his deputy editor at *The Clarion*. In 1891, a year after establishing the Manchester branch of the Fabian Society, Blatchford set up this newspaper, which rose to a circulation of at least seventy-four thousand by 1906.[3]

His increasingly patriotic and irreligious stance alienated him from some of the pacifistic Nonconformists in the Independent Labour Party (ILP). As described in David Howell's seminal *British Workers and the Independent Labour Party, 1888–1906*, the ILP at this time was a broad church, with room for a variety of socialist thought.[4] Yet Blatchford was to further antagonise the ILP when he gave funds to Victor Grayson's campaign for the Colne Valley by-election of 1907.[5] A series of articles on socialism in *The Clarion* were published in book form in 1893 as *Merrie England*; the first edition selling over thirty thousand copies. A penny edition was published in 1894, and one quarter of a million copies were ordered before publication; within a year 750,000 copies had been sold worldwide. In Britain and the United States the book would eventually sell over two million copies. In addition to this bestselling tract, the success of *Clarion* cycling groups, choirs, and sundry social clubs brought a populist socialism to a mass audience.

Blatchford and the staff of *The Clarion* had long combined a proud

---

[3] H. Richards, *The Bloody Circus: The Daily Herald and the Left*, London: Pluto Press, 1997, 10.

[4] D. Howell, *British Workers and the Independent Labour Party, 1888–1906*, Manchester: Manchester University Press, 1983.

[5] Victor Grayson was the maverick MP for the Colne Valley from 1907 to 1910.

patriotism with a radical, dissenting voice. Although in January 1901 it paid extensive tribute to the recently deceased Queen Victoria, four years earlier the newspaper had savaged the expense and frivolity of the Jubilee celebrations.[6] This was a common theme in *The Clarion*: a vigorous pride in Britain and the British coupled with a withering disregard for the class of people empowered to run the country. During the Boer War, Blatchford claimed that the cause of socialism could receive no greater blow than the fall of the British Empire, yet accused the government of gross incompetence in its prosecution of the conflict. He criticised the lack of funding for soldiers' families when money was being 'squandered on royalty', called for proper equipment and provisions to be sent to the troops, deplored Cecil Rhodes, and poured scorn on 'jingoes ... never seen at the Front'.[7] Responding to claims from the right-wing press that he wanted to 'turn people against their country', he retorted that he wanted 'to make people so fond of their country that they shall desire to possess it'.[8] This reflects another theme that runs through much of Blatchford's writing: that despite the restricted pre-1918 franchise, there was no great conspiracy to suppress the political power of labour; it was simply that millions of working-class men continued to vote Liberal or Conservative. He felt that the purpose of his newspaper, and its associated cultural movement, was to undermine this state of affairs and bring socialism to ordinary working people.

A debate concerning nationalism, militarism, and the desirability and efficacy of conscription unfolded in the pages of *The Clarion* throughout the spring and early summer of 1900. Blatchford (writing under his pen name 'Nunquam') asserted that militarism was abhorrent, and conscription its most detestable element, so that the British 'variety' of militarism – a relatively small army of professional volunteers – was infinitely preferable to continental variations.[9] In response, A.E. Fletcher argued that in reality European-style conscription was preferable to British voluntarism in *avoiding* militarism, in that every section of the population was forced to serve, thus making the military reflect society. In this he was supported by the German Marxist intellectual Wilhelm Liebknecht, who pointed out that his own son, Karl Liebknecht (future Spartacist and comrade of Rosa Luxembourg) was in the German army, along with thousands of other committed socialists. 'If the troops employed in shooting down miners at Featherstone had been mainly composed of Socialists', argued Fletcher, 'I

[6] *The Clarion*, 26 January 1901; D. Newton, *British Labour, European Socialism and the Struggle for Peace 1889–1914*, Oxford: Clarendon Press, 1985, 60.

[7] *The Clarion*, 6–20 January 1901.

[8] Ibid., 13 January 1901.

[9] Ibid., 31 March 1900.

doubt whether any damage would have been done'.[10] In response, Blatchford reiterated his stark warning that militarism was coming and a choice had to be made between 'German' and 'our kind'.[11]

At this point the Fabian playwright George Bernard Shaw entered the debate. Although a critic of British government policy in Africa, he attacked socialist supporters of the Boer republics, arguing that the Boer's cruel and racist attitudes towards black South Africans precluded their right to the support of people on the Left. For Shaw, instinctive anti-militarism was indicative of a wider problem amongst some on the Left. He explained how his fellow members of the Fabian Society were opposed to 'the familiar, seventeenth-century views of the Social Democratic Federation', and looked to capture industry, rather than to reverse economic and social change.[12] Shaw's interjection shows how the debate surrounding militarism was a component of a much larger and more profound deliberation: were the changes of the past few hundred years inherently wrong, or was it merely that the fruits of industrialisation had fallen to far too few people? Was the modern world inherently objectionable, or did advances in capitalism and technology increase the salience, plausibility, and appeal of the Left's political and economic theories? In this respect, Blatchford – once the advocate of a pre-industrial 'Merrie England' – had begun to change his views, and many on the Left seemed to be following suit. There was a great deal of scepticism and trepidation regarding 'modern Britain', but a belief that the British people would have the sense to seize the benefits of modernity for themselves.

The *Clarion* group was by no means alone in positing a 'radical patriotism' in this manner: Will Thorne, Labour MP and only member of the Social Democratic Federation (SDF) in the Commons, continued to press for the introduction of compulsory military service designed on the Swiss system.[13] For Thorne, this would ensure the permanent defeat of militarism, as every man would be trained and equipped to defend himself against both external aggression and internal oppression. Thorne felt that his 'citizen's army' would have a democratising effect on society as a whole, and awaken

---

[10] Ibid., 14 April 1900. Karl Liebknecht himself felt – in contrast to his father – that the military ethos was inimical to class consciousness, and in its 'producing and furthering the spirit of servility in the proletarian who thus submits more readily to economic, social and political exploitation'. See Liebknecht, *Militarism and Anti-Militarism*, trans. Alexander Sirnis, intro. Philip S. Foner, New York: Dover, 1972, 33. Cited in M. Mulholland, '"Marxists of Strict Observance"? The Second International, National Defence and the Question of War', *Historical Journal* 58 (2015): 636.

[11] *The Clarion*, 28 April 1900.

[12] Ibid., 26 May and 30 June 1900.

[13] *Justice*, 5 December 1903.

working people to their true power.[14] Similarly, in 1906 seven Labour MPs
– including future prominent patriots John Hodge and Charles Duncan –
signed a petition calling for the introduction of compulsory military training
in schools.[15] By no means, therefore, were leftist politics and a concern for
national defence incompatible; much less leftist politics and a more general
patriotism. Indeed, there was a longer tradition of radical patriotism and a
citizen army on the Left, stretching back through the Chartists to Major
John Cartwright and Thomas Paine.

For *Justice*, the newspaper of the SDF, as with *The Clarion*, the enemy
was not nationalism, patriotism, or militarism *per se*, but rather the control
of British foreign policy by particular interests and the domination of the
British military by a particular class. There was a particularly ugly incident
at Portsmouth in 1906 after stokers, judged to have been insufficiently
quick to obey the orders of a young lieutenant at an inspection, were
ordered to kneel in front of him. This order sparked rioting, for which
the alleged leader, a stoker named Moody, was given five years' penal
servitude. In an article entitled 'Class Rule in the Services', *Justice* railed
against the humiliation resulting from a system that would put young and
naive boys in positions of superiority to tried and experienced men, and
claimed that while, theoretically, the army and navy existed to defend the
people, 'in reality, both exist for the defence of class privilege'.[16] There
was an 'On the Knee' demonstration (named after the drill order that
had sparked the trouble) later that month, at which Harry Quelch, Pete
Curran,[17] and Will Thorne all spoke. As with *The Clarion*'s criticism of
the prosecution of the Boer War, the objection here was not against the
military as such but rather the incompetence, inefficiency, and arbitrary
decisions which resulted when appointments were made on the basis of
birth rather than talent.

At the turn of the century many figures who would become prominent
labour patriots during the 1914–18 conflict were staunch critics of British
foreign policy. In 1901 H.M. Hyndman of the SDF composed the pamphlet
The Greatness of India and her Ruin by England – a furious denunciation of
the British Empire and the motivations behind imperialism in general.[18]
Similarly, while navvies' union leader John Ward was later to become an
outspoken defender of empire, at the 1900 Trades Union Congress (TUC)

[14] P. Ward, *Red Flag and Union Jack*, 112.

[15] Newton, *British Labour, European Socialism*, 157.

[16] *Justice*, 5 January 1907.

[17] Harry Quelch was a founding member of the SDF and father of Tom Quelch; Pete
Curran was the MP for Jarrow.

[18] Serialised in *The Clarion*, 2 and 9 November 1901.

he vigorously condemned the suppression of the two Boer republics and proposed a resolution – eventually passed by a small minority – which deplored the timidity of the Parliamentary Committee of the TUC in failing to challenge the government over the South African conflict.[19] The British National Committee, set up in 1905 to represent the labour movement at the Second International, consisted of Arthur Henderson, John Hodge, Will Thorne, and Ben Tillett, all of whom would fall into the 'patriots' camp during the First World War.[20] The British labour movement was therefore at least theoretically committed to internationalism and anti-militarism: all sections of the British delegation to the 1907 Stuttgart International Congress supported the anti-war resolution, although it also reaffirmed the policy of national defence.[21]

Yet this tenuous and abstract internationalist stance was not supported by a pragmatic scheme of co-operation between the labour movements of different European nations, nor did it preclude a certain chauvinism on behalf of British trade unions. For example, it was only in 1913 that the representatives of the French and German trade unions were invited to the TUC's annual meeting, while American delegates had been invited since 1894.[22] Although there would have been practical concerns with language difficulties, assumptions of greater cultural connections and kinship with the Americans may have been a factor in this.[23] Regardless, the fact that representatives from the two leading continental economies did not attend the British TUC until the year immediately before the war gives an idea of the limited extent of co-operation between different European labour movements. Furthermore, it seems that the elites of the labour movement were rather ahead of their membership; as Douglas Newton has argued, 'most trade unionists were undoubtedly quite unaware that, through their

[19] Report of the Thirty-Third Gathering Trade Union Congress. Cited in Newton, *British Labour, European Socialism*, 103.

[20] Whilst Henderson had no truck with the jingoism which came to characterise Hodge, Tillett, and Thorne, he took up chairmanship of the PLP after MacDonald's resignation, and was instrumental to the war effort.

[21] Ward, *Red Flag and Union Jack*, 104. Marc Mulholland has argued that the language of the International before 1914 'designedly played-down the socialists' real commitment to national self-defence', and that 'Socialists of the Second International generally looked to the nation as the necessary framework for socialist construction'. See Mulholland, 'Marxists of Strict Observance', 619, 628.

[22] Newton, *British Labour, European Socialism*, 71.

[23] Neville Kirk has written about the comradeship between British, Australian, and American trade unionists. See N. Kirk, *Comrades and Cousins: Globalization, Workers and Labour Movements in Britain, the USA and Australia from the 1880s to 1914*, London: Merlin, 2003 and 'Transnational Labour in the Age of Globalization', *Labour History Review* 75 (2010): 8–19.

affiliation to the [Labour Representation Committee], they had become enrolled in something called the Second International'.[24]

There were qualifications even to the fairly ambiguous internationalism of the Edwardian years. Although a motion (sponsored again by John Ward) describing the Boer War as 'unjust' was passed at the 1902 TUC with 591,000 votes in support, 314,000 votes were still cast against, suggesting that a considerable proportion of the trade union movement found little objectionable with the conflict.[25] Although it was fairly straightforward for the Parliamentary Labour Party (PLP) to stand against the government in the debate over the naval estimates in 1909, members representing constituencies that stood to gain from increased naval funding felt this took precedence over any pacifistic or internationalist sentiment. John Jenkins and Alexander Wilkie of the Shipwrights' Union (MP for Chatham and Dundee respectively) and Charles Duncan of the Engineers (MP for Barrow-in-Furness) rebelled against the party line and voted with the government.[26]

It is perhaps not surprising that the British Left was only fitfully and temperamentally committed to proletarian solidarity in the years before the First World War, given that opposition to conflict was usually motivated not by Marxist concerns of international working-class unity, but rather by old radical, Nonconformist views. This is the argument put forward by Paul Ward, who noted that the anti-Alien Act agitation was based 'less on socialist internationalism than on traditional ideas of English tolerance and liberty'.[27] One should not necessarily be surprised by the continuity of the rhetoric expressed by Labour MPs; after all, twenty-four of the twenty-nine returned in 1906 owed their successes to the absence of Liberal opposition, and seventy-nine per cent of Labour candidates mentioned free trade, Home Rule, and reform of the Education Act in their campaign literature, seventy-five per cent also mentioning licensing reform.[28] With this liberal heritage still dominating the PLP, it naturally followed that Labour opposition to militarism owed far less to socialist internationalism than to radical liberalism.

Norman Angell was probably the most influential pacifist of the period, and Labour leader Keir Hardie was a keen supporter, praising him during a

[24] Newton, *British Labour, European Socialism*, 49.

[25] Report of the Thirty-Fifth Gathering of the Trade Union Congress. Cited in Newton, *British Labour, European Socialism*, 108.

[26] H. Weinroth, 'Left-Wing Opposition to Naval Armaments in Britain before 1914', *Journal of Contemporary History* 6 (1971): 116.

[27] Ward, *Red Flag and Union Jack*, 57.

[28] Ibid., 80.

Commons debate on armaments and offering to pay for the printing of half a million copies of his influential work *The Great Illusion*. Angell considered the idea but did not take up Hardie's proposal, apparently because he did not want to be linked 'with any one party and an extreme one at that'.[29] There is a certain irony that in 1918, with Europe in ruins, it was Angell and his prophesies of permanent peace which seemed outlandish and extreme, not to mention utterly naive and ill-founded, while Hardie's party had emerged stronger than ever and was only a few years away from government. Nevertheless, it is highly significant that Angell was a free trader and a liberal; he believed that war was impossible because the economic interests of nations were inexorably intertwined and the exigencies of international finance took precedence over the will of individual governments. His views could well be described in modern parlance as 'neoliberal' – he was, therefore, emphatically not a socialist. Howard Weinroth has drawn attention to the paradox of the Left elevating a man who quite openly cared very little about the working classes, and who had very little support amongst ordinary people. Angell's audience was narrow and confined to businessmen, professionals, and intellectuals: 'The working man ... with rare exceptions, did not fill the ranks of Norman Angellism.'[30]

This highlights a central dilemma for the Labour Party in the years preceding the First World War: whether due to its radical, dissenting heritage or Marxist economic influence, it felt compelled to at least maintain a facade of pacifistic internationalism at the same time as campaigning for the votes of working people who, more often than not, felt no such compulsion. While the trade union movement – by its very nature – and the *Clarion* group did have mass working-class support, the same could not truly be said of the SDF or the ILP, which tended to draw most of their membership from specific areas and be absent in others, or rely unduly on middle-class supporters.[31] The membership of the unions and the *Clarion* group, though regionalised and fragmented, thus better reflected the mass of working people all over Britain.

Douglas Newton has drawn attention to a remarkable incident involving Keir Hardie at Preston train station in 1898. Waiting for his train, Hardie claimed that he was so surprised to see a working man reading the *Labour Leader* (the organ of the ILP) he presumed that he must have been one of the local activists for the party. He recounted in a letter how he had walked along the platform trying to guess the identity of the man, but ultimately

[29] H. Weinroth, 'Norman Angell and The Great Illusion: An Episode in Pre-1914 Pacifism', *Historical Journal* 17 (1974): 555.

[30] Ibid., 562.

[31] This most certainly could not be said of the explicitly middle-class Fabian Society.

could not decide whether or not he knew him.[32] The image of Keir Hardie passing up and down a station platform, straining to ascertain whether or not he recognised someone whilst at the same time studiously avoiding making eye contact, is not merely amusing but also quite illuminating. Firstly, it is revealing that even a former coal miner like Hardie did not consider simply approaching the man and introducing himself, but more significant is his surprise to see a working man reading his own paper, and his assumption that he must therefore be involved with the Preston ILP.[33] This is reflected in the ultimate resignation over war and foreign policy which characterised the private beliefs, if not the public utterances, of many labour leaders during this period. Hardie, MacDonald, and other leaders could make bold speeches about the power of the workers to stop the impending cataclysm and call for general strikes to stop the war, but they knew full well that they could barely call on enough working-class support to elect a few dozen MPs. In the words of Newton, 'Hardie and the other leaders of the International were well aware of the numerical weakness of their own parties and had no illusions about the true dimensions of the power at their disposal … when their guards were down, they made candid admissions of their limited influence amongst the working class'. Indeed, Hardie apparently told a suffragette in Manchester that 'you have not the women of the nation behind you any more than we have the workman behind us. Shout less and work more'.[34]

In terms of domestic changes, Hardie need not have been so pessimistic: high unemployment and intolerable living standards led to mounting pressure for social reform, and there had been some successes in pushing municipal socialism at a local level. What the party needed to do was offer pragmatic, practical solutions to the problems faced by working people in a language they understood and based on values they accepted. In the words of Paul Ward, 'Hardie argued that the earlier anti-Parliamentarism of the movement had meant that "Socialism, in those days, was treated as a plant of continental growth which could never find lodgement in Great Britain."'[35] In this respect, the Edwardian Labour Party went to great lengths to stress

[32] Newton, *British Labour, European Socialism*, 21.

[33] It should be noted that Hardie continually misjudged the temperature of the Preston electorate: in 1900 he was convinced he stood a better chance of election here than in Merthyr, yet finished bottom of the poll, albeit with nearly 5,000 votes. A disillusioned supporter, Sam Hobson, later reflected: 'I was now convinced that Keir Hardie had not the slightest political judgment.' However, he stood successfully in Merthyr later that week and held the seat until his death. See K. Morgan, *Keir Hardie*, Oxford: Oxford University Press, 1967, 31.

[34] Newton, *British Labour, European Socialism*, 282–83.

[35] Ward, *Red Flag and Union Jack*, 87.

the very British nature of their movement. For example, Victor Fisher (who was not then the decided jingo he would become) refused to debate with the pacifist E. Belfort Bax of the SDF as he feared that 'the very worst thing the Socialist movement could do is convince the great mass of the people, who must be converted to Socialism if Socialism is to be realised, that Socialism entails anti-patriotism'.[36]

Overall, the relationship between the British Left and patriotism in the fourteen years immediately preceding the First World War was rather confused. For some elements, such as the *Clarion* group and specific trade unions – usually those connected to the defence industry such as boiler-makers and shipwrights or else in competition for jobs with foreign workers, such as sailors and dockers – patriotism was not only perfectly compatible with their political beliefs, it was an integral part of their ideology. For the Marxist SDF, the picture was more complex. Originally decidedly anti-nationalist, its position evolved in the years before the war. As early as 1903, *Justice* welcomed the *entente cordiale*, and claimed that it and the SDF had never been for 'peace at any price'.[37] Although, for most on the Left, Russia remained a paradigm of despotism – as evidenced by the outrage over the visit of the Tsar in 1906 – by 1907 *Justice* was warning that the Kaiser was the real menace to Europe, and that only the German Social Democratic Party could act as a restraining influence.[38] Ben Tillett, also writing in 1907, claimed that the Boer War had been fought 'for a rich gang of thieves and a khaki mad crowd', yet the attitude expressed towards Germany in its pages suggested that war with that country would be a different matter altogether.[39] By 1910 Hyndman wrote of 'the right and duty of this nationality to maintain its independence, even under capitalism … There is no mistake about that. If this is to be a jingo, then I am a jingo; if this is to be a bourgeois, then I am a bourgeois, if this is to be an opponent of organized Socialist opinion, then I am an opponent of organized Socialist opinion'.[40]

It is difficult to agree with Miles Taylor's claim that radical patriotism ended around the time of the Boer War, for many patriotic labour groups continued to maintain this tradition. They were critical of the British *state*, but not of the British people, and saw the nation and nationalism

---

[36] Ibid., 108. Incidentally, Belfort Bax supported the 1914–18 war, along with, in his words 'almost … all the surviving "old guard" of the pioneer Socialist body of this country'. E. Belfort Bax, *Reminiscences and Reflexions of a Mid and Late Victorian*, London: Allen and Unwin, 1918, 252. Cited in Mulholland, 'Marxists of Strict Observance', 625.

[37] *Justice*, 7 November 1903.

[38] Ibid., 9 February 1907.

[39] Ibid., 18 May 1907. See the coverage of the Kaiser's visit to Britain in the 7 September 1907 number for anti-Prussian sentiment.

[40] *Justice*, 3 September 1910.

as mechanisms to bring about change. While some on the Left had an awkward, ambiguous relationship with patriotism, feeling obliged to espouse internationalist, pacifistic rhetoric whilst privately aware that these values were not common amongst the working class, this contradiction was not a problem for others. For many on the Left, the years before 1914 were characterised by a perfectly compatible combination of left-wing and nationalist sentiment. There was no hypocrisy for men such as Blatchford, Tillett, and Hyndman in becoming decided jingos, nor in moderates such as Henderson, George Edwards, and the Webbs giving cautious support to the war effort. For the mainstream of the labour movement, the First World War did not represent a clean break with the past.

The events of August 1914 would nonetheless confuse the attitudes of some towards nationalism, patriotism, and militarism. Over the course of the war some of the most ardent pacifists became raging militarists, circumspect nationalists became committed jingoes, and men such as Blatchford sank into despair as they saw their sad prophecies realised. Describing the latest weaponry produced by modern industrial nations, he warned in *The Clarion* in February 1900 that 'These terrible weapons have never yet been used on a large scale. When they are, things will happen.'[41]

The next chapter will examine the positioning of the Left in the lead-up to the war and the choices made after 4 August. It will introduce the War Emergency Workers' National Committee, the umbrella group which co-ordinated left-wing responses to the conflict, and discuss the prominent patriots of the war years. In addition to the discussion of the elites of the labour movement, Chapter 2 will reveal some of the many millions of ordinary trade unionists and labour activists who contributed to the war effort, either at the Front or at home, many of whom committed acts of heroism and bravery that became legendary in their factories and trade union branches. Finally, there will also be an analysis of the anti-Germanism which spread on the Left. Overall, Chapter 2 will argue that labour patriotism dominated left-wing responses to the war.

---

[41] *The Clarion*, 10 February 1900.

2

'I'd sooner blackleg my union than blackleg my country' – Labour Patriotism, 1914–18

'This is not a political war. It is not a war caused inadvertently by the blunders of secret diplomacy. It is not a financiers' war, a war preventable by soft words or delicate expostulations ... It is a vast and frightful racial earthquake. It has shaken civilisation to its foundations ... These Huns are not only the enemies of France, of Britain, of Russia, of Belgium; they are the enemies of humanity.'[1]

—Robert Blatchford, *The Clarion*, April 1915

If the Left's position on international conflict was confused before the summer of 1914, it might be assumed that the rapid mobilisation of European militaries and the declarations of hostilities would have further divided and confounded the movement. Yet, on the contrary, the outbreak resulted in near-unanimous support for the war effort from across the labour movement. This chapter will examine events in August 1914, including the Left's acquiescence to the war, and how it managed to co-ordinate its response. It will discuss the principal characters in the 'patriotic labour' camp, and survey specific unions and ordinary workers who gave their support – and their lives – to the war effort. The progress of the war inevitably gave rise to anti-German hostility, and the motivations and implications of this will also be analysed. Finally, there will be a survey of ordinary trade unionists and labour activists who distinguished themselves during the conflict. In terms of both elite and subaltern levels, it will be argued that there was a decidedly united response from labour. Although *enthusiasm* for the war amongst the labour movement was rare, there was a general consensus that, once begun, it had to be seen through. Ultimately, this chapter argues that labour patriotism, rather than anti-war agitation, characterised the Left's

---

[1] *The Clarion*, 16 April 1915.

response to the war, and that the history of labour patriotism in this period has been unjustly neglected by historians.

August 1914

Most leading individuals on the British Left remained firmly against the war in the days preceding the start of the conflict. The future ultra-patriot Ben Tillett condemned the war as 'absolutely wanton and brutal in every feature', while Will Thorne lamented the 'utterly shattered' hopes of internationalism.[2] H.M. Hyndman was one of many leading leftists to have addressed a large peace meeting on 2 August, and Labour made plans to form a Peace Emergency Workers' National Committee to co-ordinate the anti-war effort.[3] Yet the invasion of Belgium and subsequent declaration of war instigated an abrupt about-turn. The Lib-Lab MP John Ward was billed to appear at a further peace meeting in Trafalgar Square on 4 August but, upon hearing of the invasion, he told his friends it would be time to talk about peace when the Germans withdrew.[4] For much of the leadership of the British Left – as with ordinary trade unionists, Labour supporters, and the British population at large – the invasion of Belgium and the subsequent ultimatum to withdraw served as a turning point, and gave a stamp of morality to the conflict. The thoughts of George Edwards, leader of the National Agricultural Labourers' and Rural Workers' Union (NALRU), doubtless chimed with the experience of many British men and women on that day:

> On August 4, 1914, the Great War commenced and, as stated, I came to the conclusion, like most of the other Labour leaders, that according to the information I had at my disposal, we had no other alternative but to enter the war. I felt that it was a struggle for our very existence, further, that we were fighting to overcome one of the greatest curses to humanity, namely the wicked spirit of militarism. I therefore decided to put what appeared to me at the time the nation's interest before any other consideration. I spoke at a good many recruiting meetings in the early stages of the war. So far did I carry my patriotism that some of my friends began to be rather nervous about me for fear I should carry it too far, but they need not have been.[5]

[2] J. Bush, *Behind the Lines: East London Labour 1914–1919*, London: Merlin Press, 1984.

[3] A. Marwick, *The Deluge: British Society and the First World War*, London: Palgrave Macmillan, 2006, 71.

[4] Labour History Archive and Study Centre (LHASC), John Ward Papers, JW/5/13: Memoirs, The Beginning of the Great War.

[5] G. Edwards, *From Crow-Scaring to Westminster: An Autobiography*, London: National Union of Agricultural Workers, 1957, 190.

Given that Edwards was from a rural, Liberal, Methodist background, his belief in the morality of the war is even more significant. Even the fiercely anti-war Marxists of the Plebs' League recognised that, whether or not the British government was utilising the invasion of Belgium as a means of securing public support for the war, the invasion itself remained an outrage:

> Whatever were the pretexts made by the British Government concerning the German invasion of Belgium, they in no way discount some good reasons why Socialists should support Belgium against this violation. And these reasons are quite consistent with international Socialism. If world-peace be an essential need of the proletariat, then the latter is certainly concerned with preserving the integrity of a state like Belgium. Otherwise the door is left wide open to invasion, to the opposite of world-peace.[6]

For the bulk of the labour leadership, the declaration of war ended weeks of tension. The awkward position of having to espouse international solidarity despite their awareness that this language did not appeal to the majority of working-class people had become ever more acutely uncomfortable in the weeks following the assassination of the Archduke Franz Ferdinand. The average Briton probably had little grasp of the multifarious combination of political, economic, and diplomatic interests which led to the First World War: there was a general will to fight if necessary, yet there was by no means anything approaching a widespread desire for war in July 1914. As Adrian Gregory has argued, pro-interventionist sentiment was a minority opinion as late as 2 August, and possibly until the actual declaration on 4 August.[7] However, once Britain had entered the conflict, it was imperative that it must not lose. In this respect, Britons fully understood the seriousness and long-term commitments entailed by the declaration on 4 August, and such a decision could only be morally vindicated if all other options were seen to have been exhausted.

The German invasion of Belgium confirmed that Britain had no honourable option other than to fight. The quick end to equivocation and the solidification behind the war effort – and the role of Belgium in this conversion – has been well summarised by Gerard DeGroot: 'For the British [in reality], this was a conflict about empires, capitalism, trade and food, democracy, honour, civilization or the defence of the trusted friends.

---

[6] *Plebs*, January 1915.

[7] A. Gregory, *The Last Great War: British Society and the First World War*, Cambridge: Cambridge University Press, 2008, 16. See also *idem., A War of Peoples, 1914–1919*, Oxford: Oxford University Press, 2014; M. Mulholland, '"Marxists of Strict Observance"? The Second International, National Defence and the Question of War', *Historical Journal* 58 (2015): 615–40.

But when Germany attacked poor little Belgium, a war of markets became a war of morality.'[8] Since the war was pitched as a question of morality, public opinion quickly painted complex issues in stark, contrasting colours. While only months previously British attitudes towards Germans had been rather ambiguous, soon – aided by tales of atrocities committed in Belgium – Germany became the symbol of everything immoral, and everything 'un-British'. In Gregory's words, 'it was the war that massively increased anti-Germanism' and popular militarism – rather than these sentiments pushing the country into the conflict.[9] *The Co-operative News*, like most left-leaning newspapers, had counselled against war in the months leading up to 4 August, but German aggression and reports of atrocities visited upon Belgian civilians convinced the editors that the war had to be fought; in a September 1914 editorial entitled 'Our Attitude to the War', the paper confessed: 'Late in the day we have realised what dream has possessed the Prussian mind.'[10]

One suspects that many at the elite level of the movement were looking for something which would validate the inevitable war and allow them to give their assent to the conflict without being accused of warmongering. In the words of Arthur Marwick, there was a great sense of 'relief' when the Germans ignored the ultimatum to withdraw (as, of course, everyone knew they would), and while 'the opposition to the war was striking, [it was] no more striking than the speed with which the bulk of it dissolved'.[11] Raynor Taylor, a trade unionist born in Oldham in 1898, concurred with this view: 'Strangely enough I think before war broke out we sensed it, everybody sensed it, that war would break out because the newspapers … were full of it … As I remember it there was a sense of … relief … it sounds strange to say, but it's true'.[12]

In his 1992 book *Labour at War*, John Horne spoke of the 'choice of 1914', the idea that the British labour movement ultimately judged its country and its society preferable to that of Germany, and so committed itself for the duration of the conflict.[13] Yet Horne underestimated the extent to which this choice was made for the labour elites by working-class opinion. The mainstream of the labour movement was well aware that it could not afford to oppose the war once British entry was a reality. At the first Labour

[8] G. DeGroot, *Blighty: British Society in the Era of the Great War*, New York: Longman, 1996, 7.

[9] Gregory, *The Last Great War*, 39.

[10] *The Co-operative News*, 12 September 1914.

[11] Marwick, *Deluge*, 73 and 72.

[12] Imperial War Museum, Catalogue No. 11113, Raynor Taylor, interviewed 1990–92.

[13] J.N. Horne, *Labour at War: France and Britain 1914–1918*, Oxford: Clarendon Press, 1991.

Party conference held since the outbreak, in January 1916, James Sexton put forward a resolution, passed by 1,502,000 votes to 602,000:

> this Conference, whilst expressing its opposition (in accordance with previously expressed opinions) to all systems of permanent militarism as a danger to human progress, considers the present action of Great Britain and its Government fully justified in the present war, expresses its horror at the atrocities committed by Germany and her ally by the callous and brutal murder of non-combatants, including women and children, and hereby pledges the Conference to assist the Government as far as possible in the successful prosecution of the War.[14]

J. Stokes of the London Trades Council, supporting the motion, argued that 'If ... the resolution was turned down what would be the position of the Labour Movement so far as the great mass of the British people were concerned[?] ... they would say that the Conference was against the country. That was a point the Conference must remember if they desired unity when the War was over'.[15]

The Workers' National Committee and Labour Support for the War

Once British participation in the European conflict was a concrete reality rather than a distasteful abstraction, the Labour Party was able to transform itself, from awkward Jeremiahs wringing their hands on the sidelines into practical men and women of action, ensuring that the interests of British workers were protected. Immediately the Peace Committee transformed into the War Emergency Workers' National Committee (WNC) – a body that was to ensure Labour Party cohesion, relevance, and achievement throughout the long and draining years of the war. Significantly for its survival and success, the WNC was an honest reflection of the eclectic nature of the Edwardian Labour movement. The TUC sent Charles Bowerman, Harry Gosling, and James Seddon; the General Federation of Trade Unions sent William Appleton, Ben Cooper, and the ultra-patriot Ben Tillett. The Labour Party was represented by William Anderson, John Hodge, and Arthur Henderson. The Fabian Sidney Webb was to have considerable intellectual influence on the committee; Susan Lawrence represented the Women's Labour League,[16] John Hodge served as President,

---

[14] Report of the Fifteenth Annual Conference of the Labour Party.

[15] Ibid.

[16] Susan Lawrence was a Labour councillor in London and later MP for East Ham North from 1926 to 1931. See M. Bellamy and J. Saville, *Dictionary of Labour Biography III*, London: Macmillan, 1976.

and Jim Middleton worked tirelessly as Secretary. By no means were these people all of one mind, in terms of the war or the direction of the labour movement. Representatives included those known for their continued opposition to the conflict, such as Anderson and later Robert Smillie; those who initially opposed the conflict but put aside ideological objections for pragmatic contribution, such as Henderson and Middleton; and outspoken labour patriots, such as Tillett and Hodge. This led Royden Harrison to ponder, 'How was any practical collaboration possible between, say, W.C. Anderson or Fred Jowett, on the one hand, and Henderson, Bowerman and Appleton on the other?'[17] Crucially, then, the inclusive nature of the WNC served to unite, rather than divide, the disparate strands of the labour movement.

After MacDonald's resignation from the chairmanship of the Parliamentary Labour Party (PLP) over its support for the government's prosecution of the war, an electoral truce was agreed between all parties on 29 August 1914, and new Labour leader Arthur Henderson joined the Parliamentary Recruiting Committee.[18] The patriotism of the labour movement was echoed by the women's suffrage movement; Emmeline and Christabel Pankhurst joined the war effort, as did Millicent Garrett Fawcett. In the words of J.M. Byles: 'Mrs Fawcett's attitude towards the pre-war militants and war-time pacifists is contradictory, but she clearly believed patriotism and militarism took precedence over the emancipation issue for the duration of the war.'[19] There was no hypocrisy in the exhortations of senior Labour figures for young men to enlist: although their age and their role in the war effort at home prevented the likes of Henderson and George Barnes from fighting, they respectively had three and two sons with the colours, and both would lose a son during the course of the war.[20] Similarly, the Socialist intellectual R.H. Tawney enlisted – as a sergeant – in November 1914, and was involved in the Battle of the Somme on 1 July, an experience recounted in his essay 'The Attack'.[21] Following – and in many cases, moving well ahead of – their leaders' example, several high-profile Labour figures threw themselves into the recruiting effort. Navvies' Union leader

[17] R. Harrison, 'The War Emergency Workers' National Committee, 1914–1920', in A. Briggs and J. Saville (eds), *Essays in Labour History 1886–1923*, London: Macmillan, 1971, 217.

[18] On MacDonald see D. Marquand, *Ramsay MacDonald*, London: Jonathan Cape, 1977; D. Howell, *MacDonald's Party: Labour Identities and Crisis, 1922–1931*, Oxford: Oxford University Press, 2002.

[19] J.M. Byles, 'Women's Experience of World War One: Suffragists, Pacifists and Poets', *Women's Studies International Forum* 8 (1985): 475.

[20] *The Co-operative News*, 9 January 1915.

[21] T. Wilson, *The Myriad Faces of War*, Cambridge: Polity Press, 1986, 327.

John Ward acted as a self-appointed recruiting sergeant up and down the country, collecting 1,400 navvies within three weeks.[22]

Following its formation in May 1915, three Labour leaders were invited to join Asquith's first coalition government (an idea which would have seemed absurd only a few years earlier): former ironworker Henderson was appointed President of the Board of Education; William Brace, a Welsh miner, was made undersecretary at the Home Office; and print worker and Norwich MP G.H. Roberts became a government whip.[23] Although the PLP originally opposed entry into the government, the National Executive Committee (NEC) and Henderson himself believed that, for strategic and moral reasons, it was proper for the party to join the coalition. While the unions were important to this decision, there was no clear division between them and the PLP on this issue, and several Labour MPs supported the decision to join the government. Henderson was later included in the War Cabinet formed in December 1916, a decision later ratified by the NEC, while Hodge became Minister of Labour and Barnes was appointed Minister of Pensions; three other Labour MPs (Brace, Roberts, and James Parker) all received minor posts.[24]

Who Were the Labour Patriots?

The background of labour patriots in this period leaves us in no doubt as to the sincerity of their commitment to leftist politics. Ben Tillett, for example, may well have gone on to espouse extreme xenophobia, and had always been an anti-Semite, but from the 1889 dock strike onwards he was a giant of the British labour movement. Born in Bristol and starting work at a brickyard at the age of eight, he became apprenticed to a bootmaker at twelve years old, not long before joining the Royal Navy. He left the navy due to disablement and served with the merchant marine for a number of years before settling in East London. In 1889 Tillett and the union he helped to found – the Dock, Wharf, Riverside and General Labourers' Union – rose to prominence during the East End dock strike: a crucial moment in the history of the labour movement, it witnessed unprecedented co-ordinated action by unskilled workers and co-operation between craftsmen and labourers. Tillett then later played a prominent role in the dock strikes of 1911 and 1912, before forming the National Transport Workers' Federation in 1910 with ultra-patriot Havelock Wilson of the Seamen's Union. A Fabian

---

[22] JW/5/13. It should be noted that Lib-Lab MPs such as Ward, although of working-class origins, did not take the Labour whip.

[23] Marwick, *The Deluge*, 99.

[24] Ibid., 124.

and a founding member of the ILP, Tillett subsequently joined the Social Democratic Party (SDF) and was eventually elected to Parliament for Salford North in a by-election in 1917.

Amongst the Tillett papers at the Modern Records Centre, a letter from E.A. Rogers recalled how policemen would march Tillett off to Seetham Lane police station as soon as he stood up to speak on the parapet of Tower Hill.[25] A further letter claimed that: 'Ben Tillett had the indefinable gift; in common with the greatest of the old time music hall performers and actors generally of being able to do anything with an audience with a look or a gesture.'[26] An anecdote from S.F. Whitlock neatly encapsulates the differences between the rambunctious, demagogic Tillett and the sober and abstemious gentlemen more typical of the Labour leadership: 'At a Labour Conference the headquarters was in a large hotel. In the lounge sat Ramsay MacDonald, Arthur Henderson, Philip Snowden + other self righteous leaders, when in comes Ben Tillett, with one of the gayest birds in town, + went upstairs with her.'[27] Tillett's ultra-patriotism during the war and concern for self-enrichment – it was reckoned he was earning up to twenty pounds a week for his music hall recruitment performances – led to a fall from grace after 1922, and towards the end of his career he may have received donations from Conservative Central Office.[28] Certainly there was a fundraising campaign in the hard-right magazine *John Bull* in the 1920s to pay for his retirement to a healthier, tropical climate in order to assuage his health concerns.[29] Yet Tillett's history in the decades before the war meant that he, like other labour patriots here, cannot be dismissed simply as 'socialists of circumstance' whose real convictions were revealed by the war. Victimised at work, attacked by the police, and prosecuted by the state, Tillett had both literally and metaphorically fought for his beliefs for decades and did not adopt socialism as a convenient cover for his jingoism.[30] Like most of the men and women of the Left – in the PLP, the trade unions, the affiliated societies, the Co-operative movement, and

[25] Modern Records Centre (MRC), MSS.74/6/2/81-117 – Papers Relating to Ben Tillett, letter to Ian Mackay from E.A. Rogers, 22 January 1951.

[26] MSS.74/6/2/81-117 – Papers Relating to Ben Tillett, letter to Mackay from Graham W. Thompson, 22 January 1951.

[27] MSS.74/6/2/81-117 – Papers Relating to Ben Tillett, letter to Mackay from S.F. Whitlock, 22 January 1951.

[28] A. Thorpe, 'Labour and the Extreme Left', in A. Thorpe (ed.), *The Failure of Political Extremism in Inter-War Britain*, Exeter: Exeter University Press, 1989, 13.

[29] MSS.74/6/2/81-117 – Papers Relating to Ben Tillett, letter to Mackay from S.F. Whitlock, 22 January 1951.

[30] MSS.74/6/2/81-117, Papers relating to Ben Tillett, Letter to Mackay from Rogers, 22 January 1951.

the labour press – labour patriots such as Tillett combined a genuine zeal for social and economic change with a natural patriotism that often served as an important component of their left-wing political beliefs.

That patriotism need not act as a restraint on radical leftism is perhaps best encapsulated by Victor Grayson. Grayson (christened Albert Victor Grayson after the eldest son of Edward, Prince of Wales) was claimed by his biographer, the hard-Left historian Reg Groves as the 'first, and last' socialist elected to sit as a Member of Parliament for the Labour Party, and was something of an Edwardian maverick. Selected in 1907 to stand for election in the Colne Valley against the odds, the local ILP refused to endorse him publicly.[31] A bombastic and demagogic speaker, he did not look to secure votes through promises of incremental reforms, but rather through emotive appeals to a future promised land: 'One thing is for sure', wrote Groves, 'Grayson won no support by promises of immediate benefits. On the contrary he told them that socialism was something they'd probably never see: "It won't be in your time, not even perhaps in your children's time."'[32] In the year after his election he became the most popular speaker on the British Left, touring the country to perform before great crowds and espouse the virtues of 'pure revolutionary socialism':[33]

> I am looking forward to the time when the British soldier will emulate his brother of the National Guard of France and, when asked to fire on the people who are fighting for their rights, will turn his rifle in the other direction. We are making a socialist now of Tommy Atkins by propaganda work in the Army ... We are making Socialists there by the dozen.[34]

After repeated breaches of parliamentary procedure and refusals to give way during a debate, Grayson was forcibly removed from the Chamber of the Commons by the Sergeant-at-Arms and expelled from the House. He then declared that 'the Parliamentary game is played out ... We need something unconstitutional to agitate the ponderous brains of modern legislators'.[35] He moved closer towards Hyndman of *Justice* and the SDF and Blatchford of *The Clarion*; two men who offered a different approach to that of Keir Hardie and the ILP, and who were also, by now, pronounced anti-Germans. Soon

[31] R. Groves, *The Strange Case of Victor Grayson*, London: Pluto Press, 1975, 21. See also D. Clark, *Labour's Lost Leader: Victor Grayson*, London: Quartet, 1985.

[32] Groves, *The Strange Case of Victor Grayson*, 35.

[33] Ibid., 37.

[34] Ibid., 55. It should be noted that Grayson was blustering here, and there is no evidence that hard-Left attempts to infiltrate the army met with any success. See D. French, *Military Identities*, Oxford: Oxford University Press, 2005, 133–35.

[35] Groves, *The Strange Case of Victor Grayson*, 67.

Grayson was declaring that 'the maintenance of the British Empire offers the best conditions for the world's march towards socialism', and came over to labour patriotism.[36]

Groves explained the patriotism of Grayson and others thus: 'The war had donned the armour of a righteous war, a guise made credible by the invasion of Belgium by a powerful, predatory and arrogant Prussian militarism. This it was that moved multitudes to volunteer, including many who had seen in this war the same opportunity for service and self-sacrifice to high aims that they had hitherto found in the rebel causes.'[37] He was undoubtedly correct in identifying the invasion of Belgium as a key motivator for many on the British Left, both high and low, in addition to the attraction of subsuming one's own desires and identity for a broader cause. Yet for many there was a vague idea that, whatever the flaws of British society, it was infinitely preferable to that of Germany, and British culture inherently superior to German *kultur*. In Grayson's own words: 'I am a hard-shelled socialist, but I must confess that our peers and privates are fighting for something more elusive than beer and skittles. Some folk call it patriotism ... religion ... God. Whatever they may call it, they are at present weaving out of the world's tangled skein, the warp and woof of a new era.'[38] According to Blatchford, 'Nobody was more in favour of prosecuting the war than Victor. In 1918, he was as great a patriot as any.'[39] He ended the war in khaki, fighting with a New Zealand unit, and apparently hero-worshipped the aristocratic officers he met when deployed overseas.[40]

Critics of Grayson might suggest, improbably, that he was always a 'Tory stooge' whose true colours were revealed by the war. Less kindly but more feasibly, they may suggest that the sort of juvenile demagoguery and hyperbole utilised by Grayson transferred easily from the far-Left to ultra-patriotism. Both of these interpretations are wide of the mark. For a brief period after his election in 1907, Grayson was the most dynamic and inspiring individual on the British Left; there was no insincerity in him – on the contrary, he was rather *too* earnest, too easily driven to hysterics in the House by the poverty and deprivation he saw. His patriotism during the war does not suggest a *change* of viewpoints, but rather highlights the compatibility of hard-Left politics and pronounced patriotism at the time of the First World War.[41]

[36] Ibid., 114.
[37] Ibid., 151.
[38] Ibid., 153.
[39] Ibid., 176.
[40] Ibid., 178.
[41] See J. Gorman, *Images of Labour*, London: Scorpion Publishing, 1985, 105.

This compatibility was present not only amongst those on the extremes of the labour movement, but also many moderates. Clement Attlee, writing in his war memoirs, revealed the intellectual process by which he dismissed his initial objection to the war:

> I could not persuade myself that there were no circumstances in which I would not possibly feel bound to fight and therefore I had to consider whether or not the present occasion was one where it was my duty to take up arms ... On the one hand my whole instincts as a socialist were against war and I had no illusions. I could not accept the ordinary cry of 'Your King and Your Country Need You', nor was I convinced of Germany's sole guilt. On the other hand it appeared wrong to me to let others make a sacrifice while I stood by, especially as I was unmarried and had no obligations.

He finally concluded: 'I attended sundry ... conferences where *the self righteous* [sic] *pacifism* of some of the members rather strengthened my intentions already half formed [sic] of joining. I think that I was finally persuaded by the wanton invasion of Belgium and by the German actions therein'.[42] If a Haileybury and Oxford socialist such as Attlee found the exhortations of the peace camp to be self-righteous, how much harder it must have been for working-class men and women – whether on the Left or Right – to be impressed by the language and manner of middle-class radicals, even if they agreed with the substance of their arguments.

Workers and Trade Unions

There was a certain contradiction in the British attitude towards conflict and imperialism. On the one hand, there was a belief that militarism was inherently un-British and that warfare should be avoided at all costs, yet this co-existed with an empire built on conquest and military campaigns. Indeed, this common belief that the British were singularly un-warlike, especially in comparison to some of the autocratic regimes of the Continent, had served as a tenet of the belief in British exceptionalism and superiority. As Adrian Gregory has put it, British 'heritage says that war is totally wrong, yet that heritage and its values must be defended to the death'.[43] Perhaps the main failing of historians when considering the attitudes of British workers – and British trade unionists and left-wingers in particular – to the First World War is a failure to grasp just how prevalent and pervasive patriotism was in Edwardian society. The British not only believed themselves to be culturally

---

[42] C. Attlee, *Memoirs*, 2. Emphasis added.
[43] Gregory, *The Last Great War*, 4–5.

and 'racially' separate from others, they considered themselves to be markedly superior, and this attitude was to be found among those on the Left just as on the Right. An October 1914 edition of the *Wheatsheaf*, a cultural periodical attached to the Co-operative movement, featured a 'Map of Racial Europe'. The map is notable for its specificity: it delineates between not only 'French' and 'German' peoples, but also 'Western Slavs', 'Eastern Slavs', 'Anglo-Irish', and 'Irish'.[44] This attitude was organic and self-replicating and not the result of top-down propaganda from the government; in fact, E.H. Reisner, an American historian of nationalism and education, claimed in the 1910s that the English hardly used schools at all as a means of incubating nationalist sentiment.[45]

Outside of the school system, organised youth movements have been accused of stoking nationalist and militarist sentiments among the Edwardian working class, but the extent of this – and the reach of such groups – may have been overstated. In his discussion of youth organisations, M.D. Blanch concluded that the Boys' Brigade and the Scouts were ultimately for the 'better sort' of youth – Boy Scouts were required to be teetotallers and non-smokers – and not massively patronised by working-class children.[46] John Springhall concurred with this, claiming that class, cost, and church or chapel attendance were the most important variables in determining membership of an organised youth group. A survey of 1911 found that only a fifth of working-class children attended Sunday school and only one per cent remained after the age of fourteen.[47] At least two of the labour activist ex-servicemen of the Imperial War Museum's archive were members of youth groups: Frederick Orton was born in Nottingham in June 1892, the youngest of ten children, and would later go on to become a leading trade unionist. He was in the Boy's Brigade from the age of twelve, trained with wooden rifles and lances, and noted that it was very religious and 'definitely militaristic'.[48] In contrast, Jack Dorgan, born in Ashington in 1893, joined the Church Lad's Brigade aged fourteen, mainly because his friends had joined. He recalled that there was no religious instruction, just constant drilling, with very few overtly militaristic aspects.[49]

---

[44] *Wheatsheaf*, October 1914.

[45] According to E.H. Grainger, *Patriotisms: Britain 1900–1939*, London: Routledge Kegan Paul, 1986, 30–31.

[46] M.D. Blanch, 'Imperialism, Nationalism and Organized Youth', in J. Clarke, C. Chritcher, and R. Johnson (eds), *Working-Class Culture*, London: Hutchinson, 1979, 105–09.

[47] J.O. Springhall, 'The Boy Scouts, Class and Militarism in Relation to British Youth Movements 1908–1930', *International Review of Social History* 16 (1971): 139–43.

[48] Imperial War Museum, Catalogue No. 10411, Frederick James Orton, interviewed 1988.

[49] Imperial War Museum, Catalogue No. 9253, Jack Dorgan, interviewed 1986.

Whether or not it was incubated through education or youth groups, in many areas of the country 'imperialist and nationalist sentiment obtained real roots in working-class opinion'.[50] Even where troops had been used in industrial disputes, there does not seem to have been the same resentment towards soldiers as to policemen: Edward Spiers has argued that at Tonypandy in 1910, for example, it was the police, especially from forces drafted in from outside the area, such as the Metropolitan Police, who bore the brunt of the strikers' animus.[51] Indeed, Gervase Phillips has noted how some Glamorgan soldiers, billeted in an English town during the war, recognised some of the constables who had kept order during the strikes of 1910–11 and were delivered of an unexpected and delayed revenge.[52] That a great mass of the population was willing to fight was demonstrated by the hundreds of thousands of men who came forward, both during the opening weeks and months of the conflict, and in a more or less steady stream throughout, until the introduction of conscription. As Anne Summers has argued, if 1.5 million volunteers could be found in a period of little over a year, there must have been a deep-seated comfort with militarism and warfare, even if it was not of the continental variety.[53] While some men enlisted to escape unemployment and absolute poverty, this cannot be said of any more than a minority, and volunteers came from buoyant industries as much as from depressed trades, including many from protected occupations where demand for labour was high, jobs secure, and wages competitive.[54]

A great deal of literature has concentrated on possible motivations for men enlisting in the autumn of 1914, but it has perhaps been undermined by an assumption that it took a great weight of motivation for a man to join the army. Certainly, they realised they were signing up to fight and possibly die, and the extent to which people genuinely believed it would be 'over before Christmas' is doubtful. Yet for many British men, serving with the armed forces would not represent a great departure from their ordinary life, even in terms of the risk of death, disease, and disablement. For example, a notice in the *Railway Review*, the newspaper of the NUR, claimed that seventy members had been killed in the war by November 1914, but a notice on the facing page informed readers that 108 railway staff

---

[50] Blanch, 'Imperialism and Youth Organisations', 119.

[51] E.M. Spiers, *The Army and Society*, London: Longman, 1980.

[52] G. Phillips, 'Dai bach Y Soldiwr: Welsh Soldiers in the British Army, 1914–1918', *Llafur* 6 (1993): 103.

[53] A. Summers, 'Militarism in Britain before the Great War', *History Workshop Journal* 2 (1976): 105.

[54] Wilson, *The Myriad Faces of War*, 519.

and customers had died in accidents on the tracks in the three months leading to June 1914.[55] Ordinary life could be just as risky as war, whether the threat came from childhood illnesses or workplace accidents. As Ian Beckett has commented: 'Subordination and tedium were commonplace in British industrial society, while popular culture made light of hardship and enabled men to normalize their emotions under stress. In effect it comes down to the characteristics of the British working-class civilian soldier – perhaps a phlegmatic acceptance of fate or sheer bloody-mindedness but always with a sardonic humour.'[56] The reaction of most Britons to the hardships and inequalities that characterised most of their lives was a sort of ironic acceptance and a determination to muddle through – an attitude which transferred well into life under military discipline. Gervase Phillips has argued of Welsh soldiers at this time that 'industrial workers ... displayed a tendency to view their service in the Army as an extension of their peace-time situation, only now instead of iron-masters and pit-bosses there were Captains and Colonels'.[57]

In his study on working-class enlistment, David Silbey argued that a broad spectrum of motivations caused men to volunteer, but one cannot help notice that many of the reasons given – 'I got patriotic', or 'We were being patriotic. Or young and silly', are very similar to the motivations for marriage revealed in music hall comedian Dan Leno's sketch *Young Men Taken in and Done For*. For example, one man woke after a night of drinking to find that he had pledged himself to a woman, although he did not have any memory of it: 'She said, "Yes you do, you spoke about it last night, when you'd had a little drink." Well, I thought, if [*sic*] I did say so, I suppose I did, so I came downstairs half asleep (in fact I think every man's asleep when he's going to be married).'[58] In the Imperial War Museum's audio archive of interviews with war veterans collected in the 1980s, William Gillman – who would later go on to be a prominent Labour and trade union activist in West Ham – recalled how he 'thought it was great' when war broke out, as he 'wanted to fight the Germans', 'like we all did, us youngsters'. He did not realise at the time how long the war would last, nor the number of casualties; he 'look[ed] at it in a different way', when he was eighteen, and saw only the potential for adventure and heroism.[59]

---

[55] *Railway Review*, 13 November 1914.

[56] I. Beckett, 'The Nation in Arms, 1914–18', in I. Beckett and K. Simpson (eds), *A Nation in Arms*, London: Tom Donovan, 1990, 25.

[57] Phillips, 'Dai bach Y Soldiwr', 103.

[58] Quoted in G. Stedman Jones, 'Working-Class Culture and Working-Class Politics in London, 1870–1900: Notes on the Remaking of a Working Class', *Journal of Social History* 7 (1974): 492.

[59] Imperial War Museum, Catalogue No. 9420, William Gillman, interviewed 1986.

Frederick Orton recalled that his friends' joining up was important to his decision to enlist, but the most attractive factor was a week's holiday once a year. He also noted that the medical examination was very 'sketchy' and not particularly thorough; Orton's parents owned a sweet shop and were not too strict on young Frederick sampling their wares – by the time he enlisted he had lost all his teeth, yet was still passed as fit to serve.[60] Jack Dorgan was a particularly militant worker; as a teenager he earned a reputation for standing up to pit bosses when older men were afraid to do so, yet he joined the Territorials three years before the war: 'We were intensely loyal, you know, nationalistic ... the Union Jack was something to be treasured in those days.' He recalled that he and his friends 'never knew or cared about Germany ... [we] didn't really know or care [about] anything outside of Northumberland'. They understood and accepted that 'the people in charge of the country' had declared war on Germany; there were no celebrations or outbursts of patriotic fervour, 'it was just accepted'.[61]

Describing the English working class, E.P. Thompson has written that 'what mattered to people was, not whether it was capitalism but whether it was a ruthless or a tolerable capitalism – whether men were hurled into wars, subject to inquisitions and arbitrary arrests, or allowed some freedom of person and of organization', and clearly most Britons felt that British capitalism, while uncomfortable, *was* tolerable, that Britons were amongst the freest people in Europe, and that this tolerable standing of living and degree of personal freedom was worth fighting for.[62] The everyday aspects of British working-class life – boredom and tedium only interrupted by the occasional tragedy of a child miscarried or still born, an infant death, a workplace accident, with the occasional exhilaration of a win on the horses or in the football pools, all made bearable by constant cups of tea and the odd Woodbine – were not too different from everyday aspects of warfare, and just as men were determined to muddle through their lives as best they could, so too they determined to fight through the war to its grim conclusion.

In the words of John Bourne, 'The British working class was well adapted to the challenge of war. Working-class culture provided the army with a bedrock of social cohesion and community on which its capacity for endurance rested. The existential realities from which this culture evolved were remarkably similar to those of military life'.[63] Martin Middlebrook

---

[60] Imperial War Museum, Catalogue No. 10411, Frederick James Orton, interviewed 1988.

[61] Imperial War Museum, Catalogue No. 9253, Jack Dorgan, interviewed 1986.

[62] E.P. Thompson, 'The Peculiarities of the English', *Socialist Register* 2 (1965): 350.

[63] J. Bourne, 'The British Working Man in Arms', in H. Cecil and P. Liddle, *Facing Armageddon: The First World War Experienced*, London: Leo Cooper, 1996, 341.

recounted the tale of an officer who claimed that a recruit informed him: 'I don't think my trade union would permit me to work the number of hours we are working now'.[64] Similarly, Gervase Phillips has argued: 'Here is the continuity, the strikers of 1911, the grumbling citizen-soldiers of 1916 and the strikers of 1926 were often the same men.'[65] People joined the army for much the same range of reasons that led to marriage: an initial burst of excitement, a courage and sense of purpose born of alcohol, a vague sense of duty, peer pressure, financial pressures, a desire for adventure. Whatever their original motivations – and these soon faded into irrelevance – men were resolved to see through their obligations until the end, and knew full well that they were involved 'for the duration'.

One of the most telling signs of the priority accorded to patriotism by the ordinary worker *vis-à-vis* the struggle to advance their own lives and working conditions was the immediate industrial truce which came into effect on 25 August 1914, and was formalised in the Treasury Agreement of March 1915.[66] The years preceding the war had been amongst the most tumultuous in British industrial history, yet no sooner had the great Triple Industrial Alliance of railwaymen, miners, and transport workers – representing some of the most militant groups of the three decades leading up to the war –been formed than it voluntarily shackled itself for the duration of the conflict. As DeGroot has observed: 'The trade unions immediately surrendered their most effective weapon – the strike – without extracting anything significant in return. The only conceivable explanation for this cooperation is simple patriotism, strengthened by a conviction that a thankful government would reward the workers when peace returned.'[67] The majority of trade unionists saw absolutely nothing incompatible between their political beliefs and their patriotism; indeed, very often the two worked together. An example of the intersection of patriotism and self-interest can be found in the formation in March 1915 of the Liverpool Dock Battalion. This formation consisted of trade unionists willing to submit themselves to organisation along military lines in exchange for a guaranteed minimum of 35s. per week and the promise from Lord Derby that 'the force will adhere strictly to Trade Union rules and under no circumstances will be used as a strike breaking battalion'.[68] While this may not have been possible in more militant areas such as the Clyde or the Tyne, it illustrates how many workers were willing to make temporary

---

[64] M. Middlebrook, *The First Day on the Somme*, London: Allen Lane, 1975, 20.

[65] D. Phillips, 'Dai bach Y Soldiwr', 104.

[66] J. Hinton, *The First Shop Stewards' Movement*, London: Allen and Unwin, 1973, 50.

[67] DeGroot, *Blighty*, 110.

[68] K. Grieves, 'The Liverpool Dock Battalion: Military Intervention in the Mersey Docks, 1915–1918', *Transaction of the Historical Society of Lancashire and Cheshire* 131 (1982): 148.

sacrifices in terms of their power to strike for reasons of patriotism and material gain, and the battalion was vastly oversubscribed.

By 14 August 1914 it was estimated that fifteen thousand postmen had left for the services,[69] and by January 1915 *The Post* calculated that fifteen thousand gasworkers and general labourers, thirty thousand Durham miners, and 1,434 postal sorters of the Fawcett Association had enlisted.[70] By mid-1915 around 230,000 miners had volunteered nationwide.[71] In addition to organised workers in regular employment, casual labour also streamed forward to enlist, with John Ward of the Navvies' Union raising four battalions; in Birmingham alone it was thought that one thousand navvies had joined up: 'I often feel proud to know that I am an old navvy's son', claimed one, 'because I know that there is not another class who have answered the call to the flag for home and beauty as our navvies have done.'[72] Similarly, in Merseyside, as many as eight thousand dockers, the majority of whom were members of the Dockers' Union, joined the army between August 1914 and March 1915. Given that so many of their members joined up, some trade unions immediately decided that they would not be eligible to pay subscriptions during their time with the colours.[73]

Alan Howkins has discussed the relatively low number of recruits from agriculture, for many of whom it was 'business as usual', and reckoned that only a tenth of farmworkers – still around 123,000 – had enlisted by 1916.[74] Howkins argues that paternalism was important in rural recruitment, that economic motives were clearly very important for some, and that enlistment rates fell when trade picked up. Yet he ultimately concludes that 'for most countrymen who joined the New Armies it is clear that a vague sense of patriotism, personal or collective, was the overwhelming reason for taking the shilling'.[75] Nick Mansfield has recalled how a parochial language specific to each locality was utilised to encourage rural farmworkers to enlist: Newmarket men were warned of the spectre of 'Uhlans riding down the High Street', and soon enough Rolls of Honour detailing the patriotism of each village were compiled.[76] Labour pacifism was virtually

---

[69] *The Post*, 14 August 1914; *Co-Partners' Magazine*, March 1916.

[70] *The Post*, 29 January 1915.

[71] R. Holmes, *Tommy: The British Soldier on the Western Front 1914–1918*, London: Harper Perennial, 2005, 149.

[72] D. Sullivan, *Navvyman*, London: Coracle, 1983.

[73] See the *Railway Review*, 21 August 1914.

[74] A. Howkins, *Reshaping Rural England: A Social History 1850–1925*, London: Routledge, 1991, 256.

[75] Ibid., 258.

[76] N. Mansfield, *English Farmworkers and Local Patriotism, 1900–1930*, Aldershot: Ashgate, 2001, 97–98.

unknown in the countryside, and in Norfolk the recruits consisted mainly of the labouring poor, many of whom had been involved with NALRU.[77]

Although there was a neutralist minority within NALRU, like the Workers' Union, which also organised agricultural workers, it 'behaved splendidly' in terms of recruitment.[78] 'In the absence of a lead from farmers', wrote Mansfield, the union 'assumed the mantle of patriotism, thereby legitimising their own activities, which had previously been regarded as unacceptable'.[79] Mansfield concurs with J.G. Fuller in arguing that while local and county loyalty was an important aid to recruitment – many men were moved more by exhortations to fight for their family, their village, or for Norfolk than by abstract appeals to king and country – military service was to have a 'nationalising' effect on men who served with the forces, broadening their horizons and bringing new issues to their attention.[80]

The Engineers, later to acquire a reputation for using their position to avoid conscription and workshop fractiousness, were at first no less committed to the conflict than the rest of the union movement. A letter in the *Monthly Journal* of the Amalgamated Society of Engineers (ASE) from February 1915 attempted to surmise the moral justifications for the war: 'Let us stand to our guns, my brothers, without flinching, and then we will retain our glorious freedom, relieve hundreds of millions from a vile military despotism, and our Sunday dinner of English beef, instead of German polony'.[81] The substitution of 'English' for British – particularly careless given the number of ASE men in Scotland, Wales, and Ireland – was commonplace at this time. If it usually elicited an angry response from members elsewhere in the British Isles, it was not reflected in the correspondence pages. Later in the war the editor of the ASE journal, eager to dispel rumours of engineers dodging military service, noted that since late 1916 large numbers of ASE men had voluntarily enlisted, and that the union leadership had come to an agreement with the government for combing out skilled men for the mechanical corps of the army.[82] In *Armies of Freemen*, Tom Wintringham paid tribute to the ASE men who piloted the tanks in the last years of the war:

---

[77] Ibid., 101.

[78] Ibid., 113.

[79] Ibid., 113.

[80] Ibid., 117.

[81] ASE, *Monthly Journal and Report*, February 1915. There was a long tradition of radical patriots using food to distinguish themselves from continental Europeans. Hugh Cunningham has highlighted an early nineteenth-century poem: 'But for liberty, roast beef, plum pudding and beauty / Everyone to their liking – Old England for me!' See H. Cunningham, 'The Language of Patriotism, 1750–1914', *History Workshop Journal* 12 (1981): 11.

[82] ASE, *Monthly Journal and Report*, March 1917.

A high proportion of the officers were rankers, but not just any sort of ranker. Skilled engineers to the last finger-nail, men who had come out of the shipyards and fitting-shops in the middle years of the war, they had taken to the new mechanical soldiering the minute it offered [*sic*]. With the matehood of the lathe and bench and the union branch in them, regarding a man as worthy or unworthy according as he turned out his job of work, watching for weakness or inefficiency with eyes trained to the micrometer, riding to death-tests with their men in their early 'suicide-club' machines.[83]

Other soldiers often thought they were Australians, such was their egalitarianism. 'They came from Birmingham and Liverpool and Sheffield', wrote Wintringham, 'from the big centres of the engineering industry and the engineering unions, and they didn't care a damn for anyone.'[84]

One of the more nuanced analyses of the war came from the editor of the *Boilermakers' Reports*. The Boilermakers professed a loyalty to the country that did not extend to the elites who ran the country; nor was there any animus towards ordinary German troops. Sounding an optimistic note due to near-full employment and the rude health of the union, the editorial of December 1914 proclaimed:

> Our strength is in the loyalty of our members. When the call came for volunteers our members responded in such numbers that special posters had to be printed by the Admiralty to persuade our members on warship construction and other munitions of war that their duty lay at home … in volunteering for the front most of our members have exchanged good paying work for a soldier's pittance, and have thus given the best of all proofs that the getting of money is not their first consideration.[85]

The union's patriotic credentials were further extolled at the beginning of 1915:

> With the present demand for labour there should come, according to the economists, a demand for higher wages, but our members' loyalty is such that, having the means of a very moderate subsistence, they devote their attention to the creation of records in putting warships quickly into commission. If there is any such loyalty amongst employers or financiers it has not so far been in evidence.[86]

The war confirmed and deepened suspicion and resentment of the ruling

---

[83] T. Wintringham, *Armies of Freemen*, London: Labour Book Club, 1940, 126.
[84] Ibid., 126–27.
[85] *Boilermaker's Reports*, January 1915.
[86] Ibid.

elite among most on the Left, and made them all the more determined to change the existing order once the guns fell silent.

Even Robert Smillie, the Scottish miners' leader and pacifist, called in July 1915 for 'every effort [to be made] by the owners and workmen alike, to secure the greatest possible output of coal in the interest of the nation during the period of the war'. After criticising exaggerated reports of workers' 'shirking' in the right-wing press, Smillie admitted: 'it is clearly proved, and admitted to on our side, that there is a considerable amount of absenteeism which is not caused by illness or accident, but might be prevented, and ought to be prevented in the present crisis'. After noting that mining was not only dangerous but also laborious and uncomfortable, he continued:

> But I believe it is my duty as President of the Miners' Federation, as a miner myself, and as a man who has done some work in connection with the organizing of our people – organizing them to fight the employers, mark you; do not let there be any mistake about it, and if necessary to fight the Government under certain conditions – I say it is my duty to appeal to our people that in this national crisis every miner should be at the pit every day that the pit is open, if he is physically able to be there at all.

Miners' leader and MP for Wigan Stephen Walsh concurred:

> I think there never was a meeting in the whole history of trade unionism such as the meeting that has taken place in this hall to-day ... I am convinced that it is not possible to find in the whole length and breadth of the United Kingdom a body of people more imbued with a sense of their high responsibility in this great national emergency than are the Miners' Federation of Great Britain.[87]

Anti-Germanism

On 11 October 1914 a manifesto was issued which placed the blame for the war squarely at the feet of the German Junkers; this was signed by most labour leaders, but Ramsay MacDonald remained conspicuous in his refusal to sign.[88] After the atrocities and military setbacks of the initial months of the conflict, anti-Germanism overpowered any pre-war internationalism; *The Co-operative News*, which had initially opposed the conflict, argued in February 1915 in favour of starving Germany into submission: 'We have to remember that we are fighting a nation of armed assassins, and all

[87] Working Class Movement Library (WCML), 'World War 1 Box 2'. Pamphlet: 'Coal and the War: National Conference of Representatives of the Mining Industry at the London Opera House, 29th July 1915'.

[88] C. Howard, 'Macdonald, Henderson and the Outbreak of War, 1914', *Historical Journal* 20 (1977): 887.

these things should be taken into consideration when we are discussing the question of the humbling of Germany by the process of economic starvation.'[89] Speaking at the Co-Partnership Committee of London Gas and Electric Light Company in December 1915, Will Crooks gave an impassioned plea for British perseverance in the conflict: 'I do not call this a capitalists' war: I do not call it a Government war. By the living God that created me I believe it is a people's war for the liberty and virtue of our own homes.'[90] As the intractable nature of the conflict and the huge amount of men and money that would be required to prosecute it became more apparent, spirits became bleaker but resolves hardened. Writing in April 1915, Blatchford was unequivocal about the weight of the issues at stake and the place of the conflict in history:

> This is not a political war. It is not a war caused inadvertently by the blunders of secret diplomacy. It is not a financiers' war, a war preventable by soft words or delicate expostulations. It is not a war comparable to any other war of which we have knowledge. It is a vast and frightful racial earthquake. It has shaken civilisation to its foundations ... These Huns are not only the enemies of France, of Britain, of Russia, of Belgium; they are the enemies of humanity.[91]

The sentiments of Havelock Wilson will have been shared by many on the British Left. Although he ended the war as fearsome and committed a jingo as any, Wilson had not always been so inclined. Although incorrigibly racist – he had led a campaign against Lascar sailors serving on British merchant ships – he, like many on the British Left, had interacted with German Socialists before the war in a context of friendship and solidarity. He thus felt somewhat disillusioned by the apparent connivance of the German Left in atrocities committed by that country, specifically the U-boat campaign against merchant shipping which resulted in the deaths of non-combatants from neutral countries. In a letter to Hermann Jochade, the Secretary of the International Transport Workers Federation in Berlin, he claimed that:

> My object in writing is to call to the attention of the Central Committee of the International Transport Workers in Berlin the ruthless murders that have occurred on the high seas to peaceful British merchant seamen, who are members of the National Sailors' and Firemen's Union, and incidentally members of the International Transport Workers Federation ... For over 18 months British merchant seamen have been done to death in the most cruel and wicked manner.

---

[89] *The Co-operative News*, 27 February 1915.
[90] As recorded in the *Co-Partners' Magazine*, December 1915.
[91] *The Clarion*, 16 April 1915.

Although he conceded that German workers did not have the same freedom to influence their government as their British equivalents, he noted that the German Social Democratic Party was able to secure some four million votes, held a majority in the Reichstag, and therefore must have had some influence over the German government: 'It is, therefore, difficult for me to come to any other conclusion than that some responsibility for what has happened rests with the Central Committee of the International Federation.' While his union had provided for interned German seamen who were members during the war, the 'treatment of the British seamen interned in German camps has been <u>disgraceful</u>'. 'As a result of the deliberate murders that have been committed at sea on merchant seamen and the scandalous treatment accorded to our prisoners in Germany a very bitter feeling has been created in this country against the German workmen, which, if I may judge aright, will remain for many years.' This bitterness had been further exacerbated by the execution in July 1916 of Captain Charles, a Merchant Navy captain alleged to have attempted to ram a German U-boat the previous year. After his capture he was court-martialled and sentenced to death despite being a civilian non-combatant, which caused widespread outrage. Wilson concluded that while the German working men may have had no influence, it would be very difficult to convince the British working man of this, especially the British seaman.[92]

An indication of the extent to which the British working class – and the working-class Left – quickly became staunchly patriotic and anti-German is the vilification of supposed pacifists. While their words may have fallen on sympathetic ears in the days leading up to the war, as soon as Britain entered the conflict pacifists' viewpoints became treasonable and intolerable. Keir Hardie was 'howled down' at Aberdare on 6 August 1914, and this was in his own constituency of Merthyr Tydfil, emphatically not a working-class Tory stronghold.[93] Further, on 20 October 1914 miners at Lewis Merthyr Lodge walked out, and stayed out, until a Mr Sholback – a German head electrician – was dismissed.[94] Perhaps the most vivid example of the anti-pacifism which gripped the British working class and much of the British Left during the early years of the war is the result of the by-election in Merthyr triggered by the sudden death of Hardie in September 1915. The official Labour candidate, James Winstone, a Baptist lay minister, was no pacifist: he had presided over recruiting meetings and his own son was at the

[92] MRC, MSS.159/3/B/78 – Havelock Wilson Papers. Letter from Wilson to Jochade, 15 August 1916.

[93] Wilson, *Myriad Faces of War*, 155.

[94] C. Pennell, *A Kingdom United: Popular Responses to the Outbreak of the First World War in Britain and Ireland*, Oxford: Oxford University Press, 2012, 100.

front. Yet he was so damaged by the support of well-known (and temporarily despised) anti-war figures such as Ramsay MacDonald and Fred Jowett that Charles Stanton, the 'patriotic labour' candidate, was able to take the seat. Stanton was no Tory stooge – he has been described by Gwyn Williams as 'literally a pistol-packing syndicalist' at one point.[95] In an article entitled 'Keir Hardie's Successor' in the *Bradford Pioneer*, T. Russell Williams argued that Stanton owed his victory to being a local man (Winstone was from Monmouthshire) and praised him as 'one of the greatest fighters that ever went onto a political or industrial battlefield', noting that he had taken the side of his own Aberdare men against the South Wales Miners' Federation over unofficial strike actions, and could have been the candidate for Merthyr in 1900, but chose to stand aside for Hardie.[96]

This victory of the 'patriotic' candidate over the official nominee perfectly encapsulates the strength of nationalistic sentiment amongst the grassroots of the British Left at this time, and this was in Merthyr, in the famously militant industrial heartlands of South Wales.[97] Similarly, at a by-election held in North Ayrshire in October 1916, only two candidates stood: the Reverend Chelmers, a pacifist and opponent of the war, and Lieutenant-General Hunter-Watson, leader of VIII Corps on the Somme. The General received 7,419 votes; the Reverend only 1,300. In the same year, Noel Pemberton Billing won Hereford on an air defence programme and patriotic labour stalwart Ben Tillett was finally elected to the Commons for North Salford in 1917 on a decidedly pro-war campaign.[98] This electoral trend was to continue into the 'khaki election' at the end of the war, when all the notable anti-war figures on the Left such as MacDonald and Philip Snowden – in addition to men who had been instrumental to the war effort such as Arthur Henderson – lost their seats. While MacDonald and Snowden were deliberately targeted by labour patriots and Conservatives, Henderson had only resigned from the war cabinet a year earlier, and so his defeat by National Democratic Party member Clem Edwards in East Ham South was particularly surprising, yet labour leaders who failed to retain the 'Coupon' fared poorly across the board.

Almost immediately the ILP – associated fairly or otherwise with pro-Germanism – came under attack from editorials in patriotic journals

[95] G.A. Williams, *When Was Wales?*, London: Penguin, 1985, 244.

[96] *Bradford Pioneer*, 5 November 1915.

[97] See B. Doyle, 'Who Paid the Price of Patriotism? The Funding of Charles Stanton during the Merthyr Boroughs By-Election of 1915', *The English Historical Review* 109 (1994): 12–17.

[98] J. Lawrence, 'The Transformation of British Public Politics after the First World War', *Past & Present* 190 (2006): 194.

such as the *Railway Review*. The anti-war Left was painted as being blinded to the realities of the world through an obsession with abstractions: 'We differ from the doctrinaire Socialists now', wrote Alex Thompson in *The Clarion*:

> As we have always done, in insisting that peace cannot be established on the pretentious multiloquence, Pleasant Sunday Afternoon fuddles, and ready-made reach-me-down comradeship, whose canting unreality and manifest incompetence have done so much to discredit and ridicule the virile creed of Socialism. Where we have differed from the lollipop Socialist is not in loving peace less than they, but in loving it more practically; not in hating war less than they, but in realizing its approach and striving to prevent it.[99]

This hostility towards 'pacifism' lasted some time: at the 1915 TUC only two delegates voted against the Labour Party's continued involvement in recruitment, and seventeen voted for a settled peace with Germany. Furthermore, 'the [pacifistic] Union for Democratic Control resolutions in respect to peace terms were laughed out of court'.[100] Nor was this sentiment confined to the elites of the unions. Trevor Wilson has recounted how, at a munitions factory in June 1917, fifty tool setters and labourers threatened to strike after a conscientious objector was promoted to foreman – the matter was only resolved when the offending workman was sacked.[101]

If the invasion of Belgium had provided the catalyst for British left-wing opinion (and, indeed, the opinion of the country as a whole) to move behind intervention, the development of a visceral hatred of Germany and all things German helped to mobilise opinion for the continuance of the war and a fight to the finish. David Silbey has recounted how one individual wanted to enlist simply to 'hammer the Kaiser'; he did not express any positive reasons for wanting to fight for his own country, he merely wanted to fight *against* Germany, and in particular against the personage of Wilhelm II, who had come to represent everything he despised in the world.[102] Similarly, Ruth Armstrong of Tilshead recalled after the war how 'My mother used to say that if he, the Kaiser, was to come over here and take England, "I would kill you all and kill myself. I won't live under Germany."'[103]

---

[99] *The Clarion*, 22 January 1915.

[100] *Railway Review*, 17 September 1915.

[101] Wilson, *Myriad Faces of War*, 522.

[102] D. Silbey, *The British Working Class and Enthusiasm for War, 1914–1916*, London: Frank Cass, 2005, 8.

[103] Quoted in R. van Emden and S. Humphries, *All Quiet on the Home Front*, London: Headline, 2003, 158. William Gillman, in his IWM interview, noted that he and his friends considered the Kaiser very much 'the villain of the piece'. See Imperial War Museum Interviews, Catalogue No. 9420, William Gillman, interviewed 1986.

Arthur Henderson captured this spirit in a speech at Easter 1918, when he claimed that 'by their offensive, the Kaiser and the war lords had drawn the British people together in a consecrated and determined effort to secure the destruction of militarism'.[104] Similarly, attacks from sea and air on the British mainland were to relegate any thoughts of peace and internationalist sentiment in the minds of Britons. As Gregory has argued: 'Destroying architectural treasures, burning homes and killing civilians in Belgium was clearly reprehensible, but destroying homes and killing men, women and children in *Britain* was far worse for [people] to contemplate.' A co-operative warehouse in Scarborough was hit by a German shell and *The Co-operative News* published a picture of the damaged building in the aftermath. The sinking of the *Lusitania* and attacks on Scarborough, Hartlepool, and London were to cement the Germans as malevolent foes in the minds of British workers far more vividly than the crude and hysterical propaganda in *John Bull* and the *Daily Mail*.

Labour Heroes

Labour movement activists fighting in the trenches were keen that their patriotism and sacrifice not be misused and that the men and women who remained at home continued to uphold the cause. Said one co-operator serving on the Western Front: 'I'm proud to be serving under the British flag, and I hope that dad is keeping the cooperative flag flying till I come back.'[105] *The Post* of July 1915 carried a photograph of a Post Office Maxim Gun section, 8th (Post Office Rifles) Battalion, City of London Regiment, but the editorial of the same edition reiterated the belief that the 'class war' had merely been postponed, and that the movement's members must remain vigilant and prepared to resume the fight at a moment's notice.[106]

The Clarion of 20 August 1915 contained a letter from John Costello, a soldier fighting at the front:

> [Receiving *The Clarion*] will cheer a few mates with whom I have come into contact, and who are, according to themselves, advanced Socialists. Many a rough time they give me as I am only an I.L.P., whereas they are S.D.P. men. However, it is war we are on now, so we sink our differences till some future time, when we will settle the matter at some street-corner meeting. But we have to settle Kaiser Bill first, then we will tackle the economic question.[107]

---

[104] Quoted in Wilson, *The Myriad Faces of War*, 633.

[105] *The Co-operative News*, 5 December 1914.

[106] *The Post*, 16 July 1915.

[107] Letter from John Costello, *The Clarion*, 20 August 1915.

Figure 1. 'Post Office Maxim Gun Section, 8th City of London Regiment,
British Expeditionary Force.' *The Post* 16 July 1915.
Photo with permission of Labour History Archive and Study Centre,
People's History Museum.

While Bernard Stevenson wrote in January 1916:

> We are only a small draft, attached to a mixed unit, doing digging and
> other indispensable work behind the growing British fighting force, but I
> know of two or three convinced Socialists within our number. One with
> whom I have often shared a bed in hutment camps was formerly secretary
> of the junior section of the I.L.P. in Nottingham, and while I mention
> these initials let me say how proud and thankful we all are of the victory
> of **sane Socialism** at Merthyr Tydfil. Men and lads of all classes, trades,
> and occupations mix here on terms of perfect equality.[108]

Another letter of encouragement typified the response from working-class
labour activists serving with the colours: 'Good old Clarion staff, – Go on!
You are fighting for the truth. It is hard, but worth it. Your teaching taught
me my duty, and I am fighting in my tin pot way for the five kiddies I left
behind me. If I go West, I go as a Socialist, not as a "Sloshialist". Good luck!
You will never die.'[109] Another indication from the newspapers themselves

---

[108] Letter from Bernard Stevenson, *The Clarion*, 7 January 1916.
[109] Letter from S. Clapperton, Royal Engineers, *The Clarion*, 29 October 1915.

as to the views of their readership is the advertisements placed in them. It was – and is – even more crucial for advertisers than editors to accurately gauge the opinions of the readership, and the adverts placed in labour papers during this period leave no doubt that companies felt that readers were patriotic and that patriotism sold.[110] Products such as clothes, boots, food, and drink all stressed their British origins and were often accompanied by photographs of bulldogs and lions.

We have seen how hundreds of thousands of trade unionists served in the military or worked in the munitions factories during the war; some served with distinction and offer clear examples of how a vigorous commitment to the war effort did not involve a compromise of principles. One of the most famous *Entente* air aces of the war, Edward 'Mick' Mannock, was a committed socialist and the secretary of his local Labour Party, but this did not prevent him from shooting Germans out of the sky in record numbers. According to his biographers, he would hold mock Parliaments: 'When the parliament was in full session the words came hot and strong. His speeches were based on the platform of Socialism, and so eloquently did he lambaste Tory members that the uproar attracted the attention of passing officers.' Yet 'it did not take long for him to reject the idea of ministering to wounded Germans. The only good one, he told himself, was a very dead one. There was no niche for a cosy-minded humanist when it came to fighting the Hun.'[111]

Soon enough notices of the death or wounding of working-class activists and trade unionists began to appear in the press. Private Jones of the Bedford Regiment fought in five large engagements in the autumn and winter of 1914, including twelve bayonet charges, until being wounded in the head and neck. His comrades said of him: 'He was a very active and loyal member of the [Manchester No. 4] branch [of the NUR], and if he proves as good a soldier as he was a Trade Unionist the Germans will not land in England yet. We are proud of our comrade and wish him God speed and a safe and glorious return to his country, wife and children.'[112] A letter in *The Clarion* of November 1915 told of the death of another activist with the colours: 'Clarionettes in South London will be grieved to learn that our dear comrade Jack Reed has been killed in action. His genial kindness and serenity endeared him to all, and there are some who knew

---

[110] A point made in D. Clampin, '"The War has Turned Our Lives Upside-Down": The Merit of Commercial Advertising in Documenting the Cultural History of the British Home Front in the Second World War', *Visual Resources* 24 (2008): 145–58.

[111] F. Oughton and V. Smyth, *Mannock, VC: Ace with One Eye: the Life and Combats of Maj. Edward Mannock, VC*, London: Frederick Muller, 1963, 63.

[112] *Railway Review*, 29 January 1915.

him intimately who will learn of his death with a dreadful pang. We loved old Jack.'[113] A further missive of August 1916 lamented: 'My only chum is gone: "Alec," as he was affectionately known in the old West London Fellowship, is on the Roll of Honour ... Once – how incredibly long ago it seems – he stood up manfully against a special meeting of the branch and defended his position as a Socialist and a Territorial. To think that in those days some of us considered the two things incompatible!'[114] Nor was it only working-class men of the Left who volunteered to fight; in March 1916, 'For the seventh time on account of the war the flag at Ruskin school is at half-mast'; Frank Southgate, the art master, had become the latest of the Ruskin faculty killed in action.[115]

An edition of the *Railway Review* of June 1917 told the story of Sergeant Harry Cator, a member of the Yarmouth branch of the NUR and a Lewis gunner in the East Surrey Regiment, who had been awarded the Victoria Cross.[116] Meanwhile, two NUR men had won the Military Medal: W.H. Binge, one time secretary of the South Eastern District Council and Hither Green branch, and A. Lodge, member of the Manchester No. 5 branch and formerly a carter of the Lancashire and Yorkshire railway.[117] Sergeant H.J. Sheppard, formerly Secretary of the Barry Socialist Society, was awarded the DCM in November 1916.[118] The journal of the ASE reported in January 1917 that Sergeant A. Warham of Crewe No. 4 Branch and the Royal Engineers had been given the Military Medal; while from the same regiment Lance-Corporal James Coupe of Barrow Fifth Branch was mentioned in dispatches and presented with the French Medaille Militaire.[119] In January 1918 the engineer Harry Coverdale – a sergeant in the Manchester Regiment who had enlisted in September 1914 – was awarded a Victoria Cross to complement the Military Medal he had won earlier in the war.[120] A Glaswegian ASE member and lance corporal in the Royal Scots' Fusiliers won the DCM; as did Sergeant Major John Broderick (of Jarrow No. 3 Branch), for carrying a wounded officer to safety on his back whilst under heavy fire near Armentieres on 9 December 1915; and the following year Joseph Wilson, a riveter of Hebburn No. 2 Branch was another ASE man honoured with the DCM. Corporal C. Andrews, a stretcher-bearer of London No. 11 Branch and the Royal West Kent was also

---

113 Letter from Jack Wilmot, *The Clarion*, 5 November 1915.
114 Letter from W.G.N., *The Clarion*, August 1916.
115 Ibid., 17 March 1916. Ruskin was a socialist school in Norfolk.
116 Ibid., 15 June 1917.
117 Ibid., 8 June 1917.
118 Ibid., 10 November 1916.
119 ASE, *Monthly Journal and Report*, January 1917.
120 Ibid., January 1918.

garlanded with the Belgian Croix de Guerre to complement his DCM.[121] The Military Medal was awarded to Private W.C. Orr of South Shields No. 1, Jack Naden of Sunderland, Joseph Vaughan of Gateshead, and Joshua Horsley of Hartlepool.[122] The final year of the war saw Corporal Ernest Goulding of the 7th Lincolns and Lincoln No. 1 Branch, who had enlisted in August 1914, awarded the Military Medal for conspicuous conduct and gallantry in bombing a pillbox.[123]

A notice in *The Co-operative News* of April 1915 proudly proclaimed that the son of a co-operator had been awarded the Victoria Cross. Lance Corporal Fuller of the 1st Battalion, Grenadier Guards, captured fifty German soldiers single-handedly at Neuve-Chapelle. His delighted father, a member of the Mansfield and Sutton society, 'was in the central shop yesterday telling us all about it', according to the latter's manager.[124] By June 1915 fifteen Co-operative Wholesale Society workers had been killed, the last falling at La Bassée: Lance Corporal M'Conville, of the City of Liverpool society, who was a former president of the Liverpool branch of the Postmen's Federation, a member of the Edge Hill ILP, and an unsuccessful candidate in the 1913 municipal elections.[125] In November 1916 *The Co-operative News* boasted of the first 'Co-Operative V.C.'. Sergeant William Ewart Boulter – whose very name gives the lie to any easy polarity between leftist political beliefs and patriotic conviction – came from a family of old co-operators, worked in a shop of the Kettering society, and enlisted during the first few weeks of the war. According to a gushing report in the *News*: 'His response to the call to arms was not so much a headstrong desire for adventure as a serious answer to patriotic duty. Once in the Army, the same eager spirit which had carried him forward in his work as a co-operative employee very soon carried him to the sergeant's mess.'[126]

The issue of war badges serves as another demonstration of the average worker's concern to appear patriotic. For example, one correspondent to the *Railway Review* of May 1915 inquired: 'In many of the munition factories the men have been supplied with these badges; then why have not the railwaymen been supplied with them? We have been stopped from enlisting, and told we are doing just as much to help our country by sticking to our jobs. If this is so, I think we deserve to have such a small form of recognition

---

[121] *Boilermakers' Reports*, April 1918.
[122] Ibid., March and May 1917.
[123] Ibid., May 1918.
[124] *The Co-operative News*, 24 April 1915.
[125] Ibid., 12 June 1915.
[126] Ibid., 11 November 1916.

extended to us.'[127] Meanwhile a column in the same newspaper from October of that year complained:

> It has been mentioned in these columns that war badges are indiscriminately distributed to all and sundry employed in railway shops, without regard to age or ability to serve in H.M. Forces, and it certainly does seem unnecessary and incongruous that greybeards should be seen proudly disporting themselves in this decoration, and thus claiming immunity from the blandishments of the recruiting sergeants.[128]

Furthermore, a leaflet circulated in 1915 by the WNC explained how any man who had attested under the Derby Scheme but not yet been called up could 'show his friends that he is a soldier' through an armlet marked with the Royal Crown.[129] Many of these survive to this day, and there are several in the collections of the People's History Museum, Manchester.

Above all, it was felt imperative not to be seen as a 'shirker'; on 27 August George Wardle, Henderson, George Roberts, William Mosses of the Patternmakers, James Brownlie of the Engineers, and Frank Smith of the Cabinet Makers visited France and Belgium, and upon their return assured the workers that:

> It is upon them, as well as upon the men at the front, that the responsibility for procuring victory rests. The lives of our own kith and kin, the desolated homes, the devastated villages, the ruined towns cry aloud for a supreme effort to end quickly this horrible nightmare, and the way to end it is to speed up the supply both of guns and ammunition, until the invader has been driven from his trenches and chased across the Rhine.[130]

Writing from the front to *Co-Partner's Magazine*, a correspondent identifies as 'F.C.B.' claimed:

> I would rather risk it all again than be a slacker. I rejoice to think that I am not that. We are at present resting in a dear little village; as I write I am sitting in a comfortable room, with a full belly and a nice cigar; and if it was not for the thoughts of my dear old pals we have left behind I would be perfectly happy. I understand some of the boys of East Ham are knocking things about. It would be better for everyone if they came out here. If I had a brother, and he was a slacker, I would never speak to him again.[131]

There was a widespread hostility towards those suspected of not pulling their weight: David Langrish has claimed that the Middlesex Appeals Tribunal

---

[127] Letter from G. White, *Railway Review*, 7 May 1915.
[128] *Railway Review*, 22 October 1915.
[129] LHASC, WNC.8/8/8/24: The Group System. Questions and Answers.
[130] *Railway Review*, 10 September 1915.
[131] *Co-Partners' Magazine*, July 1915.

received unsolicited letters from people accusing their neighbours of shirking and demanding that they not be exempted.[132]

Will Crooks neatly captured this attitude in a speech he gave to the Co-Partnership Committee on 2 November 1915: 'To begin with I am known as Bill Crooks. I have never risen from the ranks; I remain in the ranks still, and I do not intend to get out of them, either. We will get to close quarters, and ask ourselves what this war has to do with us.' After ruminating on the travesties and inequities of Imperial Germany for some time, he continued:

> I do not expect men to do something for nothing. You work for all you can get; I am not going to deny that. But when I was in the trenches and at the base, where I saw hundreds of thousands – literally hundreds of thousands, and I know what I am saying – of your brothers, of your sons, and of your nephews, we talked about things at home. Some of the men think about home and how they are doing at home, as this little story will illustrate. On the last night I told them: 'I attended a school where the little children are who give you the greatest anguish given to anyone – the physically deficient; and I said: "Now I am going to see your daddies and your big brothers; shan't I tell them something from you?" And one little piping voice said "Tell them, Mr Crooks, we can sing *God Save the King* as good as they can."' Tommy cheered it to the echo; it brought him home … They are our people. You are working and toiling, sometimes too hard, and you want to lose a quarter, and you want to lose half a day. I know you are working for wages, you are working for your daily bread – but there is sometimes a little more to be done – another turn for love.

Crooks then rhetorically asked what he had done that a wounded soldier, who had been left out for four days, should shed blood for him:

> Work too hard? Sugar too dear? Tea too much? Taxes too high? … The war is no business of us working folk? I do not want to test it beyond saying that I do not call this a capitalists' war: I do not call it a Government war. By the living God that created me I believe it is a people's war for the liberty and virtue of our own homes.[133]

This chapter has attempted to assess the nature and extent of left-wing support for the First World War. It has concurred with Adrian Gregory and others in arguing that – as with the British population generally – there was no enthusiasm amongst the Left for the war, and the weeks and days before the outbreak saw attempts to prevent the conflict. This lack of desire for bloodshed did not, however, preclude left-wing patriotism after

---

[132] D. Langrish, 'Conscription, Tribunals and Sacrifice: The papers of the Middlesex Service Appeals Tribunal', paper given at 'Labour and the First World War' Conference at Anglia Ruskin University, 3 May 2014.

[133] *Co-Partners' Magazine*, December 1915.

August 1914, committed support for the war effort, and occasionally virulent anti-Germanism. The vast majority of the Edwardian Left – trade unions, socialist societies, the PLP, the Co-operative movement, and women's groups – supported their country's participation in the First World War, conditionally but faithfully, for the duration of the conflict. There was no demand for war from the labour movement; quite the opposite. There was a great deal of criticism of the institutional and ideological factors which had precipitated the conflict, but once Britain was involved there was no question that the war effort should be supported. It is a tragedy of all wars that, the more lives are lost and resources squandered, the greater the need for the conflict to be prosecuted to an absolute victory, to vindicate the sacrifices made. So it was with the Left and the First World War: the deprivations and setbacks only strengthened the resolve that the war must not be lost and that Britain must be different after the war.

In the next chapter we will turn to anti-war agitation and resistance of the state. This includes the anti-war minority within the Left, the debates surrounding military and industrial conscription, the nature of wartime strikes, and the apparent 'pacifistic turn' of 1917. It will argue that whilst the anti-war agitation played an important role in adhering certain elements of the Left to the post-war labour movement, and was highly significant for the post-war development of the party at a national level, the anti-war group was always an isolated minority, especially during the most perilous times when the outcome of the war seemed to hang in the balance.

3

'Middle-class peace men?'
– Labour and the Anti-War Agitation

Whilst the mainstream of the labour movement supported the war effort throughout the four years of the First World War, this narrative is qualified by acute episodes of resistance to the state and battles against wartime deprivations. Further, especially in the final two years of the war, a radical anti-war movement began to gain momentum and, whilst remaining a minority within the Left as a whole, developed an internationalist and pacifistic ideology which would largely be adopted by Labour in the 1920s. This chapter will examine opposition to the war from the Left. It will first discuss the issue of conscription in 1915–16, the periodic strikes that threatened to cripple industries during the war, the soldiers' strikes and mutinies after the Armistice, the anti-war movement and centres of supposed resistance to the patriotism of the war years, and finally the Leeds and Stockholm conferences of 1917, which seemed to herald a break from the government line and a demand for an early peace settlement.

Conscription, 1916–18

Contrary to the qualified support for the war effort across most of the labour movement, on the issue of conscription there was near unanimous opposition. This owed as much to traditional British opposition to 'militarism' and the constraint of individual liberties as it did to a tremendous and genuinely held fear that conscription might be used to curb hard-won trade union rights. In August 1915 the General Federation of Trade Unions declared that virtually every trades council in the land had issued resolutions against conscription, and a unanimous resolution was passed against the measure at the Trades Union Congress (TUC) annual meeting of the following month.[1] In September 1915, Jimmy Thomas told the House of Commons

---

[1] *The Co-operative News*, 21 August 1915; *The Post*, 24 September 1915.

that the railways would strike if conscription were introduced,[2] and as late as January 1916 – when conscription was effectively a *fait accompli* – delegates representing 2,121,000 unionists voted against the measure at a special conference in Westminster.[3] The TUC of that year called on the Parliamentary Labour Party to 'lose no opportunity after the war to press for the repeal of all Acts of Parliament imposing economic, industrial, and military conscription upon the manhood of the nation'.[4]

Nor was opposition confined to the trade union movement. Outspoken Labour patriots such as Alex Thompson and Robert Blatchford argued against conscription in 1915, and editorials in *The Co-operative News*, though vigorous in their support of the war, held that conscription would be a dangerous and unnecessary step.[5] Labour patriots generally felt that while it was imperative for Britain to succeed in the conflict, success that came through conscription risked replicating the despised 'Prussianism' in Britain, which would tarnish any victory. An editorial in *The Post* of February 1916 claimed that the spectre of Prussianism and militarism at home posed an even greater threat than that of military defeat.[6] In an article entitled 'The Duty of Labour', Tom Quelch, son of Social Democratic Federation (SDF) founder Harry Quelch, explicitly compared the struggle against conscription in Britain to the conflict in the trenches:

> Not only must we – the organised workers – do our duty to our comrades who have gone to the front by providing them with everything which is likely to add to their comfort or lessen their peril, but we must also do our duty to those who are not in the Army or Navy but are doing equally necessary and in many cases, equally hazardous work at home. Take the conscription menace for example. We can well understand men, obsessed with the problems and dangers confronting our comrades in France and Flanders – especially if they have relatives (and who has not?) amongst those risking their lives in the trenches, being keen on seeing them receive as much support as possible, and on that account ready to lend a willing ear to the specious pleas of the conscriptionists. But that should not blind them to what conscription really means.[7]

Given the absolute and near unanimous nature of the objections to conscription, one might wonder how it was introduced without serious

---

[2] *The Co-operative News*, 25 September 1915.

[3] *The Post*, 28 January 1916.

[4] Report of the Forty-Eighth Annual Gathering of the Trades Union Congress.

[5] *The Clarion*, 8 January 1915 and 22 January 1915; *The Co-operative News*, 31 October 1914 and 5 June 1915.

[6] *The Post*, 11 February 1916.

[7] Ibid., 21 April 1916.

upheaval. As with jingoism and anti-German sentiment, the progress of the war itself served to change attitudes, as this letter to *The Co-operative News* indicates:

> I am an anti-militarist, and, ipso-facto, opposed to war. But many precon-ceived notions and cherished ideas have been shattered by this terrible war, not the least of which was the opinion held by hundreds of thousands that a great war was impossible. Now the seemingly impossible has happened, peace-lovers are in a quandary ... Much as I am opposed to militarism, I would prefer honest, straightforward conscription to the insidious private attempts to that end; I mean the prevalent practice of threatening discharge as an alternative to enlistment ... If the evil of conscription is necessary, then let us have it fairly and squarely, so that the youth of the upper classes are forced as much as the youth of the poorer. Let us hold the balance evenly. Finally, if conscription come (and it well may), we of the co-operative body, as well as all democrats, will have to be very vigilant lest we be enslaved by the militarists ... I sincerely hope that conscription will not be necessary; but every thoughtful person knows that if our military governors brought it forward as essential, it would pass at the present time.[8]

As with so much else, the war had transformed attitudes and ideas which were once the preserve of minorities into articles of faith for much of the population. An editorial in *The Co-operative News* of July 1916 noted: 'Before war was declared men who advocated conscription were almost hated. The tables have now been completely turned: the enemies of the country are those who actually oppose conscription, or who even calmly and coolly criticize it.'[9] Certainly there was a shift in public opinion in favour of compulsion; it was not something imposed on an unwilling population by an autocratic government. Will Thorne of the SDF (who had been advocating military service from a Marxist perspective for some time) noted this point when he argued at a meeting of the TUC that 'as there would have to be an election within six months of the end of the war, it would be the workers' own fault if they returned a Parliament pledged to conscription'.[10] On the issue of conscription, the mass of public opinion moved from opposition to support, and the British Left was forced to acknowledge this.

The main thrust of the conscriptionists' argument was that it was a military necessity. Labour patriots countered by claiming that there was no shortage of willing manpower, but rather a lack of efficient organisation and utilisation of resources at the highest levels of government. Those in favour of

[8] Letter from Frank Birch, *The Co-operative News*, 23 January 1915.
[9] Ibid., 1 July 1916.
[10] Ibid., 16 September 1916.

conscription had to persuade a reluctant public – and an especially reluctant Left – that compulsion was indeed absolutely necessary if Britain were to avoid defeat. In this respect the Derby Scheme – which requested civilian men of military age of to 'attest' their willingness to serve – was presented as a litmus test of the feasibility of voluntarism. In the words of one *Railway Review* editorial, it was 'the only effective way to defeat conscription'.[11] If not enough men were willing to attest, then compulsion would have to be introduced. This is reflected in the editorial of *The Co-operative News* concerning the Derby Scheme:

> We believe that Lord Derby could easily recruit the required men if but the whole of the Press would give him their loyal support. Lord Derby himself believes in conscription, but he is a patriot first and a conscriptionist afterwards. We warn our conscriptionist friends that if they do not follow the lead of Lord Derby, if they do not do all in their power to make this new recruiting campaign a success, and if conscription is resorted to as a result, that upon them will rest the responsibility of dangerously splitting the country at a time when it is vitally important that it should be united. We contemplate that possibility with utmost alarm. Conscription might provoke a general strike, it might lead to a social revolution, which would mean that our soldiers would be used to suppress riots in our own country, instead of being sent away to fight Germans.[12]

When the Derby Scheme failed to secure enough men, compulsion was proffered as the only available course of action; a pragmatic response to a real need which would neither outlast the war nor represent a sea-change in British culture or ideology. It was this argument that Percy Redfern, a correspondent with *The Co-operative News* and later a historian of the Co-operative movement, warned against: 'There is a belief, too, that this is a temporary measure of military necessity destined to end with the war … Conscription is not an ordinary political proposal. It is, even in its present limited form, a measure which marks a revolution in English political history.'[13] By this point the more zealous of the labour patriots had been converted. Writing in *The Clarion*, Alex Thompson argued that: 'We are all against Conscription. But necessity compels the temporary sacrifice of dogmas, as of other things. Wise men distinguish between that to which they aspire and that which immediate needs compel.'[14]

In addition to the argument of necessity, another compelling factor in favour of conscription was the idea that it would be a fairer system, resulting

[11] *Railway Review*, 26 November 1915.
[12] *The Co-operative News*, 23 October 1915.
[13] Letter from P. Redfern, Ibid., 29 January 1916.
[14] *The Clarion*, 21 April 1916.

in greater equality of sacrifice. While the upper and middle classes had actually volunteered for the military in proportionately greater numbers, there was a widespread feeling that certain sections of the population were holding back, and not being asked to sacrifice either their lives or their wealth. There are the old clichés regarding the 'British sense of fair play', but very little attention is paid to the reverse effect of this 'sense of fair play'; the idea that someone is not pulling their weight or contributing their fair share can send ordinarily tranquil people into apoplectic rage. (Adrian Gregory has described how 'The feeling that someone, somewhere, but of course never oneself, was failing to sacrifice adequately was becoming widespread by 1917.')[15] Trevor Griffiths relays an anecdote relating to the 1921 coal strike which neatly encapsulates this: 'Poor Law authorities in Wigan and Leigh advanced loans to miners' families. Following the settlement of the dispute, the Leigh guardians received a number of anonymous letters naming recipients of relief who were thought to be undeserving.'[16] No doubt community solidarity amongst unionised miners was high, but this mutuality could often reinforce the importance of shared commitment. The belief that everyone should pull their weight translated to military recruitment. As Bonnie White has noted in her analysis of recruitment in Devon, men justified staying at home by claiming that they would go 'when the farmers' sons go', 'when the Germans invade', or 'when compelled'.[17] Thus conscription was advanced as a means of ensuring that everyone contributed to the war effort. As a letter to *The Co-operative News* had it: 'By all means, let us introduce conscription; but let us make conscripts of those who have something to protect ... Let us be done with the current system of volunteering, where we have to cajole and threaten our manhood to enlist to fight our battles, while we allow those parasites – the landlords, shippers, &c – to stay at home'.[18] Similarly, a soldier serving at the front argued in his letter to *The Clarion:* 'I think [Blatchford] ought to advocate conscription. It would be the fairest way for everyone. There must be a lot of men who would be only too willing to join if they did not know that there are others who would hang back. When is our Government going to wake up?'[19]

Many trade unionists and Labour activists felt that 'shirking' from one's duty was comparable to betraying the labour cause; a railwayman writing to

---

[15] A. Gregory, *The Last Great War*, Cambridge: Cambridge University Press, 2009, 114.

[16] T. Griffiths, *The Lancashire Working Classes c.1880–1930*, Oxford: Clarendon Press, 2001, 209.

[17] B. White, 'Volunteerism and Early Recruitment Efforts in Devonshire, August 1914–December 1915', *The Historical Journal* 52 (2009): 649.

[18] *The Co-operative News*, 30 January 1915.

[19] Letter from 'Harry', *The Clarion*, 28 May 1915.

The Clarion claimed that he 'would sooner blackleg my union than blackleg my country'.[20] These sentiments were related by the 'Special Commissioner' of *The Co-operative News*. Writing in an article entitled 'Our National Duty. Can we save ourselves from military or industrial conscription? Probably our last chance', he related how:

> I met [a soldier] in Liverpool the other week, who had been wounded in Flanders, and was expecting to be sent back in the course of a day or two. 'I should go back more willingly', he said, 'if I thought everybody else was doing his duty. It hurts us soldiers, after what we've seen out yon, and what we know is to be done, to see your streets still filled with young men who could be doing something!'[21]

After the passage of the first Military Service Act in January 1916, the focus of opposition to conscription shifted: military compulsion may have been conceded as a necessity for the nation's survival, but industrial compulsion could only be intended as a means of shackling labour, and needed to be resisted at all costs. In April 1916 the Labour Party's Executive announced that: 'This meeting of the Labour Party, whilst anxious to co-operate with the Government in all matters of military necessity, cannot with the information at present in its possession agree to any extension of the principle of compulsion'. A committee was set up to investigate any instances of industrial compulsion, consisting of George Wardle, Charles Duncan, and Stephen Walsh.[22] These fears were aptly conveyed by a cartoon in the *Railway Review*, which depicted a robust-looking working man, an emaciated businessman with a Union Jack in his lapel, and a cross-shaped torture rack marked 'Industrial Compulsion'. The caption has the worker asserting to the businessman: 'I will willingly put on khaki if necessary to save my country, but I'll *never* place myself in your power by taking *that* on'.[23] This cartoon highlighted the reluctant acquiescence of the proud, patriotic working class to conscription as a means to avert military disaster, coupled with a determination that further liberties not be taken with hard-won trade union freedoms by unscrupulous employers utilising patriotism to further their own interests. These fears remained for the rest of the war, and were only assuaged a little by the promise of Director of National Service Sir Auckland Geddes in October 1917 that there would be no industrial compulsion during the war.[24]

[20] Letter from J. Gillone, *The Clarion.*, 4 February 1916.
[21] *The Co-operative News*, 24 July 1915.
[22] Report of the Fifteen Annual Conference of the Labour Party: Parliamentary Report.
[23] *Railway Review*, 5 May 1916.
[24] Speech of Sir Auckland Geddes on national service, quoted in *The Co-operative News*, 13 October 1917.

One factor which may have worked to persuade the Left to accept compulsion was the muted response when it became a reality. Writing in *The Clarion* in August 1915, the socialist economist R.B. Suthers predicted great strife if conscription was introduced;[25] after Parliament had decided in favour of conscription by a great majority, and the TUC reiterated its opposition by a similar majority, *The Co-operative News* hoped that there would be no revolutionary action by labour.[26] An editorial of the *Railway Review* carried a similarly apprehensive tone: 'We venture to say that any attempt to fasten conscription of one kind or another to the workers of this country will have to reckon with forces which are powerful enough to defeat it, and that any such attempt will be met with a stubbornness born of indomitable will.'[27] In the spring of 1916, as attested men who were married or in starred occupations began to be called up ahead of single men who had not attested, the editor of *The Post* made the usual dire predictions of serious discord.[28] Yet the predicted mass protests against conscription never materialised: by January 1916 public opinion had largely been convinced of the necessity of compulsion, and although the Non-Conscription Fellowship was formed to agitate for the repeal of the Military Service Act, the anti-conscriptionist Left was forced to accept the new reality. Even leaders of the Engineers, such as the President Robert Young and the General Secretary Robert Brownlie, had 'evolved' in their position on conscription by the end of 1915; perhaps calculating that sustained opposition would be impossible and counterproductive; perhaps reckoning that the Amalgamated Society of Engineers' (ASE) protected status would spare their men from the front. Nonetheless, it was the ASE – particularly at a shop-floor level – which organised the most serious of the wartime strikes that periodically ignited from 1915 onwards, and it is to these disputes that we now turn.

Wartime Strikes, 1915–18

Although the outbreak of war served to halt the near continuous waves of industrial strife that had characterised the years preceding 1914, rapid price increases forced many workers to break the official industrial truce and go out on strike. The first high-profile strike of the war occurred in South Wales in May 1915, with the South Wales Miners' Federation looking to force coal owners to concede wage increases commensurate with the rise in the cost of living. Predictably, the miners were vilified in much of the press,

---

[25] *The Clarion*, 27 August 1915.
[26] *The Co-operative News*, 12 January 1916.
[27] *Railway Review*, 4 February 1916.
[28] *The Post*, 24 March 1916.

and with the navy dependent on coal to stave off invasion, thousands of soldiers dead, and price increases being felt across the country, there was very little sympathy for their cause amongst the public. Yet this strike was not the result of any absence of patriotism, but rather the impossibility of paying rent and food bills in 1915 on pre-war wages. At a crisis conference held in June 1915, Asquith conceded to miners' leader Robert Smillie that 'the miners are very patriotic men. They are one of the most patriotic people in the country'. 'Yes', responded Smillie, 'but they cannot live without wages'.[29]

One of the most important episodes of community agitation and unrest during the war occurred with the Glasgow Rent Strike. Sparked in November 1915 by incessant increases in the cost of living – in Govan and Fairfield, rent had increased by between twelve and twenty-three per cent from July to October 1915 – by the end of the month up to twenty thousand tenants were refusing to pay rent'.[30] Given the mass support and community solidarity evident in the rent strike, in addition to its coincidence with the engineers' strike and the Clyde Workers' Committee, it has often been cited as an example of radical anti-war agitation. Yet banners from the strike bore slogans such as 'Government Must Protect Our <u>Homes</u> from Germans & Landlords', and 'Our Husbands, Sons and Brothers are fighting the Prussians of Germany We are fighting the Prussians of Partick *only alternative* MUNICIPAL HOUSING', so during the rent strike in Glasgow we can still see the synthesis of anti-Germanism and demand for social and economic reform that characterised much of the Left in this period.[31]

The industry subject to the greatest amount of turmoil was civil and military engineering. A combination of exemption from conscription, indispensability to the war effort, soaring living costs, and conflict between union officials and shop-floor workers ensured that the engineering sector remained volatile for the majority of the war. Yet the nature of engineering strikes varied depending on time and location. The Glasgow strikes have attracted perhaps the greatest amount of scholarly debate due to the divisions between the men on the shop floor and the hierarchy of the ASE, yet it is debatable how far these strikers were representative of the wider community. The Glasgow engineers first walked out *en masse* in February 1915, demanding an extra two pence per hour in wages. This was expressly against the wishes of the ASE leadership, who promptly cut strike pay for the Clydeside men.[32] The divergence between the position of the ASE executive – which stressed the primacy of the war effort – and rising militarism on the ground produced

[29] As recorded in *The Post*, 4 June 1915.
[30] J. Hinton, *The First Shop Stewards' Movement*, London: Allen and Unwin, 1973, 126.
[31] I. McLean, *The Legend of Red Clydeside*, Edinburgh: John Donald, 1983, 165–69.
[32] Hinton, *The First Shop Stewards' Movement*, 50.

the Clyde Workers' Committee in October of 1915. Between then and April 1916, two to three hundred delegates – representing minority militant groups rather than the established workshop organisation – met every weekend in Glasgow.[33] Some have seen in this the seeds of a radical, revolutionary defeatist policy, but leader David Kirkwood was, by the winter of 1915–16 at least, a bitter opponent of the revolutionary anti-war movement.[34] Similarly, far from impeding munitions production, the Glasgow socialist paper *Forward* refused to mention the strikes until they were concluded – although this may well have been to avoid prosecution.

The source of discontent in Glasgow lay in a combination of unbearable pressures on the cost of living, a sense of being betrayed by the union executives, and a fear of being 'combed out' into the services. Although this made for a volatile atmosphere in the engineering shops of the Clyde, it was isolated from the wider community and did not spread across the whole of Glasgow. One of the reasons for this was that dilution was specifically a problem of skilled engineers, and given the craft-consciousness of the Clydesiders, unskilled men and craft men from other industries were unlikely to sympathise with them. Further, Iain McLean has argued that the strikers were inspired more by religious than Marxist rhetoric; steeped in the tradition of Protestant Covenanters, the sectarianism of the revolutionaries isolated them as much as their craft status: one-fifth of Scotland was Catholic at the time, yet apart from Harry McShane and John Wheatley, none of the Clydesiders were.[35] Indeed, David Kirkwood later described himself and fellow Clydesiders as 'Puritans', noting that 'We were all abstainers. Most of us did not smoke'.[36] This religious aspect of Scottish radicalism has gone underappreciated by scholars who have revisited this period subsequent to McLean. For example, William Kenefick has described the 'ILP quest for international peace [as having] a near-religious quality about it', yet he has little to say about Catholic Scots in this period.[37]

Finally, the industry, craft, and religious isolation were compounded by a hesitancy to follow leaders from industrial to political action. This resulted in a fragmented response to dilution which, along with a wave of deportations, undermined the unity and efficacy of the strikers, and James Hinton's ultimate verdict was that the Committee was a general failure.[38]

[33] Ibid., 120.

[34] Ibid., 120.

[35] McLean, *The Legend of Red Clydeside*, 97.

[36] Quoted in Ibid., 98.

[37] W. Kenefick, *Red Scotland!*, Edinburgh, Edinburgh University Press, 2007, 155. A point made by A.G. Newby in his review: 'Review: Red Scotland!', *English Historical Review* 125 (2010): 1023–25.

[38] Hinton, *The First Shop Stewards' Movement*, 158 and 161.

Similarly, McLean described a diminution of revolutionary fervour through successive meetings of the Glasgow Trades Council after March 1916: 'In 1916, as later in 1919, the government and the revolutionaries were united in seeing far more revolutionary potential than actually existed.'[39] While recent scholarship has challenged some of the arguments made by McLean, they do not fatally undermine his claims. For example, in *Red Scotland!*, Kenefick did little to challenge McLean's analysis of Glasgow and its environs, but rather looked to highlight radicalism elsewhere in Scotland.[40]

After the subsidence of the Glasgow agitation, there was a six-day strike of seven thousand engineers at Barrow at the end of June 1916 over dilution, but this was relatively swiftly resolved, before a major incident in Sheffield threatened once again to launch unofficial strikes potentially capable of destabilising the war effort.[41] Leonard Hargreaves had been a fitter at Vickers and was conscripted into the army with the connivance of the company, who viewed him as a firebrand and agitator.[42] In response, twelve thousand ASE men came out on 16 November and eventually won reinstatement for Hargreaves. Crucially in Sheffield the less-skilled men were better organised, and co-operation and co-ordination across craft and industry lines were possible.[43] A similar strike was threatened at Barrow in February 1917, and on the sixth day of the seven-day ultimatum the man concerned was released from the army and returned to work.[44] During the Hargreaves strike the government drew up the Trade Cards Scheme, giving exemption from military service to craft union members engaged on munitions work, although it excluded workers outside of craft unions no matter how skilled. This came into effect in February 1917, but by April of that year the government wanted yet again to revise the rules concerning exemption, and introduced a Schedule of Protected Occupations. On 5 May the unions extracted an agreement that no skilled men would be taken before dilutees of military age were called up; and and thus reassured the Schedule. Yet no sooner had agreement been reached in May 1917 than the largest wave of strikes of the war began in Manchester: over two hundred thousand engineers were out for over three weeks; one and a half million working days were lost, and over forty-eight towns were involved at some point.[45] In many ways the unrest which sporadically gripped

---

[39] McLean, *The Legend of Red Clydeside*, 83–86.
[40] Kenefick, *Red Scotland!*
[41] Hinton, *The First Shop Stewards' Movement*, 186.
[42] Ibid., 171.
[43] Ibid., 167.
[44] Hinton, *The First Shop Stewards' Movement*, 187.
[45] Ibid., 197.

engineering throughout the war reflected a struggle between the leadership of the union and local activists on the ground. During the most serious strikes in May 1917, former ASE General Secretary George Barnes – by then cabinet minister – urged the union leadership to recognise and work with shop committees, but the executive of the ASE refused to do this throughout 1917.[46]

The government took steps to win over the more militant workers in skilled, protected occupations such as mining and engineering: by 1918, three hundred such people were sent on trips to the front to see how fellow workers lived and suffered and thus encourage the men back home to accept their lot. Yet the government's attempts to incubate concern for the war were largely unnecessary; the speed with which all industrial strife ceased during the German advance of the spring of 1918 demonstrated the workers' priorities: low pay, dangerous conditions, and poor living standards could all be tolerated – indeed, they represented the only life many had known – but the idea of Britain suffering defeat in the conflict was both literally and metaphorically unthinkable for most of the working class. As Brock Millman has accurately observed: 'If the government feared that domestic enemies would seek to exploit foreign defeats, they profoundly underrated the residual loyalty of even the most intransigent dissenters.'[47]

The nature of wartime strikes were adroitly summarised by an editorial in *The Co-operative News* from May 1917, at the height of the nationwide engineers' strike, which also served as a fair representation of the attitude to these disputes of most of the Left:

> There was no item of news in last Sunday's papers that brought a greater feeling of relief all over the country than that the Engineers' Strike was practically settled ... On the whole, the workers of this country have responded magnificently to the imperative need of unity. They have sacrificed hard-earned privileges; they have postponed a settlement of many wrongs. They have given of their life's blood on the field of battle; they have worked early and worked late in supplying those munitions of war so necessary for the defeat of the enemy. Before conscription came, they rallied to the colours by the million; and since conscription came they have waived their repugnance to [sic] military compulsion for the good of the common cause. They have patiently borne with rising prices in the face of indisputable evidence of profiteering, and have postponed the day of settlement with the profiteers. Unfortunately, the record of the governing classes has not been nearly so praiseworthy.[48]

46 Ibid., 213–14.
47 B. Millman, *Managing Domestic Dissent in First World War Britain*, London: Frank Cass, 2000, 357.
48 *The Co-Operative News*, 26 May 1917.

Such labour disputes as occurred during the war were not due to want of patriotism, much less deliberate attempts at destabilising the war effort, but rather pragmatic attempts to improve pay and conditions. Perhaps the best overall summation of the attitudes of the unionised working class towards the war is found in remarks made to literary critic Walter Raleigh. Looking to ascertain the opinion of people in Lancashire and Yorkshire towards the war, he was told that: 'They mean to win it, and they mean to make as much money out of it as ever they can.'[49]

The Anti-War Movement, 1915–18

Dissent from the labour patriot viewpoint was rare, especially in the first two years of the war, and generally took one of two forms. The minority dissenting tradition was that of orthodox Marxists such as the Plebs' League who, unlike most of the SDF and the *Justice* group, remained bewildered by mass enthusiasm for the war and positioned themselves in principled opposition to the conflict. To say that this position did not command mass support is an understatement. Writing on 'The European Crisis' in *Plebs* – the organ of the Plebs' League – a commentator expressed his astonishment that 'The arch anti-militarist, [the French socialist Gustave] Herve, asked for a gun, and other pacifists of eminence have actually shouldered one. In England, the Liberal Cabinet has received the backing of the Labour Party. What strange force is at work which thus makes friends of enemies and enemies of friends?'[50] While the Plebs' League's members were shocked and dispirited by the mass support for the war and the upsurge in popular patriotism which followed, they made no attempts to *deny* the strength of patriotic feeling; they felt it was irrational and absurd, but nonetheless very real. A letter to *Plebs* from James Millar – who would still be running the organisation in his nineties in the 1970s – in February 1915 elucidated this dilemma: 'If we believe that war, at the bottom, is a struggle between two groups of Capitalists for a market that threatens to become too small for both, how can we take part in the bloodshed? It has been argued, on the other hand, that if we Socialists do not identify ourselves with the working-classes [sic] in this war we can hardly hope to win their confidence.'[51] This newspaper carried occasional messages of support for its dissenting stance, sometimes from men serving in the trenches, as in October 1916: 'Just received *Plebs* – the best yet! It's like a ray of sunshine to a man out here – only more dependable, as it comes more regularly … Enjoyed the jab at the

[49] Quoted in Gregory, *The Last Great War*, 212.
[50] *Plebs*, November 1914.
[51] Letter from James P.M. Millar, Musselburgh, Scotland, *Plebs*, February 1915.

Clarion Royal Family. Why don't they bury themselves – they've been dead long enough?'[52] Yet these exceptions proved the rule of mass support for the war as much amongst the grassroots of the labour movement as among the working class more generally.

The majority strand of opposition to the war centred on the Union of Democratic Control (UDC). Created immediately upon the outbreak of hostilities on 4 August 1914, Arthur Henderson joined its committee in November 1914, and only resigned his post when included in Asquith's coalition cabinet in May 1915. While the Marxists of the Plebs' League were aware of mass support for the war, even as they were confounded by it, the same cannot be said of the intellectuals of the UDC. Writing to Arthur Ponsonby in May 1915, Charles Trevelyan – a Liberal MP later to defect to Labour – demonstrated his misjudgement of popular sentiment in Britain and France when he claimed that 'Germany cannot suffer complete defeat, short of a four or five years' war, and ... none of the allied peoples will stand that'.[53] Nonetheless the Union did proceed cautiously in the early years of the war, and tried 'to demonstrate to the working class that they were not trying to hamper the war effort', despite their opposition to the conflict.[54] Marvin Swartz has claimed that the Union 'bridged a gap between rich Liberal Quakers and the socialist Independent Labour Party [ILP] that on domestic issues alone might have remained unbridgeable'.[55] While it is fair to see the UDC as a vital link between disillusioned Liberals and the Labour Party (and this connection will be discussed in more detail in Chapter 4), the extent to which it acted as an ideological connection between pacifist Liberals and ordinary Labour activists is highly questionable. For an example, an ex-councillor in West Ham stated that he had 'no confidence in the middle-class peace men', and that they would turn their backs on the labour movement as soon as it had served its purpose. Soon after this the West Ham trade council disaffiliated from the UDC and, according to Swartz himself, this suspicion was representative of trade union opinion in general.[56]

---

[52] Letter from A.D.B. (B.E.F., somewhere in France), *Plebs*, October 1916.

[53] Quoted in M. Swartz, *Union of Democratic Control in British Politics during the First World War*, Oxford: Clarendon Press, 1971, 68. Arthur Ponsonby was a Liberal who joined Labour after the war and was elected for Sheffield Brightside in 1922. See J. Bellamy and J. Saville (eds), *Dictionary of Labour Biography VII*, London: Macmillan, 1984. Charles Trevelyan was one of the foremost Liberal opponents of the war in 1914 and left the party, standing unsuccessfully as an independent Labour candidate in 1918. He won Newcastle Central for Labour in 1922.

[54] Swartz, *Union of Democratic Control*, 149.

[55] Ibid., 94.

[56] Ibid., 148.

A year into the conflict, as opposition to the war lost some of the treasonous associations it had earlier held, membership swelled from fifty affiliated organisations in June 1915 to 107 in November of that year, with a theoretical membership of over three hundred thousand. By the end of the war, the Union could boast of three hundred affiliated bodies and a membership of 650,000.[57] It acted as a link between the anti-war sections of the ILP, who were strongest in the towns of West Yorkshire, East Lancashire, South Wales, and Scotland that had a radical, dissenting culture and a high degree of religious nonconformity, and among the metropolitan radicals and intellectuals of London.[58] As it had more of a broad base and considerably greater support than those opposing the war from a Marxist perspective, it was able to exercise greater influence on the mainstream of the Labour movement. In 1917 Henderson expressed 'full sympathy' with the four main points of the Constitution of the Union, and six out of the seventeen members elected to the Labour Party's Executive Committee in January 1917 had been members of the UDC at some point.[59] Yet the momentum which eventually developed behind organisations such as the UDC should not obscure the fact that they held very much minority positions, both within the population generally and within the British Left, especially at the grassroots level.

Perhaps a high point for the anti-war movement was the ILP conference at Leeds in 1917. Resolutions were passed calling for an end to the war and for the formation of workers' and soldiers' councils along Russian lines. Yet Ben Tillett's assessment that the convention 'did not represent working class opinion and was rigged by a middle class element more mischievous than important' is accurate, if a little paranoid.[60] The fact that the 1918 election swept members of the UDC from the House of Commons (although many returned within a few years, with several featuring in the first Labour government), suggests that even by the end of the war the Union commanded very little mass support.

There is a great deal of evidence to support the allegation that the labour movement was merely the means to an end for some of the radical intellectuals of the UDC. As Swartz noted: 'Although he thought it possible within a few years to nationalize land, coal mines, and railways, Morel in the summer of 1916 did not consider socialism (with which he identified the Labour Party) to be a viable political force.'[61] Furthermore,

[57] Ibid., 61.
[58] Ibid., 89.
[59] Ibid., 148 and 154–55.
[60] G. DeGroot, *Blighty: British Society in the Era of the Great War*, New York: Longman, 1996, 149.
[61] Swartz, *Union of Democratic Control*, 103.

in July 1917 Morel attacked the 'fatuous tradition [of British Labour] which insists that its political representatives must not be men of education, but men who have actually served their time in factory or workshop, mine or mill'.[62] One cannot avoid the impression that for men like Morel the working class were an obstinate, ignorant mass unaware of their own best interests, who prevented the elevation of men of education (such as himself) to their deserved prominence. It is notable how few of the Liberals and intellectuals who joined the UDC had a history of concern for the well-being of the British working classes, and so it remained during the war; the Labour movement was ultimately merely a vehicle through which to pursue their pacifistic aims. They were pacifists first, their interest in social reform was only incidental. Whatever one may think of the excessive jingoism of some of the Labour patriots, the same accusation cannot be levelled against them. One may argue – and with some justification – that the more extreme Labour patriots provided, in embryo, the combination of economic populism, cultural and racial exceptionalism, and reverence of the state that was to take root in Italy and Germany with such devastating consequences, yet their patriotism was always an aspect of their genuine concern for the betterment of the British people. Not only were the anti-patriots disingenuous; their beliefs regarding the impact of the war were fundamentally mistaken. Morel had claimed that 'the politicians are preparing a worse world for our children than the one they were born into', but the reality was that a child born in the 1920s could expect a higher standard of living than a child born in the 1900s (similarly, and even more counter-intuitively, a child born in the 1950s would enjoy a more prosperous lifestyle than one born in the 1930s).[63] Not only did labour patriotism ensure that the Labour Party was not toxified in the eyes of the working class; labour participation in the war laid the foundations for a world unimaginable in the 1900s (as discussed in Chapter 5).

Even on the pacifistic hard-Left, the advent of war precipitated a moral dilemma which was to cut through groups such as the ILP. Writing in the *Bradford Pioneer* – a newspaper later to become a staunch opponent of the conflict, based in a city associated with anti-war radicalism – shortly after the declaration of hostilities, local activist Jessie Cockerline outlined her personal conundrum: 'Speaking as a Socialist and, more than that, as a woman, I sincerely and honestly affirm that I hate and detest war. I

---

[62] Morel to Leech, July 1917, quoted in Swartz, *Union of Democratic Control*, 144. E.D. Morel was a Liberal who had come to prominence through his outspoken opposition to Belgian atrocities in the Congo. A founding member of the UDC, he joined the ILP in 1918 and served as MP for Dundee 1922–24.

[63] Ibid., 81.

realize only too well that we women will in so many cases have our fathers, husbands, brothers, sons and lovers taken away from us.' After emphasising that she had no prior quarrel with Germany, she continued:

> But the time for philosophical utterances has gone ... We must realize, however much we may declaim against our Government, yet it is better than that which a continental despotism would inflict upon us as a vanquished nation ... Germany has too long held the role of an armed bully and we re-echo the words of a leader in a great German newspaper, 'Better an end with terror than terror without end'. Comrades, the German boast is to be put to the test and now that Great Britain, deplorable as we all admit it to be, is drawn into the conflict then may we each of us firmly do our duty, great or small, for what is to each of us 'My country, right or wrong'.[64]

Although he had resigned the Labour Party leadership over the war, in August 1914 even Ramsay MacDonald echoed the sentiment that the war, once begun, had to be seen through.[65] Also in that month Fred Jowett, fellow ILP luminary and later one of the leaders of the anti-war movement, told a crowd of five thousand spectators: 'I want this country to win', and called for the defeat of German militarism and militarism at home. The *Pioneer* reported that both statements were greeted with enthusiastic cheers.[66]

Writing in the Glasgow ILP paper *Forward* under the pen name 'Rob Roy', Dr Sterling Robertson, a long time socialist activist in Scotland, criticised MacDonald and Hardie for not taking part in recruitment, despite their assurances that the war must be won and German militarism crushed:

> I am not going to stand aside and see [labour men taking part in recruitment] traduced because they face the facts, and don't think, talk and act as if the Socialist States of Europe were in existence or could be had for the grasping ... The working classes generally, even where they had the power, left it in the hands of War Lords, Capitalists and Diplomatists, and they are reaping the terrible fruits ... It doesn't help me to snipe at the present Government, supplied by the good sense of the British people, which I have had a free opportunity to influence and bring round to my point of view.[67]

The military itself felt that the pages of the *Bradford Pioneer* could be a possible recruiting ground, placing an advert in the paper in October 1915 for men for the Royal Garrison Artillery.[68] The City of Bradford

[64] *Bradford Pioneer*, 14 August 1914.
[65] Ibid., 14 August 1914.
[66] Ibid., 4 September 1914.
[67] Quoted in *Bradford Pioneer*, 1 January 1915.
[68] Ibid., 1 October 1915.

Co-operative Society also advertised that it was taking orders for cigars, cigarettes, tobacco, and pipes for 'Boys at the Front'.[69] A large advert told of 'St George's Flag Day' on Saturday 6 May, in aid of the 'Lady Mayoress' War Guild. War Hospital Supply Depot. Personal Comforts for Wounded Soldiers. All Proceeds go to the Benefit of our Sailors and Soldiers. Give Generously and Wear a Flag.'[70] There was a further 'Lifeboat Flag Day' on 5 August,[71] and a two-column advertisement just before the Armistice appealed for funds for 'Gun Week': 'The Guns are coming to Bradford on Monday. BE ready to give them a rousing welcome! ... It is to THE GUNS that our advancing armies look, to blast the way to Victory ... Millions of pounds are needed to shatter the Hun defences'.[72]

Even in the last months of the war, it was felt appropriate to advertise fund-raising drives such as Gun Week in one of the most pacifistic newspapers, in one of the most pacifistic towns in England – and these fund-raising drives were particularly successful, raising thousands of pounds. Adrian Gregory has said that the success of war loans and funding drives such as Tank Week 'suggest[ed] an unseemly rush to secure excess profits rather than patriotism', but while this may have been true for large investors, it is doubtful that working people investing a few shillings or pounds were primarily motivated by a return on their investments. John Hill, General Secretary of the Boilermakers, certainly felt that higher interest rates motivated large subscribers, but that his members had more honourable intentions:

> I never had greater pleasure than we had in offering a loan of £30,000, all of which has been accepted ... The people who have lent money on this occasion have been lauded in the newspapers as patriots, but there is not much patriotism in investing in gilt-edged Government securities on a certain 4 per cent when most other investments are in a state of paralysis or collapse. In the circumstances, however, it was a duty, and in this, too, we have done our share.[73]

Gregory's further point that 'the strongest correlation between high subscription and any other variable [was] size of the urban centre and a distinct sense of civic identity' is more salient for the working classes of towns such as Bradford.[74] The success of funding drives in such places did not necessarily reflect patriotic fervour in the national sense, nor love of

---

[69] Ibid., 26 November 1915.
[70] Ibid., 5 May 1916.
[71] Ibid., 4 August 1916.
[72] Ibid., 8 November 1918.
[73] *Boilermakers' Reports*, December 1914.
[74] Gregory, *The Last Great War*, 227.

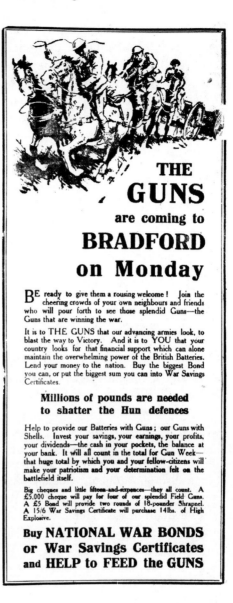

Figure 2. 'The Guns are
Coming to Bradford',
Bradford Pioneer,
8 November 1918.
Permission of Working
Class Movement Library.

'King and Country', but rather a local pride and patriotism that could be
radical and progressive rather than reactionary and conservative.

Hector Munro, a prominent Bradford ILPer went to France with an
ambulance wagon at the outbreak, as did Alderman J.H. Palin. Jowett
admitted that: 'British victory over "Prussianism" had to be won and ... he
could not agree to a peace settlement which did not include the "restoration
of Belgium to complete sovereignty"'; Alderman Arthur Taylor, an ASE
leader and 'doyen of the Halifax ILP' claimed that the war had been

inevitable and that England was the best of a 'bloomin bad lot'. James
Parker, ILP MP for Halifax, became a prominent patriot, and claimed
when pleading for more recruits that if the Germans won, the working
class would have 'everything to lose and nothing to gain'. Of the 461 young
men in the Bradford ILP, by February 1916, 113 were in the trenches, 118
were in training in England, six were in the navy, and 207 had attested
under the Derby Scheme. By 1918, of the 442 members eligible for service,
351 were serving while 48 were conscientious objectors or doing national
war work.[75] In London, prominent anti-war activist George Lansbury
wrote in the revolutionary newspaper *The Women's Dreadnought* in August
1915: 'The women of the East End have sent their men to fight. Those of
us who hate and detest war know that these men must be armed and fed,
and while the war lasts we shall do our best to see that is done.'[76] Similarly
Fred Montague, London Organiser of the ILP, joined the army, served
in France, and was commissioned in the army education department. He
addressed recruitment meetings in his lieutenant's uniform and would go
on to become the MP for West Islington in, 1923–31 and 1935–47.[77]

While this book concentrates on England, it is worth making reference
to places such as Clydeside and certain parts of Wales, where it is
sometimes assumed that opposition to the war was greater than elsewhere
in Britain. In his discussion of Welsh soldiers in the First World War,
Gervase Phillips noted that 272, 924 men – or 21.52 per cent of the
population – enlisted into the services, and that 145,205 of those – that
is to say, over fifty per cent – were volunteers.[78] Furthermore, Phillips
claimed that there was no widespread opposition to conscription, and that
a broad social mix served in the ranks.[79] While there does seem to have
been a disproportionate tendency for Anglicans to join up – there were
only 9.1 per cent Anglican communicants in Wales pre-war, yet twenty-six
per cent of Phillips's sample were Anglicans – there was no discrepancy
between Welsh speakers and English speakers. 'It would seem', wrote
Phillips, 'that men in predominantly Welsh speaking counties were no less
likely to enlist than in counties where the English language predominated'.
Anecdotally this is supported by Robert Graves, then an officer in the
Royal Welch Fusiliers, who recorded that from 1915 onwards there was

[75] K. Laybourne and Reynolds, *Liberalism and the Rise of Labour*, London: Croom Helm,
1984, 184–89.
[76] *Women's Dreadnought*, 21 August 1915, quoted in K. Weller, *Don't Be a Soldier!*, London:
Journeyman, 1985, 27.
[77] Weller, *Don't Be a Soldier!*, 28.
[78] Phillips, 'Dai bach Y Soldiwr', 945.
[79] Ibid., 95 and 98.

a flood of Welsh speakers into the regiment until Welsh and non-Welsh speakers were equally represented.[80]

Dai Egan has argued that 'the extent of the anti-war movement in South Wales … has so far been vastly underestimated by historians', but even he conceded that it did not begin to grow until 1917.[81] Furthermore, Egan illustrated his point with the results of a South Wales Miners' Federation ballot in November 1917 to authorise strike action should the government attempt to introduce a comb-out scheme, but surely they undermine it. The results were 98,948 against striking if the government attempted a comb-out and 28,903 for. Egan adds: 'Although *no single District voted in favour of strike action*, the vote was very close in the Western Aberdare and Merthyr Districts.'[82] If a strike ballot to resist the combing-out of unionised miners in South Wales could not succeed, after the Russian Revolution, after the horrors of the Somme and Passchendaele, and after years of intolerable rises in the cost of living, then one wonders in what context it might succeed. Egan's statistics, far from strengthening the case for trade union opposition to the war, give more evidence, if such were needed, that the majority of British workers meant to see the conflict through to the end. As Phillips concluded, the general population was convinced that this was Wales' war: 'The socialists' antipathy to his employer, the non-conformist's independence from the whims of the establishment were forgotten as the war was made their war, as their struggles were identified with the struggle against Germany.'[83]

William Kenefick has argued that Scottish radical opposition to the war has been underappreciated, yet he did not deny the isolation of the sentiment. Kenefick quoted Bruce Glasier as saying, of a tour of Scotland: 'For the present the ILP Branches are almost as sharply isolated from the surrounding population as were the Christian communities of Ephesus, Galicia, and Corinth in Apostolic days … The ILP is nonetheless regarded with grave suspicion as a pestilentially pacifist faction … a noxious shrub in the glowing flowerbed of British patriotism'.[84] Glasier was not given to

---

[80] Ibid., 100.

[81] D. Egan, 'The Swansea Conference of the British Council of Soldiers' and Workers' Delegates, July, 1917: Reactions to the Russian Revolution of February 1917, and the Anti-War Movement in South Wales', *Llafur* 1 (1972–76): 178.

[82] Ibid., 179. Emphasis added.

[83] Phillips, 'Dai bach Y Soldiwr', 102. It was not only the First World War that stirred militarism in South Wales. Kenneth Fox has noted that during the Boer War, schoolchildren sang patriotic songs and miners queued to enlist: 'In Merthyr, as elsewhere, the war was a source of excitement, and "pro-Boer" was there as much a term of bitter castigation as in the rest of the country.' K.O. Fox, 'Labour and Merthyr's Khaki Election of 1900', *Welsh Historical Review* 2 (1965): 351 and 358.

[84] Kenefick, *Red Scotland!*, 139.

pessimism: indeed, in his review of *Red Scotland!*, Ewen Cameron noted how on an earlier tour, 'the Glasiers were more visionary' than tough and pragmatic and likely to understate the difficulties of bringing Socialism to Scotland.[85] Kenefick argued that 'the jewel in the ILP and [Non-Conscription Fellowship] crown was without doubt Dundee', yet this was a city represented by labour patriot Alexander Wilkie and Winston Churchill.[86] Even at the 1922 election, when Labour made a substantial breakthrough in Dundee, the Communist and old Clydesider Willie Gallagher polled in last place out of six candidates.[87]

In Edinburgh, of the three Labour councillors for whom information exists, one was stridently pro-war, and the other two volunteered for the military, even though all three were members of the ILP.[88] In Glasgow, only two of the nineteen ILP councillors came out against the war, and J. O'Connor Kessack, a leading ILPer and vice-president of the Scottish Trade Union Congress, was killed in action. The three Scottish Labour MPs supported the war throughout, and none of them voted against the conscription bill.[89] Meanwhile, of the Clyde strike leaders who stood for election in 1918, only Neil Maclean was successful, in Govan; John Wheatley lost in Shettleston by seventy-four votes to Admiral Adair, the work's manager at Parkhead, who had stood as a Coalition Unionist, and the only other success for the Left was George Barnes in the Gorbals, who was officially a Coalition Labour candidate.[90] Iain McLean reckoned that Labour 'wilted' under the burden of its 'pacifism'; James Stewart, the defeated candidate in St Rollox admitted that his defeat was due to his opposition to war indemnities and expelling Germans from Britain – if this was the result in the West of Scotland, it is not hard to imagine the electoral consequences for Labour in 1918 had it not supported the war.[91] By way of contrast, the Aberdeen TUC had been resolutely pro-war, and Aberdeen North was one of the few Scottish seats won by Labour in 1918.[92]

---

[85] Ewen A. Cameron. 'Review: *Red Scotland!*', *Journal of British Studies* 47 (2008): 983.

[86] *Red Scotland!*, 154.

[87] Ibid., 170. It should be pointed out that the two victors in Dundee, Edwin Scrymgeour and E.D. Morel, were both noted pacifists.

[88] J. Holford, *Reshaping Labour: Organisation, Work and Politics – Edinburgh in the Great War and After*, London: Croom Helm, 1988, 152.

[89] I.G.C. Hutchinson, 'The Impact of the First World War on Scottish Politics', in C.M.M. Macdonald and E.W. McFarland, *Scotland and the Great War*, East Linton: Tuckwell Press, 1999, 49.

[90] McLean, *The Legend of Red Clydeside*, 154.

[91] Ibid., 156.

[92] Hutchinson, 'Impact of the First World War', 49–50.

The Leeds and Stockholm Conferences

The Leeds conference was convened by the ILP and the British Socialist Party (BSP, formerly the SDF/SDP and now divested of its patriotic wing) and held on 3 June 1917. This hailed the Russian Revolution and called for the establishment of workers' and soldiers' councils around the UK. To some this has served as an indicator of a break in the labour patriot consensus and a symbol of how the British labour movement had become radicalised by the war, yet this is serious misjudgement of Leeds and its significance. Firstly, elements within the ILP and BSP had been sceptical of the war for some time, and were not late converts to the pacifistic cause; secondly, the conference represented only a minority of the labour movement, and the attempts to establish workers' and soldiers' soviets were an embarrassing failure. Ben Tillett justly claimed that the conference did not represent working-class opinion, whilst the Dockers' Executive went further, claiming that the conference was convened 'at the instigation of moneyed and middle-class people whose mischievous exploitation of the labour movement is disruptive in character'.[93] The Executive of the Labour Party stated on 18 July that it had 'nothing to do' with Leeds, and asked that no local organisation affiliated to the party should convene local conferences or set up the proposed councils.[94] The full National Soldiers' and Workers' Council finally met in the third week of October 1917 – almost five months after Leeds – and it was to be the last ever meeting.[95] The Dockers' Union Executive's accusations were hyperbolic and unfair but there is no doubting the divisive effect of the Russian Revolution on the Left; while the hard Left and the anti-war movement remained only a minority, there was increasing concern that the anti-war pacifists could destabilise both the war effort and the progress of the British Left. The South Wales labour paper *Llais Llafur*, for example, warned Russia against the dangers of Leninism and not continuing to prosecute the war, while a mob led by Charles Stanton – MP for Merthyr and Welsh miners' leader – broke up a labour council in Cardiff formed in the aftermath of Leeds.[96] The conference held at Swansea on 29 July faced a similarly vicious assault, with up to five hundred people in the mob.[97]

[93] T. Wilson, *The Myriad Faces of War*, Cambridge: Polity Press, 1986, 522.

[94] Egan, 'The Swansea Conference', 170.

[95] Ibid., 159.

[96] Ibid., 164–69.

[97] Ibid., 173. It should be noted, however, that there is some debate as to the true 'spontaneity' of the mobs which attacked peace meetings. John Hope has claimed that the National War Aims Committee empowered the British Empire Union and the British Workers' League to attack pacifistic and hard-left meetings. See J. Hope, 'British Fascism

In the same year as the Leeds conference came the ill-fated attempt to convene a conference of the various socialist and labour parties of the combatant nations in Stockholm. On 9 May the Labour Party Executive had voted against attendance at the mooted conference, and although he too was initially opposed, Henderson's first-hand experience of the Russian Revolution (he had spent several months of the summer of 1917 in Petrograd; MacDonald was meant to accompany him on this trip but Seafarers' Union sailors refused to sail with him on board) convinced him of the need to avoid further turmoil in Russia and keep that country in the war.[98] He felt that Stockholm would clarify British war aims and thereby refute Bolshevik arguments about nature of the war.[99] Thus he envisioned that Stockholm would strengthen the hand of the Provisional Government, keep the Russians fighting and the *triple entente* intact. The Labour Party Executive voted nine to four in favour of Henderson attending Stockholm, yet the government initially opposed a member of its War Cabinet attending the conference and intended to refuse him a passport. Henderson's threatened resignation persuaded the government to relent, and he was given approval to travel.[100]

A special conference of the Labour Party was scheduled to discuss the issue on 10 August: the conference endorsed Stockholm, but some unions, in particular the Miners, argued that the delegation should be limited to twenty-four: eight from the Labour Party, eight from the trade unions, and eight others selected by the conference. Hildamarie Meynell has argued that the intention here was to limit the influence of the socialist societies, presumably as they were viewed as being more inclined towards a lenient peace.[101] According to Meynell, it was this issue – minority representation – which dominated the Stockholm debate. The initial vote on 10 August was 1,846,000 to 550,000 in favour; given the conflict of interests of a member of the War Cabinet attending a peace conference while the war continued, Henderson resigned from the Cabinet the following day. In the meantime, the largely Webb-penned Memorandum on War Aims was presented to the special conference on Stockholm, providing for the first time in codified form exactly what labour thought it was fighting for. The conference reconvened on 23 August, where the ILP pressed for separate

and the State, 1918–1928: A Re-Examination of the Documentary Evidence', *Labour History Review* 57 (1992): 78.

[98] J.M. Winter, 'Arthur Henderson, the Russian Revolution, and the Reconstruction of the Labour Party', *Historical Journal* 15 (1972): 753–73.

[99] Ibid., 767.

[100] H. Meynell, 'The Stockholm Conference of 1917', *International Review of Social History* 5 (1960): 206.

[101] Ibid.

representation in Sweden, in addition to the twenty-four argued for by the Miners. Robert Smillie offered a compromise: if the ILP dropped the claim for separate representation, the Miners' Federation of Great Britain would waive the bloc vote and allow its members to vote individually. Philip Snowden protested, and this deal came to nothing. Despite the loss of the Miners' support, the second vote came out a narrow 1,234,000 to 1,231,000 in favour; a separate amendment proposed by the ILP to allow separate representation was defeated.[102] The decline in support for Stockholm at the vote emboldened the government to state yet again its opposition and threaten to withhold passports, although this threat was never realised as the proposed conference collapsed due to intractable divisions among the European labour movement. Rather than marking any great turning point in the war, it should be viewed as an embarrassing distraction.

As Trevor Wilson has argued: 'The Labour debacle over Stockholm showed that, however well Henderson had assessed the situation in Russia, he had misjudged the temper of British workmen.'[103] Yet despite the government's attempts to foster division in labour ranks over Stockholm, the party did not divide over the issue: the Memorandum of War Aims received wide support and on 28 December 1917 Labour declared it would only continue to support the war if it was certain that it was being fought to make the world safe for democracy and if there was an end to secret diplomacy.[104] Lloyd George spoke to the TUC on 5 January 1918, trying to convince the Congress that these pacifistic and internationalist aims were indeed what Britain was now fighting for, and three days later Woodrow Wilson gave his famous 'Fourteen Points' speech to the US Congress, which was seized on by the Labour press as embodying the very values for which the labour movement was fighting.[105]

This chapter has attempted to ascertain the limits to the labour patriot consensus during the First World War. While vociferous anti-war movements existed, and grew in size and reach after 1917, they were never more than minority movements. In a recent article on the anti-war movement in Manchester, Alison Ronan concedes that:

> Anti-war women, who were increasingly marginalised by their position, developed complex, albeit narrow, circles of friends within their overlapping groups of association ... Many of the activist families were already marginalised by their socialist politics or non-conformist beliefs ... became of this

---

[102] Ibid., 217.

[103] Wilson, *Myriad Faces of War*, 525.

[104] See Millman, *Managing Domestic Dissent*, 214–15.

[105] D. French, 'Allies, Rivals and Enemies: British Strategy and War Aims during the First World War', in J. Turner (ed.), *Britain and the First World War*, London: Unwin Hyman, 1988.

marginalization and isolation, friendship and association between activists became even more essential.[106]

Historians such as Cyril Pearce and Karen Hunt have argued passionately for the need to appreciate local radicalism and strident opposition to the war in certain areas, and while knowledge of such groups enriches our understanding of labour history, they should not disguise the existence of a patriotic majority. Indeed, it is surely the atypical and distinctive nature of these groups which attract scholarly attention in the first place.

While the agitation against conscription, shop-floor strikes, and the anti-war movement may not have characterised the Left's response to the war, these experiences were an important part of left-wing wartime experience, and these minority trends should not be discounted. The anti-war agitation did make an important contribution to the type of labour movement that emerged after 1918: as the fervent nationalism of the war years gave way to regret and recrimination, Labour was able to highlight wartime dissent as evidence of its radical and progressive nature, in the same way its war record secured patriotic credentials. The next chapter will consider how Labour used its war record in the five years between the end of hostilities and the coming of the first Labour government. It will discuss the immigration into Labour of many former Liberals (and some Conservatives) during the 1920s, the appeals to soldiers and ex-servicemen made by the Left, and the role of the war in bringing Labour closer to working-class culture. It will argue that while the pacifistic, internationalist streak was highly important in attracting Liberal activists and voters to Labour, overall the patriotism displayed during the war was vital in convincing working-class voters and trade unionists that Labour shared their values.

[106] A. Ronan, 'Fractured, Fragile, Creative: A Brief Analysis of Wartime Friendships between Provincial Women Anti-War Activists, 1914–1918', *North West Labour History* 37 (2012–13): 22.

4

'Our Platform is Broad Enough and our Movement Big Enough' – The War and Recruits to Labour

'Come along with us, our platform is broad enough and our Movement big enough to take you all.'[1]

—Arthur Henderson, Labour Party Conference, 1918

'Your sensible remarks about the war have made me and my mates think more of your queer ideas about Socialism and Determinism. We think there's something in them.'[2]

—'A London Working Man', *The Clarion*, February 1915

This chapter deals with the question of how the war impacted on Labour's electoral fortunes after 1918. It begins with the post-war influx of Liberals who felt that Labour was now the real home of the radical Liberal tradition, and argues that – having proved its patriotism during the war – the party could show a more radical face over Ireland, India, and disarmament. The second section will address the experiences of soldiers and ex-servicemen specifically, and argue that while the war did not create a long-term radicalisation of veterans, the labour movement made a concerted effort to appeal to soldiers, and many ex-servicemen moved towards labour after the war. The third and final section describes the most significant breakthrough for Labour, concentrating on the extent to which the Left made 'cultural' appeals to voters: as Englishmen and women, as Britons, as patriots, as Anglicans, as Catholics, and as individual people. This chapter will argue that support for the war was critical to the successes of Labour in the interwar period. Not only did it prevent a parliamentary annihilation in 1918, it secured patriotic credentials to counterbalance the

---

[1] Report of the Seventeenth Annual Conference of the Labour Party.
[2] *The Clarion*, 19 February 1915.

influx of middle-class radicals; prevented a break with the trade unions; and facilitated Labour's appeals to a working-class culture based on family, neighbourhood, pubs, and patriotism. It will be argued here that this cultural appeal to the wider working class allowed Labour to win support from beyond both the heavily unionised skilled workers and the Nonconformist tradition which had hitherto provided most of its support, and that the experience of the war – and labour patriotism during that conflict – was essential to this cultural appeal.

The Conversion of Liberal and Conservative Elites

While many of those who fled the Liberals for Labour in the 1920s had become disillusioned with *laissez-faire* Liberalism due to the war, economic concerns can only partly explain post-war recruitment, and moral prerogatives were the most important factor for many former Liberals. In the words of Peter Clarke, many Liberals 'changed allegiance not because they thought there was too little socialism in the Liberal party, but because they thought there was more liberalism in the Labour Party'.[3] As Duncan Tanner had it, Labour's Memorandum on War Aims was 'almost a [Union of Democratic Control] document, and was supported by many radical Liberal moral reformers. Its views on Free Trade, Ireland, conscription, the treatment of alien immigrants, and on issues of liberty and freedom raised by press censorship, attracted many radical Liberals to the Labour Party'.[4] Significantly, this did not just occur at a national level but also in individual constituencies: while some Liberals continued to support the coalition, 'Liberal moral reformists flocked to Labour in the Nonconformist strongholds'.[5] While Union of Democratic Control (UDC) members and those associated with pacifistic Labourism were ejected from the House of Commons in the khaki election of 1918 – even some men who were instrumental to the successful completion of the war, such as Arthur Henderson, lost their seats – by 1922 the 'pacifists' such as Ramsay MacDonald and Philip Snowden had returned to both the Commons and the apex of the Labour Party, and several former UDC members served in the first Labour cabinet of 1924. Stuart Macintyre has described a 'post-war influx of some leading critics of imperialism who all came from the middle-class [*sic*] and mostly from

---

[3] P. Clarke, 'The Progressive Movement in England', *Transactions of the Royal Historical Society* 24 (1974): 177.

[4] D. Tanner, *Political Change and the Labour Party*, Cambridge: Cambridge University Press, 1990, 370.

[5] Ibid., 380.

Liberal backgrounds'. Men such as J.A. Hobson, E.D. Morel, Arthur Ponsonby, Charles Trevelyan, Noel Buxton, and Leonard Woolf all came to Labour via this route.[6] The UDC thus provided an essential gateway to Labour for many, yet it was labour patriotism during the war that ensured there was a Labour Party left for them to join: had Labour opposed the war it would have been contaminated in the eyes of much of the working class, and the mooted formation of a separate, purely trade union party may have met with more success. As it was, this proposal was rejected by the TUC of September 1916, by 3.8 million to 567,000 votes.[7]

The securing of patriotic credentials and alignment with the nationalist values of the working class also provided a valuable counterweight to accusations of anti-British sympathies and revolutionary intent from the Right. As triumphalism and anti-Germanism gave way to weariness, regret, and resentment, the party was well placed to provide an 'oppositional patriotism'. The reaction against the war within Labour was fierce. A special conference held in December 1921 on unemployment and the European crisis condemned the actions of the government since the Armistice in destroying Central European trade and causing subsequent distress in Britain, while a resolution was passed at the Brighton 1921 conference instructing the Executive to strengthen links with the Second International.[8] Speeches at the Labour Party National Conference of 1922 called for the renegotiation of German reparation payments, condemned the use of force in foreign policy, and claimed that Labour 'will appeal to the working-class [sic] to support them with all its means and strength in this struggle against armaments'.[9] By 1923 non-intervention in Russia had become a central pillar of Labour's foreign policy, and the same sentiment lay behind the Barrow Labour Party and Trade Council putting forward the motion: 'That the time is long overdue for a determined protest to be made by organised Labour, backed up by an industrial stoppage, in order to awaken the public conscience to the crimes committed by the British

[6] S. Macintyre, 'Imperialism and the British Labour Movement in the 1920s', *Our History* 64 (1975): 15. See also, J.N. Horne, *Labour at War: France and Britain 1914–1918*, Oxford: Oxford University Press, 331.

[7] Report of the Forty-Eighth Annual Gathering of the Trades Union Congress. Although this vote was won by a comfortable margin, it is worth noting that, at the height of the war, a motion to split from the Labour Party could carry over half a million votes, and the agitation for a purely trade union party, though never more than a minority movement, remained throughout the war years.

[8] Report of the Twenty-First Annual Conference of the Labour Party. Curiously, while British labour was represented on the Executive of the International by the pacifistic internationalists Fred Jowett and Tom Shaw, they were joined by ultra-patriot Ben Tillett.

[9] Report of the Twenty-First Annual Conference of the Labour Party.

Government against subject races in the interests of the expansion of the Empire and for imperialistic and capitalistic ambitions'.[10]

As Jon Lawrence has described in his article 'Forging a Peaceable Kingdom', Labour began to attack what it portrayed as 'Prussianism at home', such as the Amritsar Massacre and the Black and Tan outrages in Ireland, claiming that such incidents were harmful to the spirit and soul of Britain and shameful stains upon the nation.[11] This clever positioning was designed to both curry favour with radical patriots and win over the increasingly important Irish vote; as Lawrence has claimed, 'Labour's reluctance to become involved in all-party campaigning over Ireland was no accident. Besides its determination to assert its independence, Labour rightly saw Ireland as an issue on which it could outbid the Liberals and thereby win over both traditional Radicals and the British Irish'.[12] This radicalism was applied elsewhere in the British Empire. A resolution adopted by a Joint Meeting of the General Council of the TUC and Executive of the Labour Party in 1922 declared that: 'The present policy of the Government in Egypt is producing in that country precisely the same effect as its similar policy did in Ireland', while a further resolution adopted by the National Joint Council (representing the TUC, the Labour Executive, and the Parliamentary Labour Party (PLP)) warned that 'the antagonisms now growing in India are disastrous to the future relations of the British and Indian peoples'. At the same time, it should be noted, the Council 'deplor[ed] no less the action of the Non-Co-Operators in boycotting those Parliamentary institutions recently conferred upon India, by means of which grievances should be ventilated and wrongs redressed'.[13]

The temper of the of the 1922 Labour conference – held in the context of the 1921 miners' lockout – with regard to militarism is best conveyed by a resolution put forward by R.C. Wallhead, Independent Labour Party (ILP) member and MP for Merthyr Boroughs: 'this Conference is of the opinion that the Socialist and Labour Parties of all nations should agree to oppose any War entered into by any Government, whatever the ostensible object of the war'. An amendment to this was proposed by Kirkcaldy MP and British Socialist Party (BSP) member Tom Kennedy, to be inserted after 'object to the war': 'but should be free to support any nation forced by

---

[10] Report of the Twenty-Second Annual Conference of the Labour Party: Resolutions. This is perhaps particularly significant as Barrow was a major centre for engineering and naval armaments.

[11] J. Lawrence, 'Forging a Peaceable Kingdom: War, Violence, and Fear of Brutalization in Post-First World War Britain', *The Journal of Modern History* 75 (2003): 572 and 577.

[12] Ibid., 585.

[13] Report of the Twenty-First Annual Conference of the Labour Party.

armed aggression to defend its independence or its democratic institutions'.[14] Kennedy claimed that he was 'an anti-imperialist and detested war', yet he regarded the motion as 'wholly unnecessary, purely Utopian and purely a pacifist resolution'. Fellow BSP member Councillor W. Pitt seconded the amendment, and Silvertown MP Jack Jones spoke in favour. Jones claimed he had been against the war in 1914 and 'had stood with Keir Hardie in Trafalgar Square to advocate peace', yet: 'The people who were supporting the resolution to-day believed in war. They had got a Red Army and they had invaded countries and told the people who did not believe in their policy that they had got to accept it at the point of the bayonet.'[15] Despite the support for the amendment amongst ultra-patriots and some of the general unionists, it was overwhelmingly defeated 3,231,000 to 194,000, and the resolution was passed intact. Considering that the unions controlled around ninety per cent of the conference votes, such a heavy defeat indicates that they endorsed the pacifistic turn. For middle-class radicals, such apparent unanimity helped assuage fears that the party was no more than the political arm of the unions, and that the unions themselves were unsympathetic to the aspirations which had caused Liberal recruits to defect. It was also this adoption of an internationalist foreign policy in the early 1920s that led the formerly Liberal newspaper *The Nation* to begin supporting Labour as the only real alternative to the Coalition and the true heir to Liberalism.[16]

The prominent Liberal recruits to Labour during the 1920s were complemented by a group of former Conservatives, High Anglicans, and various scions of the Establishment. For Martin Pugh: 'Those families who were dedicated to the idea of public service implicitly subscribed to a patriotic-collectivist ideology in the sense that they regarded the State as a relatively benign and positive vehicle for promoting the interests of the community as a whole.'[17] As Godfrey Elton wrote in *Among Others:* 'The principle of national control ... had saved us from losing the war ... the nation organised for war had been a nation organised for service ... I saw no reason why, after the war, these inspiring characteristics should not be reproduced in a nation organised for peace.'[18] A cynic might claim that

---

[14] Ibid. The two-member constituency of Merthyr Tydfil was split into Aberdare and Merthyr Boroughs in 1918; that the same area could elect two men as different as the pacifist Wallhead and ultra-patriot Charles Stanton demonstrates how shared socio-economic principles cut could across patriotic/pacifistic divides.

[15] Ibid. Jack Jones had been elected as a National Socialist in Silvertown in 1918, but immediately took the Labour whip.

[16] Tanner, *Political Change*, 407.

[17] M. Pugh, '"Class Traitors": Conservative Recruits to Labour, 1900–30', *English Historical Review* 133 (1998): 55.

[18] Quoted in Pugh, 'Class Traitors', 56.

these high-born recruits sensed an opportunity for advancement within a coming political force, yet, given the wealth and success already enjoyed by most of the Tory converts, this scepticism appears unwarranted. Indeed, many of the new recruits to Labour in the 1920s soon proved their value to the party: Oswald Mosley's run in East Birmingham in 1924 was an important step in weakening Conservative control of the West Midlands, and Mosley came within a few votes of unseating Neville Chamberlain himself. Herbert Morrison, Hugh Dalton, and Mosley all held office in the 1929 government; Maurice Sankey proved to be one of the most left-wing of the 1929–31 MacDonald ministry, while all three of Clement Attlee's Chancellors – Dalton, Stafford Cripps, and Hugh Gaitskell – were former Conservatives, the first two recruited during this period. The Tory recruits of the 1920s thus provided not only financial assistance and policy expertise, particularly in foreign affairs, but more significantly: 'By using middle- and upper-class converts Labour could extend its appeal into the more marginal seats where both Tory working-class and middle-class votes had to be won.'[19]

The recruitment of former Liberals and Conservatives caused some resentment in the labour movement. The maverick Lib-Lab MP John Ward – who ended the First World War fighting against the Bolsheviks in Siberia – grew increasingly jingoistic and anti-socialist, eventually standing as an independent Constitutionalist in 1924. Lamenting this loss to Labour, W.A. Appleton, the Secretary of the General Federation of Trade Unions, wrote to Ward: 'I also regret that there is not sufficient generosity or comradeship in that Labour Party which gives shelter and support to the rejected noblemen, lawyers, doctors and petit bourgeoisie [sic] of the other parties, to leave you alone.'[20] Yet clearly there was room in the labour movement for Ward, should he choose to stay there. Most of the fifty-seven[21] Labour MPs returned in 1918 were patriotic trade unionists, and the idea that the party was stolen from sensible and conservative union leaders like Ward by middle-class liberals and socialists is clearly hyperbole.

[19] Ibid., 60.

[20] Labour History Archive and Study Centre (LHASC), John Ward Papers, JW/4/15/1: Letter from W.A. Appleton, 23 October 1924.

[21] Fifty-seven official Labour MPs were elected in December 1918. In addition, two 'Independent Labour' MPs were returned in Frank Herbert Rose at Aberdeen North and Owen Thomas at Anglesey. Alfred Edward Waterson became the first Co-operative Party MP after his election in Kettering, and he subsequently took the Labour whip. The labour patriot Jack Jones was elected for the National Socialist Party in Silvertown; four MPs stood as 'Coalition Labour' – George Wardle, George Barnes, George Roberts and James Parker – and nine MPs were returned for the National Democratic and Labour Party, giving a total 'Labour' complement of seventy-four.

Indeed, Ward pays tribute to the variety of the party in his own memoirs. In *The Beginnings of my Parliamentary Career*, he noted that, before the war:

> Mr Outhwaite, and J.C. (now Colonel) Wedgewood belonged to the same group, though I could never make out what these two men held in common. Outhwaite was a denationalist and strongly anti-British, Wedgewood was a Nationalist and a patriot. Outhwaite hated the very sight of the Union Jack, Wedgewood marched and fought under it. Outhwaite's mind was such a puny thing that it could not contain more than one idea at one time, Wedgewood's mind was so facile that it could gather to its fold knowledge upon every conceivable subject under the sun, the only thing that seemed to bind them together was the sure and certain faith that the only cure for every ill in the world, from malaria to mumps, is the single tax.[22]

Yet by 1918 both Josiah Wedgewood the patriot and Robert Outhwaite the pacifist had joined Labour. This variety and heterogeneity was not to Ward's liking. Continuing in his critique of the post-war party, he wrote:

> Recently the Party threw open its doors to individual membership, and by so doing has provided a new channel into and along which the tide of the politically abnormal can flow ... The Wee Free [Asquithian] Liberals will gradually discover that their power to attract the Single Taxer, the Food Reformer, the Prohibitionist, the Anti-Vaccinationist, and the 'Anti-Everythingist' has been lost. The Wee Free has a younger, more magnetic competitor in the field claiming the allegiance of the Singular and the Particular ... The truth and force of this suggestion will be strengthened by only a casual reference to some of the men who used to stand as Liberal candidates, and have recently transferred their affections to Labour, such a perusal also proves, what I have often suspected, that a crank is not necessarily a fool.[23]

The St Helen's MP James Sexton complained in similar terms at the 1918 conference that the new constitution would let anyone in: 'He would remind those who objected to the British Workers' League that if anybody was responsible for its existence it was the cranks inside the Labour Party. Nothing had been said about the cranks inside the U.D.C. and the Council of Civil Liberties avowedly opposing the policy of the Labour Party.'[24] Of course, individual membership was essential for Labour to move beyond the trade union base and become a truly national party, yet men such as Ward still felt that their movement was being adulterated. As David Howell has pointed out, the influence of the unions in the 1920s made Labour distinct

---

[22] JW/4/23/1: Manuscript for *The Beginnings of my Parliamentary Career*.
[23] Ibid.
[24] Report of the Seventeenth Annual Conference of the Labour Party.

from other European socialist parties, yet many unionists believed that middle-class recruits were culturally alien to working-class sensibilities; while the middle-class socialists believed men such as Ward and other Lib-Labs lacked political conviction.[25] In this respect we can see the significance of the war in providing a clean break from the politics of 1906: out went the old Lib-Labs of impeccable working-class credentials; in came often newly minted socialists from various backgrounds.

This section has highlighted how labour patriotism during the war allowed for the movement of former Liberals – and some former Tories – towards Labour in the post-war era. Yet it has focused almost entirely upon politicians and intellectuals and as such has examined only the experiences of elites. In the next sections we shall turn to Labour's appeals to the masses during and after this period, beginning with an examination of the relationship between servicemen and the Left.

Labour, Soldiers, and Ex-Servicemen

The years since the war have witnessed a great deal of debate about the extent to which soldiers were radicalised or imbued with a sense of class allegiance. Further work has focused on the relationship between radical ex-service groups and the wider Left. Yet perhaps the most significant development in terms of the relationship between servicemen and left-wing politics was the transformation in the attitudes of the labour movement towards military service, and the concerted attempt to win the military vote in the post-war years. This section will survey the debates concerning radicalisation, and discuss the movement of former soldiers towards the Left after the war. It will argue that Labour's attitudes towards military service changed considerably, the party in 1918 deliberately identifying itself with the ex-servicemen's cause. Further, this change in attitude towards the military was symbolic of a wider shift in left-wing attitudes towards the working class and working-class culture more generally.

David Englander has described how petty officers led seven hundred sailors through Liverpool to protest at demobilisation delays in 1919[26] and claimed that: 'From reports compiled by Military Intelligence it was clear that class allegiance had not been transformed by the wearing of the King's uniform.'[27] Certainly there was a real fear of insurrection amongst some in

[25] Howell, *MacDonald's Party*.

[26] D. Englander, 'Jack, Tommy and Henry Dubb: The Armed Forces and the Working Class', *The Historical Journal* 21 (1978): 614.

[27] D. Englander, 'Soldiers and Social Reform in the First and Second World Wars', *Historical Research* 67 (2007): 321.

the military establishment: as late as September 1920 Sir Henry Wilson wrote in his diary that there was 'good cause for anxiety', that army and Air Force mechanics were 'much in with the Unions' and that '[Admiral of the Fleet Sir David] Beatty has Soviets in every port'.[28] Andrew Rothstein, himself a soldier and militant during the last year of the war, argued that the mood of soldiers – who were notably more restrained in Armistice celebrations that civilians in Britain – grew steadily more mutinous from the cessation of hostilities.[29] The strike movement that characterised the demobilisation period was a truly 'subaltern' agitation according to Rothstein, and began despite the best efforts of 'the great majority of the trade union leaders and most Labour MPs'.[30] Rothstein's general thesis was that the strikes were instrumental in preventing large-scale British deployment in Russia – which seems a reasonable assertion – although he equivocated over whether sympathy for the Bolshevik cause lay behind this refusal to go to Russia. However, according to the material utilised in Rothstein's book, political concerns barely featured in the demands elucidated by troops. Instead they directed their anger at more practical, everyday concerns, such as red tape and bureaucracy, food quality, compulsory church attendance, lack of leave, and the maintenance of discipline after the Armistice.[31] William Gillman – East End activist and trade union official after the war – said he felt no objection to fitting guns for use against the Bolsheviks, it 'didn't enter into it' as far as he was concerned; he saw a clear distinction between the socialism he believed in and Russian communism.[32]

Striking naval ratings in Liverpool probably reflected the general sentiment when they simply demanded that the officers treat them as 'men, not as children'.[33] The near-constant risk of death; the mud, rats, and discomforts of the trenches; the brutal discipline and field punishments were all tolerable for the duration of the war, but from the moment of the Armistice onwards, poor rations, boredom, and patronising treatment became intolerable. In Rothstein's words, 'what the citizens in uniform wanted was, above all, to go home and get back to their jobs',[34] and it is in this context that we should understand the soldiers' strikes during the demobilisation period, rather than as representations of military radicalism, or successful Leftist agitation.

[28] Quoted in K. Jeffrey, *The British Army and the Crisis of Empire 1918–22*, Manchester: Manchester University Press, 1984, 17.

[29] A. Rothstein, *The Soldiers' Strikes*, London: Macmillan, 1985, 3.

[30] Ibid., 7.

[31] Ibid., 45, 59, 62.

[32] Imperial War Museum, Catalogue No. 9420: William Gillman, interviewed 1986.

[33] Rothstein, *The Soldiers' Strikes*, 62.

[34] Ibid., 105.

Anger at bureaucracy and army inefficiency also characterised Gloden Dallas and David Gill's *The Unknown Army*. Speaking of the Etaples mutiny in September 1917, they quoted the camp adjutant claiming that the "'chief cause of discontent" was the fact that men who had already done much service at the front had to undergo "the same strenuous training as the drafts of recruits arriving from home'".[35] Similarly, the mutineers at Le Havre 'tore down a large label: "For officers only", which was posted above a comfortable waiting room. I mention this as it typifies one of the many causes of the trouble – the bitter resentment felt at the easy conditions of the officers as compared with those of the men'.[36] All manner of indignities were accepted whilst at the front, but they soon became seen as unacceptable when in the rear, and requests for leave passes to London and extensions of canteen opening hours featured prominently amongst the troops' demands.[37] Dallas and Gill described 'the tensions which resulted when a nineteenth-century discipline pressed down on several million working men', and it appears that it was these tensions between individuals and state bureaucracy, rather than general anti-war sentiment or political militancy, which powered the post-war mutinies.[38]

Michael Paris has noted how, unlike earlier conflicts, the First World War offered little opportunity for individual initiative or heroism; troops were merely single units in a great mass of men, cogs in a massive bureaucratic machine.[39] For some men this will have reflected their pre-war lifestyle, the trenches substituting for the factory or mill. Yet for others

[35] G. Dallas and D. Gill, *The Unknown Army*, London: Verso, 1985, 72.

[36] Ibid., 105.

[37] Ibid., 111 and 118. Helen McCartney has noted how an exhausted Territorial battalion was near mutinous upon the curtailment of their leave, but was persuaded by their officers that it was crucial to the war effort, and not an arbitrary decision: 'It was the illusive concept of "fairness" that lay at the heart of the unwritten contract between the authorities and the soldiers. Whilst the Territorials would have preferred a break from the trenches, they understood that the military authorities were grappling with a dangerous man-power shortage, and under the circumstances six days' leave was a fair compromise.' See H.B. McCartney, *Citizen Soldiers: The Liverpool Territorials in the First World War*, Cambridge: Cambridge University Press, 2005, 129.

[38] Dallas and Gill, *The Unknown Army*, 138.

[39] M. Paris, *Warrior Nation*, London: Reaktion Books, 2000, 115 and 134. Recent work by Gary Sheffield and Dan Todman has stressed the evolution of fighting methods towards the end of the war, which relied more upon the skill of individual infantrymen. In addition, by the end of the war, half of the officers were former NCOs. Thus, in tactics and composition, the army of 1918 was notably different to that of 1914 or even 1916 but generally a soldiers' life in the First World War did not permit much autonomy or agency. See G. Sheffield, *Forgotten Victory: The First World War: Myths and Realities*, London: Headline Review, 2002; D. Todman, *The Great War: Myth and Reality*, London: Hambledon and London, 2005.

the subordination and lack of autonomy, the sacrifices and hardship for little reward, and the lack of means for redress of grievance will have been novel experiences. To what extent did the shared experiences of trench life, coupled with post-war resentment and disillusionment, lead former soldiers towards the Left? Two years after the fighting ceased, war correspondent Philip Gibbs argued that 'many men who came alive out of that conflict were changed and vowed not to tolerate a system of thought which had led to such a monstrous massacre of human beings who prayed to God [and] loved the same jobs of life'.[40] Further, Susan Pedersen has claimed that it was not merely ex-servicemen themselves who were indelibly changed by the war: 'Soldiers' wives learned to intervene in the public sphere in their own interest: they responded angrily to charges of drunkenness, lobbied Labour organizations for increased rates, and kept up a constant stream of letters to their MPs.'[41] Most of the correspondents with the War Emergency Workers' National Committee (WNC), an organisation set up to co-ordinate the labour movement's response to the war, were women, suggesting that the conflict did bring wives and mothers into the political sphere.

One of the most important organised manifestations of soldiers' discontent was the National Federation of Discharged and Demobilised Soldiers and Sailors (the Fed), which only allowed officers to join if they had been promoted from the ranks. Members of the Fed would physically break-up right-wing meetings in Norfolk and South Wales, and acted as a conduit for soldiers towards civilian unions such as National Agricultural Labourers' and Rural Workers' Union (NALRU), the National Union of Railwaymen (NUR), and the Workers' Union; Jack Beard, President of the Workers' Union, was prominently involved with the Fed, and wore his old volunteer uniform to meetings.[42] Nonetheless the political orientation of the Fed varied across the country; in some areas it worked with the state against aliens and pacifists, and could be hostile towards strikers.[43] More radical than the Fed was the National Union of Ex-Servicemen (NUX). Formed in May 1919 by Fed members looking to organise ex-soldiers within the labour movement, it eventually constituted over one hundred branches.

[40] Quoted in E.J. Leed, 'Class and Disillusionment in World War I', *The Journal of Modern History* 50 (1978): 696.

[41] S. Pedersen, 'Gender, Welfare and Citizenship in Britain during the Great War', *The American Historical Review* 95 (1990): 1003.

[42] N. Mansfield, 'The National Federation of Discharged and Disabled Soldiers and Sailors', *Family and Community History* 7 (2004): 21 and 25.

[43] P. Burnham, 'The Radical Ex-Servicemen of 1918', in N. Mansfield and C. Horner (eds), *The Great War: Localities and Regional Identities*, Newcastle: Cambridge Scholars Publishing, 2014, 33.

The NUX flirted with continental socialists and the Third International, but had affiliated to the Labour Party by 1920.[44] Despite the initial enthusiasm for ex-servicemen's organisations in the immediate post-war period, much like the extreme patriotic labour groups such as the British Workers' League/National Democratic Party, these bodies did not translate enthusiasm into solid electoral success. The ex-servicemen's organisations nominated twenty-nine candidates in 1918, but only one was elected, and radical soldiers' groups had lost their significance within a few years of the Armistice.[45]

The relative quiescence of British veterans compared to their equivalents not just in defeated countries such as Germany, but also in ostensibly victorious nations such as Italy and France, puzzled both contemporary observers and later historians. Although Lloyd George, despite initially handling demobilisation poorly, had been forced to introduce a large-scale pension scheme, awarding 1.7 million disability pensions by 1921, for all the rhetoric, a land fit for heroes failed to emerge, and the recession of the early 1920s left many soldiers in penury.[46] Why, as Deborah Cohen asked, 'did German veterans become alienated from a state that provided them with generous benefits, while their British counterparts – despite the neglect of successive governments – bolstered the established order?'[47] Cohen's answer is that a combination of the innate conservatism of many soldiers ('Most men wanted a steady job and a secure home life, not a revolution in the East End'), the success of the British Legion (which grew from eighteen thousand members in 1921 to over three hundred thousand in the early 1930s), and the pronounced public gratitude 'shielded the state' from ex-soldiers' resentment.[48] Peter Reese has depicted a more cynical and passive reaction to the war, noting that even at its height the British Legion numbered a mere fraction of the millions who enlisted, and that it was never seen as a 'great military Trade Union which could force Governments to give them special help. They had been given the initial privilege and subsequent curse of the British fighting man, and, although service charities might help, they each had to endure their fight'.[49] In short, although the experience of war had served to anger and alienate many

[44] S. Ward, 'Intelligence Surveillance of British Ex-Servicemen, 1918–1920', *Historical Journal* 16 (1973): 186–87.

[45] Ibid., 183.

[46] I. Beckett, 'The Nation in Arms, 1914–18', in I. Beckett and K. Simpson (eds), *A Nation in Arms*, London: Tom Donovan, 1990, 25.

[47] D. Cohen, *The War Come Home: Disabled Veterans in Britain and Germany 1914–1939*, Berkeley: University of California Press, 2001, 189.

[48] Ibid., 49–50 and 189.

[49] P. Reese, *Homecoming Heroes*, London: Leo Cooper, 1992, 148.

hundreds of thousands of men, they were 'not angry enough at their fellow citizens to court the unrest that bayonets brought'; they were discontented and disillusioned, but not enough to want to bring down the state.[50]

In June 1915, one of the soldiers' letters which had become a frequent feature in the patriotic labour newspaper *The Clarion* claimed that the paper was missing an opportunity through lack of availability in barrack towns: 'In Aldershot I had some trouble in obtaining *The Clarion*, and did not see a single newsagent with the bill displayed. Were it well-advertised I think it would have a very good sale.'[51] Although there was no concerted effort by editor Robert Blatchford and his team to specifically target troops, the apparent popularity of the newspaper amongst soldiers was a common theme in the letters sent from the trenches. Corporal R. Palmer of the Royal Welch Fusiliers claimed that *The Clarion* was immensely popular in his battalion; particularly interesting as it was considered an elite unit.[52] 'Tommie', writing in July 1915, assured Blatchford that 'Whenever it arrives the boys in my section make a rush to get a look at it'; Sapper J.G. Moir claimed that it was 'greedily read' by everyone in his section, and Private Fred Vesey confirmed that 'you would be surprised at the way it is sought after by the other boys'.[53] Private A.E. Price of the 4th Hussars suggested that there was a certain amount of circumspection amongst some of those who borrowed his copy: 'I think it my duty to let you know', he wrote 'along with the other chaps who have written, of the beneficial results attained amongst the rest of the troops, who all come sneaking round for the first rub of *The Clarion* when it comes.'[54] The impression generally given is that most troops had not heard of Blatchford or his paper, yet – despite occasional scepticism about a supposed 'socialist' tract – often found much to agree with: '*The Clarion* goes round the "bhoys", and it is a study to watch a man who has never seen or heard of our paper before as he casually glances first and then gets stuck into it', as one soldier attested.[55]

Perhaps a more realistic – yet still encouraging – account of the paper's reception amongst the troops was given by Private B. Solway: 'I can assure you the paper is read till it is properly black. Old Robert is a great favourite with Tommy. There is always a lot of arguing over his comments' – an assertion echoed in an interview with a group of Glaswegian soldiers in August 1916, who spoke of the importance of *The Clarion* in barrack

[50] Ibid., 59.
[51] Letter from Corporal R. Fyfe, *The Clarion*, 4 June 1915.
[52] Letter from Corporal R. Palmer, *The Clarion*, 28 April 1916.
[53] Ibid., 2 July 1915, 21 July 1916, 2 July 1915.
[54] Ibid., 2 July 1915.
[55] Ibid., 16 July 1916.

room debates and the arguments it had caused.[56] One suspects that the combination of nationalism, populist leftism, and a concerted effort to root the paper in working-class culture was agreeable to many, especially given Blatchford's and *The Clarion*'s proud history of recruiting ordinary workers to the labour movement through cultural activities and a shared language. We cannot know the exact circulation of *The Clarion* in the trenches, nor the number of new readers who agreed with what they read. Yet the very fact that a new audience was reading the paper meant that many were being exposed to concerted leftist arguments, couched in a language of family, patriotism, the pub, and soldierly camaraderie, and edited by a former soldier. For this alone *The Clarion* played an important role as a channel for soldiers into the labour movement, much as it had done for the wider population in the decades since its launch.

Another indication of communication between the Left and men in the services came from a letter from Labour Party Secretary Jim Middleton to A.N. Field, serving in the navy: 'I am sorry that our stuff has reached you in Party envelopes, and can quite appreciate the ragging you may have got from your comrades', Middleton apologised, before continuing: 'however, it will interest you, and probably them, to know that there is hardly a mail that reaches us now without enquiries for our literature, and particularly of our Reconstruction Policy, War Aims, etc., coming from men with the colours.'[57]

Looking back on the lack of widespread revolutionary ardour among his old comrades, former Private C.A. Turner confided to Martin Middlebrook:

> One universal question which I have never seen answered: two or three million pounds a day for the 1914–18 war, yet no monies were forthcoming to put industry on its feet on our return from war. Many's the time I've gone to bed, after a day of 'tramp, tramp' looking for work, on a cup of cocoa and a pennyworth of chips between us; I would lay puzzling why, why, after all we had gone through in the service of our country, we have to suffer such poverty, willing to work at anything but no work to be had. I only had two Christmases at work between 1919 and 1939.[58]

Yet while many soldiers lost their radicalism in the years after the war, many channelled their anger through the labour movement, and former soldiers would feature prominently among future Labour and trade union leaders: Nick Mansfield has drawn attention to one Bill Curtis of Salhouse, Norfolk, one of only twenty-four from the 8th Battalion of the Norfolk Regiment who survived the Somme, who became one of the new local activists for Labour

[56] Ibid., letter from B. Solway 29 January 1915; 11 August 1916.
[57] Labour History Archive and Study Centre, War Emergency Worker's National Committee Files, WNC.15/3/5 – letter to A.N. Field, *HMS Spender*, 16 July 1918.
[58] M. Middlebrook, *The First Day on the Somme*, London: Allen Lane, 1975, 309.

after the war.[59] Similarly, the Imperial War Museum archive contains interviews with men who would become prominent labour and trade union activists after the war, such as William Gillman in East London, Jack Dorgan in Northumberland, and Frederick Orton in Nottingham.

One of the most high-profile of the recruits with no previous interest in politics who later joined the labour movement was Douglas Houghton. Houghton – who has the distinction of being the last cabinet minister born in the nineteenth century and the last veteran of the First World War to serve in the Cabinet and both Houses of Parliament – was born in Nottinghamshire in 1898, the son of a lacemaker. In 1914 he worked as an apprentice clerk, in addition to studying for the Civil Service exams. After joining the Civil Service Rifles, he fought at the Somme, served as a Lewis Gunner, and ended the war as a bayonet instructor at training depots in England. His letters to his parents prior to the war had been largely devoid of any political content and were mainly concerned with requests for cakes and clean laundry. When in France, he observed in an uncensored 'green envelop' letter that officers were granted undue luxuries and privileges, but his tone was more one of envy than outrage:

> You ask me what I think of an officer's life out here. Well, frankly speaking I only wish I had taken the opportunity of getting a Commission before I came out. The greatest consideration is … incidental comfort. They rarely have to put up with any inconvenience. Their position is least enviable when up the line but even then it's worth it. Then again officers 'work' things. As soon as the news comes than we are going up the line we find our officers going away on 'courses'. We have been up twice and the second time only one officer accompanied us that had been up the time before.[60]

Houghton clearly enjoyed army life, however, for he extended his service after the war and censured his mother when she expressed exasperation that he was not yet demobilised by April 1919: 'You are passing grave criticism about things of which you have only limited information. The army of occupation is not such a dreadful affair as you would have us believe. Life in it is not much more strenuous than in England – there are new and interesting surroundings.'[61] Later that year, whilst back in England, he opined: 'I have no desire to return to the office. I get fed up enough with long hours and exacting work and the monotonous daily routine and lack of exercise and I certainly like army life in England.'[62]

---

[59] N. Mansfield, 'Class Conflict and Village War Memorials, 1914–24', *Rural History* 6 (1995): 74.

[60] LHASC: Douglas Houghton Papers, DHO/35 – letter to mother, 18 November 1917.

[61] DHO/35 – letter to mother, 3 April 1919.

[62] DHO/35 – letter to mother, undated 1919.

Although a fan of army life, Houghton felt aggrieved by the treatment of soldiers and ex-servicemen in the period after the Armistice, and criticisms of the government feature more prominently in his post-war correspondence, particularly concerning British prisoners of war. He wrote to his father: 'I think we have made rather a tame ending to victory. Fancy the prisoners of a victorious alliance being turned adrift to fend for themselves. I would have insisted that they be sent to the frontier in 1st class carriages.'[63] After the khaki election, he noted that 'Some of the election results startled us, especially in the electorate's handling of Asquith and most of the Liberal side ... It is certainly a fact that thousands of soldiers were unable to record their vote'.[64] He witnessed the industrial disruption which followed the war at first-hand, but not from the labour side, confiding to his mother in July 1919 that 'I don't know how the leave will go. There is some uncertainty owing to the strikes. The Battn. is being held in readiness to move in connection with local colliery disputes.'[65] The preparations for the 1919 police strike, however, he considered excessive: 'Detachments were detailed, armed, equipped etc and sent to do guard duties pending the settlement of the police strike. Even Lewis Guns and 3000 rounds of ammunition per gun were mobilised. One would have thought that they were dealing with armed bandits instead of harmless bobbies.'[66] It is important to remember that at this point Houghton was not a member of a trade union or any other group affiliated to the labour movement; he was an individual, and after 1918 it was increasingly to individuals that Labour appealed.

Contrary to those commentators who felt that the war brought the Left and the military closer together, David Englander has argued that in fact 'nothing could be further from the truth ... if anything, the war had accentuated Labour's prejudice against the serviceman' and, in addition, 'during the war the Labour movement became concerned *about* the soldier, not *for* him'.[67] Furthermore, claims Englander, the Labour Party treated ex-servicemen's claims for special privileges with suspicion, and failed to develop a coherent policy on the army until 1939.[68] This lack of concern – or even disdain – for the soldier was not apparent in the language of the labour movement at the time. Almost immediately many leftist newspapers and organisations developed a preoccupation with the welfare of soldiers and sailors, particularly papers which had campaigned for better treatment of

63 DHO/35 – letter to father, undated 1919.
64 DHO/35 – letter to mother, 30 December 1918.
65 DHO/35 – letter to mother, 25 July 1919.
66 DHO/35 – letter to mother, undated 1919.
67 Englander, 'Jack, Tommy and Henry Dubb', 618–20.
68 Englander, 'Soldiers and Social Reform', 321; 'Jack, Tommy, and Henry Dubb', 621.

troops in the years before the war, such as *Justice* and *The Clarion*. As with the Boer War, the call for recruits had revealed the poor physical condition of many British workmen, and patriotic labour papers – and left-wing ones such as *The Herald* – used this to indict the economic creed of the Liberal and Conservative parties. As an example of corroborating evidence from an ostensibly objective outsider, *The Clarion* printed a letter in January 1915 from a New Zealand officer, who observed: 'There are some English Territorials here, and they look very small alongside our men. I did not know there was such a difference until I saw a regiment of each together.'[69]

As early as 1916 the Minority Report of the Departmental Committee on discharged soldiers and sailors suggested setting aside plots of land for veterans, in addition to a minimum industrial wage and high-quality affordable housing.[70] The labour movement organised a War Pensions Conference in Pontypridd on 3 June 1916, attended by over four hundred delegates from 189 trade union branches, sixty-six churches, fifteen trades councils, and six friendly societies, where the following resolution was passed unanimously:

> This Conference considers that the method of providing for our brave Soldiers and Sailors who have sacrificed so much for their country, by collections in various ways, is unworthy of the British Public; that we pledge ourselves to take every step necessary to bring pressure to bear on Parliament to make provision for the disabled Soldiers and Sailors, so that they and their families shall not suffer or be dependent on charity. And furthermore, that we, the Delegates assembled at this Conference, are prepared to advise the members of the various organisations we represent not to assist in any local efforts in furtherance of the Charity Clauses in the Naval and Military War Pensions Act, 1915, so as to place upon the Government the onus of providing all the funds required to administer the Act.[71]

By September 1917 *Co-Partners' Magazine* – organ of the London Gas and Electric Light Company – argued in an article entitled 'Hope for Disabled Soldiers and Sailors' that 'every sailor and soldier is entitled to the benefits of this [War Pensions] scheme; which is not a charity, but a part of the recompense owed by the nation to the men who have fought and bled for it'.[72] In 1917 the WNC pushed for an increase in soldiers' wages, and Jim Middleton tabled a question for Charles Duncan MP to ask the financial secretary of the War Office. 'You will be interested to know', he wrote,

---

[69] *The Clarion*, 29 January 1915.
[70] Reported in *The Co-operative News*, 8 July 1916.
[71] WNC.24/1/172.
[72] *Co-Partners Magazine*, September 1917.

'that the Workers' National Committee is going into the whole question of soldiers' rates with a view to demanding a general increase, and I will see that the remuneration of men in your position is considered.'[73]

In May 1915 the WNC decided to give assistance to the wives of British prisoners interned in Germany who 'as a result sending regular parcels of food, etc. to their husbands, find themselves in distress'.[74] The Committee also lobbied against the practice of suspending separation allowances to the relatives of men executed for desertion; Middleton wrote in a letter to J. Dawson of the Keighley and District Trades and Labour Council: 'This is a matter I took up personally with Mr Barnes in the early days of his Pension Ministry, but without success. The views of some of the permanent officials on the subject were simply detestable, while others, with whom I discussed the matter, were altogether more sympathetic. The former, naturally enough had not been in the Service, the latter had.'[75] After the war, former soldier Ernest Thurtle was one Labour MP prominent in the struggle to abolish the military death penalty, and the wider party took steps to fight for soldiers' rights.[76] In the words of Terrence Bogacz: 'Reflecting popular concern and claiming to speak for the other ranks, the Labour Party argued that among those men executed for cowardice were many who had been shellshock victims and thus had been unjustly sentenced to death.'[77]

In the spring of 1917 the WNC circulated a pamphlet entitled 'The Soldiers' and Sailors' Charter', which described the changes to pensions and gratuities introduced to Parliament by Labour's George Barnes, Minister for Pensions, on 5 March. The new rates granted a pension of between twenty-five and sixty shillings depending on rank, degree of disablement, and pre-war earnings. Full provision was made for soldiers needing treatment away from home, with pension and allowances paid to wives, children, and dependents; there was a five-shilling bonus payable for each week of rehabilitation training, and men were to be paid ten shillings a week for work missed due to medical procedures. Furthermore, in a concession to pressure from the labour movement, men who suffered disablement not directly attributable to or aggravated by military service were to be paid a £150 gratuity, where previously they had not qualified for any remuneration.[78] Another pamphlet, 'The Labour Party: For Services Rendered', carried the full text of Barnes's

[73] WNC.2/5/11/11.

[74] WNC.25/3/34 – letter from Middleton to Mary MacArthur, 14 May 1915.

[75] WNC.2/5/17/2 – letter from Middleton to J Dawson, 24 October 1917.

[76] T. Bogacz, 'War Neurosis and Cultural Change in England, 1914–22: The Work of the War Office Committee of Enquiry into "Shell-Shock"', *Journal of Contemporary History* 24 (1989): 253.

[77] Ibid., 236.

[78] WNC.23/2/3 – 'The Soldiers' and Sailors' Charter'.

speech. Describing men who would not be able to return to their old way of life, Barnes argued that 'a pension in a case like that seems to be like giving an old friend 1s. to get rid of him instead of putting him in a position to earn 2s., which is what he really needs'. He went on to praise voluntary organisations such as the Star and Garter hospitals, the Lord Roberts Workshops, and St Dunstan's, where hundreds of men blinded in the war had been rehabilitated, and many more were scheduled to follow.

Barnes proudly announced that men who had served in the army before the war, and had been claiming an army pension, were now allowed to apply for an additional disablement pension – something denied to them previously – and that this change was to apply retrospectively. Furthermore, he described the more generous arrangements for disablement not directly caused by service: 'In future if a man's disease is aggravated by service he will get his pension just the same as if it were attributable to it or caused by it; and if it arises seven years after the war he will get a pension if it is clear that it has been substantially aggravated by the war.' Barnes ended his speech on a controversial note, however, confirming that men who were passed fit for military service, but later found unfit and dismissed, would not be granted any gratuity or pension. Responding to an interjection from Edinburgh East Liberal MP James Hogge that these men should be paid their due, Barnes was unequivocal: 'These men have been passed into the Army owing to the great pressure under which doctors had to work in the early days. Hundreds of them have been passed into the Army who should never have been passed in – veritable weeds, that ought never to have been there at all.'[79] This remark caused consternation amongst some in the labour movement, and contributed to a building resentment against Barnes and other Labour figures involved with the government from those on the Left of the party.

The ILP placed a demand for a Soldier's Charter on the agenda for the Labour Party Conference of January 1918. This charter called for an increase in pay, separation allowances, and pensions; more generous industrial training for injured ex-servicemen; more 'humane' and 'comfortable' medical examinations; for the use of the death penalty to be reduced to the smallest possible margins; for the grievances of ex-servicemen to be justly represented; and for the Labour Party to pressure the government into adopting this programme.[80] The final aspect of the charter was perhaps the most significant: the ILP was pressing for the Labour Party to take up the ex-servicemen's cause; to become the party of the veteran and an agitator for equitable treatment for those who had fought and served.

[79] WNC.23/2/5 – 'The Labour Party: For Services Rendered'.
[80] Report of the Seventeenth Annual Conference of the Labour Party: Agenda.

Almost immediately after the outbreak of war *The Co-operative News* featured a hastily written and somewhat patronising homage to the pre-war army entitled 'A Tribute to the Lower Classes. The Men Upon Whom the Nation Has Had to Depend: Heroism Out of Poverty'.[81] A further article in October 1914 asked: 'Who is Tommy Atkins? Glorified in Battle, but Despised in Labour Struggles: Plain John Smith in Khaki'. The paper's correspondent concluded that the soldier represented the best values of the British working man: 'Tommy's name was not Tommy Atkins, but John Smith, the plain working man, whom Robert Blatchford addressed in those remarkable articles of his which formed the volume of "Merrie England."'[82] Will Crooks paid similar homage to the 'everyman' nature of the British soldier during a speech to the Co-Partnership Committee on 2 November 1915. After detailing reported German rapes and outrages, he contrasted them with the spirit of the British soldier: 'Tommy is not a plaster saint', Crooks claimed, 'but he is a man!'[83] This phrase encapsulated the message of the patriotic wing of the labour movement during this period: both the previously despised pre-war soldier and his New Army or conscript equivalent were now representative of the best traits of the British working man: far from perfect, fond of drink and rough amusements, coarse of language, and not given to abstract thought, but solid, dependable, honourable, indefatigable, and the source of all wealth and security and greatness of the nation. The argument that followed logically from this position was that government policy must be tailored to improve the lot of such people: it owed it to them before the war, and its obligations had been multiplied by the conflict.

A year before the end of the war, even *Punch* marvelled at the idea of these heroes returning to their old occupations after their extraordinary experiences – a cartoon entitled 'Glimpses of the Future' depicted a housemaid calling to her employer: 'Mr, Jones, Sir – Him wot killed seventeen Germans in one trench with his own 'ands 'as called for the Gas Account, Sir'.[84] There was an extended tale in a June 1915 edition of *The Post* – entitled 'Vulgar Fellows' – which is worth quoting at length as it revealed the patronising attitude of many of the elites of the labour movement towards the working class, and how this shifted during the war. There were seven men in a crowded bank-holiday carriage: two Kitchener troops off to train at trench-digging, two Yeomanry troopers, a big artilleryman, 'loaded upon us in a drunken sleep', an army doctor, and the author:

---

[81] *The Co-operative News*, 19 September 1914.
[82] Ibid., 10 October 1914.
[83] *Co-Partners' Magazine*, December 1915.
[84] Reprinted in *Co-Partners Magazine*, October 1917.

Just before the train started, however, a sturdy chap wearing the neat cap badge of the Royal Fusiliers climbed in upon us. He cheerfully rearranged the form of our gunner, and so provided himself with a seat. Then the train moved off, and as we passed the long line of faces on the platform, the weary smile of one old woman was directed towards our new arrival.

The Fusilier produced a quart bottle of beer:

After drinking himself he offered it to the Yeomen. With some persuasion one of them partook. Then, perhaps with greater honesty, certainly with greater enthusiasm, the trench-diggers helped themselves. It was then my turn. I excused myself, politely, but with decision. I have never worn the blue ribbon. It is sometimes pleasant to drink a friendly glass, seated with a good chum in a comfortably furnished lounge. It is more pleasant still, as one of the jobs of the road, to call at mine inn with 'a thirst like that of a thirsty sword.' But a quart bottle, offered by a stranger in a railway carriage on a Bank-holiday, and with one lying before me whose abnormal thirst had led him astray – certainly not!

The men began to talk, and the Fusilier related how he had been at the front since the outbreak and had survived unmarked until late January, when a shell had torn open his chest and thigh. As he was recovering, two of his brothers were killed in the trenches. Discharged from the hospital, he had been given forty-eight hours' leave to return home, and was now en route back to France:

He gazed out of the window in a thoughtful silence for a considerable time … Later, something said prompted him to tell us that the old woman who had watched our train start was the mother of a regimental comrade. She had asked him to deliver a parcel of cakes and cheap cigarettes to her son, from whom she had not heard during many weeks. He had taken the parcel and promised to deliver it because he lacked the courage to tell this mother something the War Office had failed to tell her. To his certain knowledge, her son had fallen several weeks previously. When the Fusilier told that story someone in the carriage swore audibly, and the whizzing landscape became blurred to at least one pair of eyes.

At Rugby the troopers were replaced by two middle-aged civilians, and the conversation turned to after-the-war matters, one of the civilians positing that the government would have to do something to help the workers:

'The Government!' scoffed our Fusilier. 'We can't wait for those beggars. We'll put things right ourselves.' For the first time I noticed that he looked just like that square-jawed chap on the posters who invites us to fall in and follow. No doubt he was at the moment connecting the economic future with the ugly scars over his heart, with his two dead brothers, and with the waiting mother of his lost chum. No one in the compartment had any reply for him ... Shortly afterwards the Royal Fusilier produced again his homely flask. After satisfying his own thirst he presented the bottle to me. This time I took it, and, after passing the palm of my hand over its mouth in the approved fashion, I drank. It was proffered by a man – a fighting man and a thinking man.[85]

It was precisely this type of worker that the labour movement had usually failed to reach up until this point, perhaps due to the disdain which many left-wing elites had for such men. Labour patriotism during the war was vital to making inroads into this constituency in the years that followed.

This section has demonstrated how labour patriotism allowed service in the military to become a channel towards Labour, and the significance of this to Labour's post-war success. The military identity and camaraderie engendered by this did not last much longer than the war, however, and Labour needed to formulate its appeals to the post-war working class in a language that would win through even as memories of the war faded. It is to the construction of this language, and the role which labour patriotism played in this construction, that we now turn.

The War and the Appeal to the New Electorate

This final section is concerned with how Labour's experiences during the war affected its appeal to the post-war electorate. The new franchise and new party constitution which resulted from the conflict required new methods and new ways of organising, and the war reinforced the need for Labour to appear culturally analogous to working-class voters. Here we will consider the changes to the party and its election campaigns, the relationship between unskilled workers and the party, attempts to attract new female voters, and finally appeals to voters based upon community and culture. Thus far, the labour movement had drawn its strength from areas which featured either high rates of unionisation in skilled or craft unions, or a tradition of radical Nonconformity, or very often both. After the First World War the party broke out from these bridgeheads to become a truly national party by 1945. It is argued here that the first war itself and Labour's support for it were crucial in this transformation. Labour began to win votes amongst unskilled workers, women, Catholics, patriots, and 'the football crowds' at exactly the time when it most needed to broaden its appeal. In the words of Arthur Henderson: 'Trade unionism had very little hold upon the agricultural constituencies; but there was evidence that they wanted Labour candidates. How were these people to be organised?

[85] *The Post*, 18 June 1915.

They could only do so by saying to every man and woman ... "Come along with us, our platform is broad enough and our Movement big enough to take you all."[86]

Henderson used his speech to the 1918 party conference to argue for the new constitution: 'There has been a notable increase in the general interest taken by all sections of the community in the work of the Party and its future development, and during recent months a cordial and welcome spirit of enquiry both as to our actual principles and more particularly as to our proposals for reconstruction after the War.' Hence there was to be individual membership for those unable or uncompelled to join trade unions and not prepared to join socialist societies, and similar special preparations made for organising women.[87] Arthur Peters – the National Agent – reported:

> At no time in our previous history has the vitality of the party been so manifest. Requests for advice and assistance from all parts of the country continue to be received, and during the past two months numerous local Conferences have been successfully carried through and many others are to follow. Local Labour Parties are being established upon the lines of our suggested new rules and the warm welcome accorded the proposals for individual membership afford grounds for believing that the new organisation will soon develop good and substantial machinery for the effective working of all our future elections.[88]

On the report of the Boundary Commissioners, he declared: 'The battle-grounds for the future are now defined, many handicaps being removed, and with considerably increased facilities for contests our democratic forces will welcome the opportunity for an appeal to the country immediately after the world-conflict has ceased.'[89] Chairman Frank Purdy proclaimed: 'We aim in the years coming to be the People's Party – a Party not parochial in its conception, but national in its character and broad in its aspirations; constructive in its programme; watching keenly the foreign policy and international relations of the nation; and bringing to the service of the State all that makes for the social and industrial improvement of the people.'[90]

Pre-War Labour and Working-Class Culture
In the 1960s Richard Hoggart observed that 'the more we try to reach the core of working-class attitudes, the more surely does it appear that that core is a sense of the personal, the concrete, the local; it is embodied in the idea

---

[86] Report of the Seventeenth Annual Conference of the Labour Party.
[87] Ibid.
[88] Ibid.
[89] Ibid.
[90] Ibid.

of, first, the family, and, second, the neighbourhood'.[91] When Martin Pugh wrote of 'the sentiments of a conservative working class that, in certain circumstances, was prepared to vote Labour', he cannot be said to be wide of the mark.[92] This was not lost on some Edwardian Labour leaders; in his autobiography, J.H. Thomas declared that 'the workers are more conservative than the Conservatives'.[93] While some areas such as the coalfields of South Wales and northeast England or the textile districts of West Yorkshire were home to a proud radical tradition, often arising from Nonconformity and increasingly supportive of the Labour Party, this tradition was generally absent from large areas of West Lancashire, London, the Midlands, and most southern towns. As Gareth Stedman Jones has noted, there was a distinct lack of temperance tradition amongst the radical artisans in London, and the impression conveyed by Charles Booth's survey of the turn of-the-century London poor 'was of a working-class culture which was both impermeable to outsiders, and yet predominantly conservative in character: a culture in which the central focus was not "trade unions and friendly societies, cooperative effort, temperance propaganda and politics" (including socialism) but "pleasure, amusement, hospitality and sport"'.[94] Elizabeth Ross has written of pre-war East London that 'Church goers often had to face choruses of mockers', and one convert walking with a missionary in southwest Bethnal Green in 1889 was assaulted by former drinking companions.[95] Of course we cannot make any easy assumptions and there were always exceptions to apparently homogenous cultures: Andrew Davies has noted of interwar Salford that, far from being an omnipresent background to daily life, 'people took part in pub culture when they could afford to'; and that whilst football was enormously popular amongst working-class men, very often people could not afford to attend matches featuring Manchester United or Manchester City, and to make do with more humble grassroots teams.[96]

[91] R. Hoggart, *The Uses of Literacy: Aspects of Working-Class Life*, London: Chatto and Windus, 1957, 61.

[92] M. Pugh, 'The Rise of Labour and the Political Culture of Conservatism, 1890–1945', *History* 87 (2003): 518.

[93] Quoted in M. Pugh, *Speak for Britain! A New History of the Labour Party*, London: Vintage, 2011, 170.

[94] G. Stedman Jones, 'Working-Class Culture and Working-Class Politics in London, 1870–1900: Notes on the Remaking of a Working Class', *Journal of Social History* 7 (1974): 472 and 479.

[95] E. Ross, '"Not the Sort that Would Sit on the Doorstep": Respectability in Pre-World War I London Neighbourhoods', *International Labor and Working-Class History* 27 (1985): 44.

[96] A. Davies, 'Leisure in the "Classic Slum"', in A. Davies and S. Fielding (eds), *Workings' Worlds. Cultures and Communities in Manchester and Salford, 1880–1939*, Manchester: Manchester University Press, 1992, 108 and 111.

Yet, generally, most working-class areas exhibited a culture centred around the pub, the music hall, family, and patriotism, which often inhibited leftist recruitment.

The Social Democratic Federation – the leading socialist society in London – never had more than three thousand members out of a population of more than six and a half million.[97] In London, Jones concluded that the 'republican and international culture which had been such a characteristic feature of artisan tradition in the first three quarters of the century had all but died out by 1900'. The persistence and popularity of working-class Toryism confounded and perplexed many on the Edwardian Left. Many towns and cities seemed dominated by people who, though living in conditions of terrible squalor, being independent of mind and not averse to riots and general rowdiness, continued to loyally vote Conservative.[98] Stedman Jones quoted a member of the Paddington Radical Club from the Boer War era: 'When I ventured to point out to one member that the cost of the present war would have put old age pensions on a sound basis, the answer I received was "to Hades with Old Age Pensions."'[99] Yet the Labour Party needed the support of these people: as Pugh has argued, in areas such as Lancashire and the Midlands it was not enough to absorb Liberals; the party needed to convert working-class Tories as well.[100]

'If the Labour Party could select a King', Ben Tillett had sneered in 1908, 'he would be a Feminist, a Temperance crank, a Nonconformist charlatan ... an anti-sport, anti-jollity advocate, a teetotaller, as well as a general wet blanket ... Horse-racing would vanish [and] as for music halls, they would be anathema!'[101] Tillett was voicing his frustration at the apparent dichotomy in cultural values between the wider working class and its supposed representatives: early socialists had looked to create a 'morally uplifting' popular culture, which had often served to alienate them from the wider electorate.[102] In 1918 MacDonald claimed that his

[97] Stedman Jones, 'Working-Class Culture', 481.

[98] It should be noted that Patrick Joyce has warned against portraying working-class Conservatives as a sort of 'lumpen proletariat', particularly in late Victorian Lancashire. See P. Joyce, *Work, Society and Politics: The Culture of the Factory in Later Victorian England*, Brighton: Harvester Press, 1980, 212. Similarly, work by Marc Brodie has called into question the reasons that lay behind the Conservatism of the pre-1914 East End without challenging it. See M. Brodie, *The Politics of the Poor: The East End of London, 1885–1914*, Oxford: Clarendon Press, 2004.

[99] Stedman Jones, 'Working-Class Culture', 480.

[100] Pugh, *Speak for Britain*, 45.

[101] Quoted in Pugh, *Speak for Britain*, 74.

[102] B. Beaven, 'Challenges to Civic Governance in Post-War England: The Peace Day Disturbances of 1919', *Urban History* 33 (2006): 378.

defeat in Leicester and Labour's relatively poor showing was 'the fault of the minds of the people'. 'We all know perfectly well', he further asserted in 1919, 'that electoral majorities are composed of a small minority of active politically minded people influencing a mass of people who have no fixed convictions or orientations.'[103] He also blamed his Leicester defeat on female voters, suggesting that they were more susceptible to the patriotic fervour of the khaki election than men; something backed up by chairman J. McGurk's address to the 1919 party conference: '[Lloyd George] denounced the party as Bolshevist, and frightened the electors, particularly the women, by lurid descriptions of what would happen in England if Labour came to power.'[104]

September 1915 had witnessed an oration in the House of Commons by J.H. Thomas attacking the conscriptionist press. In the speech Thomas lambasted 'Lord Northcliffe, whose cynical estimate of the intelligence of the masses of the people is indicated by the class of reading he serves up for their edification'.[105] Yet, unfortunately for Thomas and the rest of the Labour movement, Northcliffe and other right-wing, populist press barons and editors – most notably Horatio Bottomley – had a very keen understanding of the character and sensibilities of the British people; hence the high circulations of their newspapers. Blatchford, in contrast to Thomas, was aware of this. Ruminating on the issue in an article entitled 'Why Labour and Socialist Papers Do Not Pay', he asked: 'Is it because the working people don't know what's good for them; or is it because the Labour and Socialist journals do not know what the working people want? Men like ourselves ... always make the mistake of assuming that the millions of British workers have tastes, interests, habits of minds and concentration of purpose exactly like our own.' After calling for more sports coverage in left-wing newspapers, he concluded:

> I think the chief reasons why Labour and Socialist papers fail are, firstly, that they give the public too much Labourism and Socialism, and, secondly, that in the nature of things they appeal to a small minority of the people. The kind of daily paper that might succeed, if it were backed financially, is, I think, a bright newspaper of broad and comprehensive general interest with an editorial brief for Socialism or Labour.[106]

---

[103] Ibid., 483 and 485.

[104] Report of the Eighteenth Annual Conference of the Labour Party. This claim is supported by J.J. Smyth, who said of munitions workers in Glasgow that 'unfortunately for Lloyd George, shell girls did not get the vote in 1918'. J.J. Smyth, *Labour in Glasgow, 1896–1936*, East Linton: Tuckwell Press, 2000, 90.

[105] *The Co-operative News*, 25 September 1915.

[106] *The Clarion*, 11 June 1915.

If Blatchford blamed cultural differences for Labour's limited appeal, this was not appreciated by orthodox Marxists such as the Plebs' League. On the contrary, they were frustrated and antagonised by the apparent obnoxious and pig-headed nature of much of the working class. In an editorial entitled 'To Our Critics', *Plebs* magazine claimed in May 1917 that the difficulties of the labour movement to date could be overcome if only the workers spent more time studying economics, and learned to view the world from a more scientific and logical perspective.[107] A piece by Frank Jackson in August of that year went further. Discussing an article by Sir Harry Johnston in the *Cambridge Magazine*, Jackson argued: 'His contention that "the weakness of the Labour Party is that it is not as it should be, the Party of all Workers" is scarcely a criticism of the Labour Party; since the Constitution of that body makes it abundantly clear that, if it is not the Party of All Workers, then it is the Workers' and not the Party's fault.'[108] It was this contemptible argument – that workers should naturally move towards the labour movement but were too obtuse to know their own best interests – which the labour patriots fought against. They knew full well that to convert the mass of the working classes to the Left they needed to offer pragmatic and practical means to achieve palpable goals, whilst rooting their appeals in the local culture and vernacular. In the words of C. Brown, whose letter appeared in *The Clarion* in March 1916: 'What we shall need to keep before us will not be so much of Marx, or even [NUR President Alfred] Bellamy, but of [William] Morris.'[109] Further, the patriots believed the war had revealed that the labour movement was perfectly in tune with British sensibilities: an editorial in the *Railway Review* of February 1915 claimed that 'the case for Trade Unionism – loyal, patriotic, level-headed, and sane – has never received ampler justification'.[110] *The Co-operative News* welcomed the promotion of George Barnes to Labour chairman and representative in the Cabinet after the resignation of Henderson over the Stockholm affair in similar terms: 'Mr Barnes is a typical Englishman. There is nothing flashy about him. His qualities are those of sound common sense.'[111] John Clynes was on the Executive of the General Municipal

---

[107] *Plebs*, May 1917.

[108] *Plebs*, August 1917. The *Cambridge Magazine* was a prominent Lib-Lab publication; its offices were attacked during the war by an unlikely combination of university undergraduates and ANZAC servicemen.

[109] *The Clarion*, 31 March 1916.

[110] *The Railway Review*, 19 February 1915.

[111] *The Co-operative News*, 9 June 1917. This is interesting, as Barnes was born and spent much of his childhood in Dundee, and sat for Blackfriars and Hutchesontown/Glasgow Gorbals for sixteen years. He did, however, move with his parents to England and spent most of his adolescence south of the border.

Workers for thirty years from 1909, and wartime patriots Charlie Cramp of the NUR and William Hutchinson of the Engineers would go on to represent their unions throughout the 1920s.[112] Pugh has noted, 'Men like Clynes and Thomas would scarcely have achieved lasting power in their unions and in the Labour Party had they not reflected rank-and-file sentiment': the argument that cautious, conservative leaders held back the radicalism of their membership is highly implausible.[113]

In addition to providing evidence of a type of leftism easily compatible with working-class cultural values, the labour patriots lambasted the cultural distance between some of the leaders of the labour movement and the people they aspired to represent. Future NUR leader Cramp wrote a strongly worded letter to the *Railway Review* on this subject in May 1916. After asking why the people did not understand the ILP, he argued that it was because the ILP 'does not understand the people':

> One of the most important things is ... to learn that the world is not a huge cosmopolitan Sunday school, but a planet peopled with men and women who are the heirs of instincts, habits, and frailties accumulated by the race through ages of pain and striving. The Socialism which they will adopt will be as an easy-fitting garment, not a straight-jacket composed of fads intended to restrict their liberties; and all the time that ILP MP's [*sic*] run after Temperance Bills, Insurance Acts, and other Liberal nostrums, the people will not understand them.

Similarly, in April 1915 *The Clarion* thundered that 'Socialism is to the bulk of our people a novel and foreign idea. One is sufficiently handicapped by an open championship of Socialism without having Labourism, Pacifism, Little Bethelism, Teetotalism, Anti-Patriotism, Pro-Germanism, and all the fantastic vagaries and flatulent sentimentalities of the Lib.Lab. rump stuck in one's hair like straws.'[114] The newspaper continued in this vein in October 1915, when an article defending the patriotic labour viewpoint concluded with the statement: 'It is the fault of those who do not understand *The Clarion* that the very name of Socialism is despised and detested by the great mass of British people.'[115]

Yet change was on the horizon: R.H. Tawney, a Christian socialist and intellectual who had nonetheless enlisted as a sergeant and fought on the first day of the Somme, claimed after the war that he saw in Henry Dubb the 'common, courageous, good-hearted, patient, proletarian fool' with whom

---

[112] Howell, *MacDonald's Party*, 60.

[113] Pugh, 'Rise of Labour', 520.

[114] *The Clarion*, 23 April 1915. 'Little Bethelism' was a strict, Puritanical movement popular in the late Victorian period and lampooned by Charles Dickens in *The Old Curiosity Shop*.

[115] *The Clarion*, 15 October 1915.

the labour movement should be particularly concerned.[116] Even Snowden argued in the 1920s for appealing to 'matter of fact people', rather than to an intellectual elite.[117] Criticism from the Right about their internationalist, Bolshevik sympathies 'was very much in the minds of Labour leaders throughout the early 1920s and beyond, as they endeavoured to demonstrate their party's patriotism, moderation and respectability as suitable credentials for governing Britain and the British Empire'.[118] Discussing the Edwardian working class in London, Stedman Jones pronounced that 'fatalism, political scepticism, the evasion of tragedy or anger and a stance of comic stoicism were pre-eminently cockney attitudes'.[119] These were precisely the attitudes revealed by a letter to *The Clarion*, from a correspondent signing himself 'A London Working Man', in February 1915:

> The Sleepers Are Waking. Sir,-Your sensible remarks about the war have made me and my mates think more of your queer ideas about Socialism and Determinism. We think there's something in them as well, but what we cannot stand is the wishy-washy sentimentalism of some of your writers and readers about such things as pensions and coal and bread. We have got a big war on and we have got to pay for it. Well, we do not kick and you cannot make us kick. There is no unemployment worth speaking about, and, if the masters are making a bit, well, so are we. What with full-time and overtime, there is more money about than there was before the war, and many of the poor widows with fifteen and twenty bob a week that you seem to want us to make a song about, are a long sight better off than they were when the old man took half his dibs to the pub. So me and my mates thinks you might draw it mild, and wait till there's more to kick about.[120]

This brief declaration, with its acceptance of the class system as a natural phenomenon and its allusions to the pub, gives us an insight into the soul of the British working man who was untouched by either radical Noncon-formity or trade unionism. Labour patriotism during the war – either from newspapers such as *The Clarion*, unionists like Ben Tillett, or politicians such as John Clynes, George Barnes, and Will Thorne – offered a new kind of leftism to these people, and persuaded them that one could quite comfortably be both a patriot and on the Left. There was no better demonstration of these values or evidence of Labour's concord with the beliefs of the mass

[116] Quoted in S. Macintyre, 'British Labour, Marxism, and Working-Class Apathy in 1920s', *The Historical Journal* 20 (1977): 488.

[117] J. Shepherd and K. Laybourn, *Britain's First Labour Government*, London: Palgrave Macmillan, 2006, 15.

[118] Ibid., 24.

[119] Stedman Jones, 'Working-Class Culture', 460.

[120] *The Clarion*, 19 February 1915.

of British people than the Left's record during the war, and many of the candidates it fielded in the 1920s.

General Unions and the War

Even after the rise of 'New Unions' at the end of the nineteenth century, the Labour movement still counted on skilled and more prosperous workers for much of its support. In industrial towns socialism was more feasible in 'richer' areas with better organised skilled workers,[121] and in London the Social Democratic Federation and other socialist groups were 'still recruiting their activists to a striking degree from among artisans, skilled craftsmen, and other self-improving minorities, but not from the mass of the labouring poor'.[122] Furthermore, many unskilled unions, such as those representing dockers and seafarers, had a spasmodic relationship with the Labour Party, which severely curtailed Labour influence in solidly working-class port towns.[123] General, unskilled unions such as the NUR and the Workers' Union grew substantially during the war and moved closer towards Labour, and, given the patriotism of most of these unionists – at both grassroots and elite levels – we can see the significance of labour patriotism in this convergence.

During the war the National Union of General Workers grew to 302,390 – ten times the size of its membership in 1910,[124] while the Workers' Union grew from 140,000 members to 379,000 by 1918, eventually reaching a post-war peak of half a million and becoming the largest single union in the country.[125] Significantly, London and the southern counties witnessed the largest growth; of minimal importance in 1914, they accounted for fully one quarter of the membership by 1918, and one third by 1920.[126] This growth of unionism in London during the war was vital to Labour's success in the capital after the Armistice. By 1926, the Central London Labour Party had an affiliated membership of 371,260 across sixty-one constituencies.[127]

---

[121] Pugh, *Speak for Britain*, 44.

[122] G. Eley and K. Nield, *The Future of Class in History: What's Left of the Social?*, Ann Arbor: University of Michigan Press, 2007, 94.

[123] S. Davies, *Liverpool Labour: Social and Political Influences on the Development of the Labour Party in Liverpool, 1900–1939*, Keele: Keele University Press, 1996, 173.

[124] J. Marriot, *The Culture of Labourism: The East End between the Wars*, Edinburgh: Edinburgh University Press, 1994, 89.

[125] R. Hyman, *The Workers' Union*, Oxford: Clarendon Press, 79. The largest union remained the Miners' Federation of Great Britain but, as its name suggests, this was a federation rather than a single institution.

[126] Hyman, *Workers Union*, 107.

[127] M. Worley, *Labour Inside the Gate: A History of the British Labour Party between the Wars*, London: I.B. Tauris, 2005, 56.

Along with the south, the Workers' Union became particularly prominent in the Midlands – exactly the areas where industry was expanding at the greatest rate. At the end of 1914, the Workers' Union became the first general workers' organisation to become nationally recognised – 'an achievement which officials saw as final confirmation of its established status in ... industry'.[128] The new-found confidence was demonstrated by the Workers' Union alone taking a stand against the restoration of pre-war practices, which President Jack Beard criticised as irrelevant in the post-war world.[129] While the Workers' Union was to fall away – membership was down to 140,000 by 1923[130] – and eventually be absorbed by the Transport and General Workers' Union, its wartime experience reflected the more general trends taking place. Large, 'unskilled' unions such as those of railway workers, labourers, transport workers, and dockers were growing and moving towards the Labour Party. This was crucial to Labour acquiring a broader base of support than the craft unions which had traditionally provided the bulk of their support, and, given the conservative nature of many unskilled trade unionists, war patriotism was an essential element in this transformation.

Women Voters

Notwithstanding the assistance given to the wives and mothers of soldiers, at first the labour movement largely resisted the greater autonomy given to women by the war. The *Railway Review* repeatedly mocked, in print and cartoons, the very idea of women working in any position on the railways, while R.B. Walker of NALRU wrote to Labour secretary Jim Middleton concerning his belief that the WNC supported the introduction of women into farmwork, warning that 'our members protest most emphatically against the very suggestion of such a thing'.[131] Although dilution and replacement of men by women remained a cause for concern throughout the war, towards the end of the conflict the Left had largely begun to concern itself with securing wage equality to prevent undercutting. The WNC archive file '30/3 – Wages' contains numerous complaints from around the country about inconsistent wages, and resolutions from local trades councils calling for an equal minimum wage for both male and female workers.[132] There was some success in minimum wage agitation for women, at least in agriculture; Arthur

---

[128] Ibid., 89.

[129] Ibid., 122.

[130] Ibid., 128.

[131] WNC.1/4/3.5.i – letter from R.B. Walker, 22 February 1915.

[132] See, for example, WNC.30/3/40 – letter from Bolton Workers' Emergency Committee, 19 December 1917.

Balfour wrote to the WNC's Marion Philips in January 1918 promising a twenty-shilling per week minimum wage for women who could pass an efficiency test and eighteen shillings for those who could not.[133]

The change in fortunes of the general, unskilled unions was mirrored by the rise of women within the labour movement: in 1915 the NUR began to admit women for the first time, while the Workers' Union – which had admitted women since its inception – saw its female membership climb from three thousand in 1914 to eighty thousand by 1918. They took up the cause of those neglected by the craft unions; in the words of the Workers' Union's *Trade Union Worker* in 1916: 'Our special object, in a humble way, is to champion the cause of the woman worker, the labourer, the semi-skilled worker'.[134] In contrast, the ASE never allowed women to join. Nor was it only in areas featuring high levels of female employment that women's sections flourished; as Stuart Ball, Andrew Thorpe, and Matthew Worley have noted, 'somewhat ironically … given the masculine character of the miner-dominated labour movement throughout the region, notable Labour women's section minutes exist for Bishop Auckland, Durham, Seaham, Spennymoor and Sedgefield'.[135] Enthusiastic female union organisers were crucial to this change. Ellen Wilkinson, for example, spent the war as an organiser for the Amalgamated Union of Co-operative Employees, and led a drive to recruit women who had been substituted for men. Wilkinson and her contemporaries argued that if trade unionism was to prosper, the privileged position of male craft unionists needed to change – and the war provided the catalyst for this change in terms of both skill and gender.[136]

Given the likelihood, from 1916 onwards, of franchise reform after the war, it became apparent than women would form a crucial constituency for Labour in the post-war world. This was reflected in the mixture of innovation and caution in *Labour and the New Social Order* – not an appeal to the converted but to twenty million electors, ten or twelve million of whom had never voted before.[137] Sue Bruley has argued that the establishment of Labour Party Women's Sections in interwar South Wales was an important part of Labour's growth, whereas the economistic Communist party

---

[133] WNC.30/3/43 – letter from Arthur Balfour to Dr Marion Philips, 3 January 1918.

[134] G. Braybon, *Women Workers in the First World War: The British Experience*, London: Routledge, 1981, 68–69.

[135] S. Ball, A. Thorpe, and M. Worley, 'Researching the Grass Roots: The Records of Constituency Level Political Parties in Five British Counties, 1918–40', *Archives* 29 (2004): 32.

[136] M. Perry, '"Industrial Unionism for Women": Ellen Wilkinson and the Unionisation of Shop Workers, 1915–18', paper given at 'Labour and the First World War' Conference at Anglia Ruskin University, 3 May 2014.

[137] R. Barker, 'Ramsay MacDonald and the Labour Party', *History* 61 (1976), 54.

concentrated on the miner at work and did not attract women.[138] In the so-called 'housewives budget' of the first Labour government in 1924, the tax on sugar was reduced from two shillings and nine pence per pound to one shilling six pence per pound.[139] Before the 1918 general election five national women organisers were appointed, and 'endeavours were made to visit as many constituencies as possible in order that something might be done in each to organise women for election work'. In 1919 special attention was given to the Black Country, the West Riding, Lancashire, and Cheshire, 'as the results obtained in these places at the General Election were most promising'.[140]

Communities

In interwar Britain, unionised men and women were not enough; there was a need to turn to the wider community. Michael Savage has observed of interwar Preston that Catholic and Anglican social clubs came to terms with the need to provide drink, while the Nonconformist societies did not, partly contributing to their failure to develop a vigorous popular culture.[141] Local Labour was sensitive to this, and from 1900 onward all the new working men's clubs were Labour clubs; originally drinking was 'not encouraged ... but after the election defeat of 1910 the Labour Party felt that it had to reduce the hold of the licensed victuallers by providing its own drinking facilities'.[142] Having described Labour's biggest weakness before 1914 as 'its inability to develop organisations to tap neighbourhood capacities', by the 1920s popular politics were based 'mainly on neighbourhood and female support' and in 1929 Labour MPs took the two Preston seats for the first time.[143]

[138] S. Bruley, 'The Politics of Food: Gender, Family, Community and Collective Feeding in South Wales in the General Strike and Miners' Lockout of 1926', *Twentieth Century British Studies* 18 (2007): 61.

[139] Shepherd and Laybourn, *Britain's First Labour Government*, 87.

[140] Report of the Nineteenth Annual Conference of the Labour Party.

[141] M. Savage, *The Dynamics of Working-Class Politics. The Labour Movement in Preston, 1880–1940*, Cambridge: Cambridge University Press, 1987, 123. Although Andrew Thorpe has argued that during the 1930s, both communal drinking and organised religion were in decline nationwide, and Nonconformists were hit the hardest. See A. Thorpe, *Britain in the 1930s: The Deceptive Decade*, Oxford: Blackwell, 1992, 102–03. The change in Preston is perhaps especially significant as, according to Brian Harrison, it was the birthplace of the English temperance movement. See B. Harrison, 'Drink and Sobriety in England, 1815–1872', *International Review of Social History* 12 (1967): 219.

[142] Savage, *Dynamics*, 130.

[143] Ibid., 160 and 180. In this respect, Preston Labour may have been overzealous: in 1934 a man named W.H. Francis claimed he was rejected as a candidate because he was a teetotaller and local preacher. See Savage, *Dynamics*, 183. Heidi Topman found that the interwar years

Another area in which Labour greatly expanded after the war was the East End of London. In the 1919 municipal elections in West Ham the party won seven of the nine seats contested; after the 1922 election Labour held thirty-six council seats.[144] In 1923 the Labour vote in West Ham fell at a council level, but at the general election they won all four constituencies with a notable increase in their vote, and by 1924 Herbert Morrison could point to a fourfold increase in the Labour vote over just six years.[145] Significantly, Labour held on to these gains in the East End and was not affected the reversals of the late 1920s and early 1930s which damaged the party in the rest of the capital.[146] Why then was Labour so successful in this area, which had not seemed promising before the war? John Marriott has argued that the party treated voters in the East End 'as industrial workers, as mothers, as citizens, as consumers and as tenants', and that its success 'had been based on an ability to articulate the demands of an enlarged working-class electorate'.[147] Certainly, practical and pragmatic reforms to improve the lives of ordinary people were important, as was the growth in unionism and the Co-operative movement, but just as crucial was the East End electorate's acceptance of the idea that Labour was 'their' party and best able to represent the working class:

> Membership of political organisations, regular attendance at meetings to debate policy and formulate strategy, steady work in electioneering, propaganda, even voting at elections were alien to this political culture. But at the same time it was not positioned outside the boundaries of labourism. To say that support for the Labour Party was not active is not the same as saying that it did not exist. The support derived from an instinctive, traditional, commonsensical identification with the party rather than an intellectual, ethical or moral commitment.[148]

David Howell has described Silvertown MP Jack Jones as 'epitomiz[ing] in an extreme and personal fashion the politics of the General Municipal Workers in West Ham – a stress on the needs of muscular male workers, a distaste for middle-class intellectuals, a suspicion of all things foreign'.[149] Similarly, James Sexton in St Helens emphasised his patriotism and utilised

---

saw a wave of labour movement building purchase and construction across Greater London and references to the existence of at least one labour hall, club, or institute in every borough of what is now Greater London between 1918 and 1939.

[144] Marriott, *The Culture of Labourism*, 27 and 65.
[145] Ibid., 114 and 27.
[146] Ibid., 163.
[147] Marriot, 98 and 163.
[148] Ibid., 182.
[149] Howell, *MacDonald's Party*.

vitriolic anti-German language in his election addresses. For Howell, dockers' officials such as Sexton and Tillett in Salford North 'sat in the Commons not for constituencies where their members were a significant sector of the electorate, but for working-class districts where a Labour appeal rather than a socialist agenda could be attractive.'[150] Furthermore, Duncan Tanner has written:

> Whilst some of the newly captured London seats contained groups with strong Labour leanings (like railwaymen), constituencies containing large numbers of lower middle-class voters and new council and private housing developments were more numerous ... Many of the newly captured provincial seats were influenced by similar trends, and did not contain a massive concentration of trade unionists or other 'traditional' Labour voters.[151]

Patriotism was essential to this language of 'labourism', and provided a useful counterweight to the pacifism and internationalism of the PLP in the 1920s. Speaking at the 1919 party conference, Mary Bamber a BSP delegate from Liverpool (and mother of Bessie Braddock) claimed:

> If the Labour Party ... would stop trying to be statesmen, and get on with the work which the rank and file were doing outside, they would be surprised at the support they could get from the country ... With one or two exceptions it had not been possible in most of the labour speeches to draw a dividing line between the speeches of Labour Members and some of the advanced Liberals in the House of Commons ... Speaking as a woman of the working class, but a woman who understood the whole international position, she declared that there was a mighty difference in being a Labour Member and understanding the international situation. If they were going to build up a Party to dominate the thinking of workers of this country, they would have to go on definite working class lines.[152]

The Conservatives attempted to exploit what they saw as Labour's weakness in international affairs: Christopher Cook has noted how a great deal was made of Labour's links with the Second International, the Hackney Conservatives branding Labour 'a party whose policy is directed by the German Socialistische Arbeiter Internationale'; there were similar attacks in Islington South, Southwark Central, and Wandsworth Central.[153] In

---

[150] Ibid., 180–81.

[151] D. Tanner, 'Class Voting and Radical Politics: The Liberal and Labour Parties, 1910–31', in J. Lawrence and M. Taylor (eds), *Party, State and Society: Electoral Behaviour in Britain since 1820*, London: Scolar Press, 1997, 120.

[152] Report of the Eighteen Annual Conference of the Labour Party.

[153] C. Cook, *The Age of Alignment: Electoral Politics in Britain 1922–1929*, London: Macmillan, 1975, 145.

other areas, such as Battersea North, Poplar South, and rural Norfolk, the Liberals aped these tactics, accusing local Labour parties of Bolshevist sympathies. Labour made a concerted effort to fight these accusations: along with W.F. Toynbee, prospective parliamentary candidate for Chelmsford, and J.E. Kneeshaw, former agent in Rushcliffe, and Captain Edward Gill, M.C. made up a three-man propaganda team for the 1922 election, and visited over seventy constituencies between them – significantly, Captain Gill was appointed chiefly to the southern and southwestern counties.[154] Of unsuccessful Labour candidates at the 1918 election, eleven were current or former officers, including four in London: Major A.J. Lewer in Islington East, Colonel A. Lynch in Battersea South, Captain Haden Guest in Southwark Central, and Captain D. Sheehan in Stepney Limehouse. Furthermore, Lieutenant-Colonel J. Kynaston stood in Wolverhampton Bilston, Major Trestrail in Torquay, Captain Kendall in Stroud, Major D. Graham-Pole in East Grinstead, Captain E. Gill in Frome, and Captain E.N. Bennett in Westbury, Wiltshire.[155] In 1918 Labour was very careful to select appropriate candidates for each constituency. In contrast to the southern seats contested by former officers, none of the Labour candidates in Scotland had a military title, although South Ayrshire was won by the staunchly pro-war James Brown.[156]

There has been a tendency to overstate the importance of sectarian differences in undermining community solidarity, perhaps resulting from a concern to explain why class consciousness was absent from socio-economically homogenous groups. In the words of John Bohstedt, there is a need to rescue people of different religious and ethnic groups 'from the enormous condescension of labour history'.[157] Very often a dividing line in working-class communities was not so much 'religion' or ethnicity per se, but rather 'culture'.[158] For example, it could be argued that Irish Catholics

[154] Report of the Twenty-First Annual Conference of the Labour Party: National Agent's Report.

[155] Report of the Eighteen Annual Conference of the Labour Party.

[156] As opposed to forty-six per cent of the Conservative candidates, ten per cent for the Coalition Liberals and six per cent for the independent Liberals. See I.G.C. Hutchinson, 'The Impact of the First World War on Scottish Politics', in C.M.M. Macdonald and E.W. McFarland, *Scotland and the Great War*, East Linton: Tuckwell Press, 1999, 49.

[157] J. Bohstedt, 'More than One Working Class: Protestant and Catholics Riots in Edwardian Liverpool', in J. Belchem (ed.), *Popular Politics, Riot and Labour: Essays in Liverpool History*, Liverpool: Liverpool University Press, 1992, 176.

[158] Very often, religion and popular culture could coincide. According to a Catholic in Liverpool in the interwar period: 'Going to church and going to the pictures were the highlights of the week. They took you out of yourself. In church you could do a bit of thinking. In the pictures you could escape to Hollywood.' Quoted in F. Boyce, 'Irish Catholicism in Liverpool between the Wars', *Labour History Review* 57 (1992): 18.

who enjoyed the music hall, pub culture, football, the racecourse, and gambling had more common ground with like-minded Protestants than with their more sober-minded, abstemious coreligionists. Issues such as community, neighbourhood, and patriotism could cut across old divides such as skilled/unskilled and Catholic/Protestant. In the East End of London, for example, the 1889 Dockers' Strike featured an unusual alliance between Irish Catholics and Methodists;[159] while the committee established to oversee the Bethnal Green war memorial reflected the new coalition of the labour movement in the East End, consisting of representatives of the council, Christian clergy, a local synagogue, two benevolent societies, two hospital aids funds, the Union of Boot and Shoe Operatives, the Rifle Club, and special constables.[160] Similarly, the establishment of the Stepney Labour Party after the war featured intercommunity co-operation between Jewish, Irish, and indigenous communities. In Liverpool the 'trauma' of the 1911 Transport Strike had allowed for intercommunal co-operation, and Catholic councillors had co-operated with Conservatives for two decades to sustain an impressive housing programme.[161] The Liberal editor of the local *Daily Post* described the sort of people who followed demagogic Protestant preachers in pre-war Liverpool as 'good, hard-headed fellows ... [who] don't care two-pence about religion at all; but they to a man hate "Popery" intensely'.[162] This suggests that doctrinal differences were of far less importance that matters of culture, loyalty, community, and identity – issues which began to fall into abeyance after the Irish treaty was signed, when most of the Nationalists joined the Labour Party, taking their voters with them, and Labour was increasingly able to appeal to people as Liverpudlians, rather than as Protestants or Catholics.

If the central challenge for Labour after the war was to move beyond the radical artisans and highly unionised skilled workers who had previously provided the bulk of its support, and capture groups hitherto unsupportive of labour, then a constituency which served as a microcosm for Labour's cultural appeals to the wider electorate was that of the Irish Catholic diaspora in England. For many Catholics (and, for that matter, Anglicans), unlike Nonconformists, religion was a public rather than a private issue. Where for most Nonconformists, faith was a deeply personal matter involving private

[159] R. Davis, *Tangled Up in Blue*, London: Ruskin, 2011, 10.

[160] A. King, *Memorials of the Great War in Britain: The Symbolism and Politics of Remembrance*, Oxford: Berg, 1998, 29.

[161] Bohstedt, 'More than One Working Class', 212 and 202.

[162] Quoted in Bohstedt, 'More than One Working Class', 196. According to P.J. Waller, by the 1920s less than one in five Liverpudlians were church goers. See P.J. Waller, *Democracy and Sectarianism: A Political and Social History of Liverpool 1868–1939*, Liverpool: Liverpool University Press, 1981, 286.

reflection and reading of scripture, for many Catholics it was a highly public issue based around attending weekly mass, regular confessions, significant feast days, and ostentatious ceremonies. In this respect, Catholicism in England was more analogous to the ancient Roman concept of religion – which was entirely concerned with public displays of faith rather than personal belief – than the doctrinaire religiosity of the Nonconformists. As with the politics of much of the wider working class, popular Catholicism was more about identity ('socially grounded loyalties', in the words of Steven Fielding) than doctrine and ideology – hence few Catholics took anti-socialist pulpit sermonising seriously.[163] As Fielding had it, 'it had been on the level of culture, rather than explicit ideology, that the [Labour] party had made its most powerful appeal to Irish Catholic loyalties'.[164] That is to say, Labour appealed to Catholic immigrants in towns such as Liverpool through cultural identity, rather than 'class' identity or doctrinaire socialism.

Clearly breakthroughs in areas such as Liverpool were slight: the party continued to struggle on Merseyside throughout the interwar years and it was only in the 1950s that Labour took control of the council. Yet very often Labour's appeal to culture was successful: Catholics' political allegiances were increasingly won over to Labour after the war, and throughout the interwar period the Irish were amongst the most consistent Labour supporters within the working class.[165] Thus in areas without either a strong craft union movement or a radical Nonconformist tradition, we may have seen a Labour 'evolution' largely without a labour movement. In his forward to Eric Taplin's study of the dockworker's union, Jack Jones paid tribute to James Sexton, 'a man who came out of the Fenian stable but over the years became a pillar of society'.[166] Yet men like James Sexton, who saw no contradiction between Catholicism, patriotism, and trade unionism were by no means exceptional in the post-war Labour Party. The success of this strategy is personified in Jack Hayes – who became the first Labour MP to sit for a Liverpool constituency when he was returned in Edge Hill in 1923. Hayes was an Irish Nationalist and a former Metropolitan policeman who was involved in the police strikes of 1918 and 1919, yet neither his Irish nationalist beliefs nor his former career as a policeman were barriers to his involvement in the labour movement. Three of the police strikers were adopted by Labour as municipal candidates in 1919 and two of them – Hayes and Charles Burden – were

---

[163] S. Fielding, *Class and Ethnicity: Irish Catholics in England, 1880–1939*, Buckingham: Open University Press, 1993, 109.

[164] Ibid., 107.

[165] Davies, *Liverpool Labour*, 225; Fielding, *Class and Ethnicity*, 105.

[166] Forward by Jack Jones in E. Taplin, *The Dockers' Union: A Study of the National Union of Dock Labourers, 1889–1922*, Leicester: Leicester University Press, 1986, xiv.

elected.[167] Through people such as Hayes we can see how the party could have some success in presenting itself as a broad church open to all.

Seats Won by Labour before and after the First World War

English constituencies provided the vast majority of Labour's forty seats after the January 1910 general election, with only a few exceptions: George Barnes in Glasgow Blackfriars and Hutchesontown and Alexander Wilkie sharing Dundee's two seats with Winston Churchill; Thomas Richards in Monmouthshire West; and Keir Hardie, the biggest of the 'Big Four', representing Merthyr Tydfil.[168] The English seats generally represented either mining or industrial districts, or those combining a mixture of both. There was a fair regional spread, incorporating the northeast (Chester-Le-Street, Barnard Castle), northwest (Blackburn, Bolton, Manchester North and East, St Helens, Stockport, and Wigan), Yorkshire (Bradford West, Chesterfield, Halifax, Leeds East, Sheffield Attercliffe), and a small but significant foothold in London, with C.W. Bowerman at Deptford and Will Thorne in West Ham South.

Labour barely improved its standing at the next election twelve months later: George Lansbury won in Bow and Bromley, Frank Water Goldstone took one of the two seats for Sunderland, Thomas Richardson was returned in Whitehaven, and Will Crooks won back the Woolwich seat he had lost in January. Yet these gains were offset by setbacks, such as James Seddon losing Newton and Thomas Glover's defeat in St Helens; overall, Labour made a paltry gain of two seats, and the PLP was almost exclusively trade unionist in composition. They had thirty-four seats in England, five in Wales, and three in Scotland.

Despite a combination of the loss of virtually every Labour MP associated – fairly or otherwise – with the anti-war movement, and the widespread effective disenfranchisement of hundreds of thousands of soldiers, Labour added fifteen MPs to its pre-war total in December 1918. The party made important gains in London and the Midlands, capturing Wentworth, Woolwich East, Holland with Boston, Nottingham West, West Bromwich, Smethwick, and Mansfield. Furthermore, in a PLP even more dominated by trade unionists, Labour patriots were prominent: Ben Tillett took Salford and James Sexton won back St Helens. Although the Coalition Government generally vanquished candidates who did not have the so-called 'Coupon' of support, and even Labourites who had had a crucial role in the war effort

---

[167] Waller, *Democracy and Sectarianism*, 285.

[168] Election statistics and constituency results in this section taken from Labour Party Annual Reports, 1910–1924 and F.W.S. Craig, *British Electoral Facts, 1832–1987*, Dartmouth: Parliamentary Research Services, 1989.

Table 4.1: Candidates Fielded, Seats Won, and Total Votes Won by Labour
at each election, January 1910–23.

Election	Candidates Fielded	Seats Won	Total Votes
January 1910	78	40	505,690
December 1910	56	42	370,802
1918	361	57	2,244,945
1922	414	142	4,235,457
1923	427	191	4,348,379

Source: Labour Party Annual Reports, 1910–1924.

such as Henderson lost their seats, the party did not merely hold on: it
expanded. Clearly Labour patriotism during the war was essential not only
in avoiding an electoral catastrophe (which, admittedly, may have only been
short-lived) but in winning new voters and new seats.

After the opening of Parliament, Brigadier-General Sir Owen Thomas
of Anglesey, Jack Jones of Silverton, and F.H. Rose of Aberdeen North all
took the Labour whip, as did A.E. Waterson, elected in Kettering as the
first Co-operative MP, thus bringing the numbers of the PLP to sixty-one.
The first three were undoubtedly Labour patriots and Waterson's links with
Labour forged during the war were significant in his recruitment; hence
we can see the importance of labour patriotism in securing these four new
members.[169] Over the course of the Parliament, one MP withdrew from the
PLP whilst two others – originally elected as an independent and a National
Democrat – joined, bringing its strength up to sixty-two. Furthermore,
there were thirteen gains from by-elections, resulting in seventy-five Labour
MPs at the time of the dissolution.

The promising bridgeheads of 1918 were more fully exploited in 1922, when
the post-war catholicity of the party allowed expansion in labour heartlands,
London, and parts of the countryside. Labour was able to succeed in traditional
areas with a strong trade union base, taking Accrington, Barnsley, Batley and
Morley, Bradford Central, Bradford East, Crewe, Derbyshire North-East,
Dewsbury, Doncaster, Eccles, Elland, Gateshead, Ilkeston, Jarrow, Keighley,
Leeds South, Newcastle-upon-Tyne Central, Newcastle-upon-Tyne East,

---

[169] See the entry for Alfred Waterson in K. Gildart and D. Howell, *Dictionary of Labour
Biography XII*, London: Macmillan, 2004.

Newcastle-upon-Tyne West, Oldham, Rochdale, Sedgefield, Sheffield Attercliffe, Sheffield Brightside, Sheffield Hillsborough, and Wrexham in 1922. Crucially, the party also made big breakthroughs in London, capturing Bermondsey West, Bow and Bromley, Camberwell North, Limehouse, Stratford West Ham, Walthamstow West, Whitechapel, and Poplar South.

It is after 1922, and the return of the Labour 'pacifists', that we can see the variety of the post-war party. Pre-war ILPers and Liberals such as Jowett in Bradford, Lansbury in London, Snowden in the Colne Valley (former seat of maverick labour patriot Victor Grayson), Josiah Wedgwood in Newcastle-under-Lyme, Arthur Ponsonby in Sheffield Brightside, and Charles Trevelyan in Newcastle-upon-Tyne Central were elected to stand alongside ex-servicemen such as Clement Attlee in Limehouse, WNC executives such as Sidney Webb in Seaham, and ex-serviceman future First Lord of the Admiralty and Defence Minister A.V. Alexander, who was returned as Co-operative MP for Sheffield Hillsborough.

There were sixteen by-elections in between the general elections of 1922 and 1923, and Labour contested twelve of them, making a net total of two gains. J. Chuter Ede gained Mitcham, Surrey from the Conservatives by 8,029 votes to 7,196, fighting against Sir A. Griffith Boscawen, then the Minister of Health. This was the first time the constituency had been contested by Labour, and Chuter Ede was helped by Griffith Boscawen being parachuted in from Taunton, where he had lost his seat at the general election, and by a four-cornered contest: E. Brown, an Independent Liberal, took 3,214 votes and J.T. Catterall, an Independent Conservative, took 2,684. Similarly, Major Hills – another minister, defeated at Durham in the general election – fought Edge Hill, and was defeated in a straight fight by Labour's Jack Hayes (10,300 votes to 9,250): 'The victory is the first breach which the Party has been able to make in the walls of this Conservative stronghold.'

At the general election of 1923 the party fielded 427 candidates; there was a seventy-four per cent turn-out, and the total Labour vote increased to 4,348,379. Of 144 seats held, 128 were retained, only sixteen were lost, and sixty-three further gains; 101 MPs were returned under the auspices of trade unions, thirty as ILP candidates, the same number were nominated by district Labour parties, four were from the BSP, two were Fabians, and six were Co-operative party members. In addition, fourteen women were returned. London accounted for fifteen of the sixty-three gains, and these successes were not confined to the East End heartland; seats were won in South and even West London (Hammersmith North). New areas where seats were won for the first time included Bristol and Reading, and there were victories in several diverse southern constituencies: Dartmouth, Gravesend, Ipswich, South Norfolk, Norwich, southeast Essex, and Maldon. Labour success in established heartlands increased: all three seats in Salford were won, all four in West Ham, and both East Ham seats were taken. Further, Wakefield, Huddersfield, Northampton, and Coventry – which had all been fought continuously for twenty years – now yielded victories.

The low number of losses in 1923 was encouraging: in 1922, when defending seventy-nine seats, Labour had lost nineteen; but defending 144 seats in 1923 they lost only sixteen. Of these, thirteen were due to local pacts between Conservatives and Liberals, including against Henderson at Newcastle East and C. Roden Buxton at Accrington. The other three were lost by small majorities – by only six votes in Sedgefield.

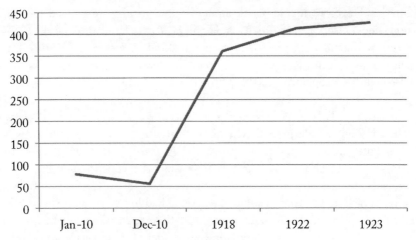

Graph 4.1: Candidates fielded by the Labour Party at each general election, January 1910–23

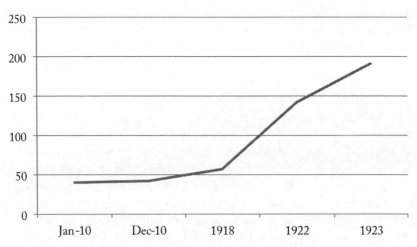

Graph 4.2: Seats won by the Labour Party at each general election, January 1910–23

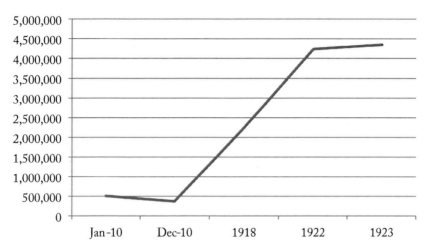

Graph 4.3: Votes won by the Labour Party at each general election,
January 1910–23

This chapter has described the significance during the First World War of
labour patriotism in opening up new channels to the labour movement from
disparate groups previously strangers to Labour. To be sure, after the war
Labour looked to move away from its belligerent stance during the conflict:
by 1922 the 'pacifists' of the war period had returned to the party leadership
and the party as a whole espoused decidedly anti-war views throughout the
1919–35 period. Yet, in terms of the recruitment of former soldiers, 'cultural'
appeals to the broader working class, and counterbalancing the post-war
influx of Liberals and other middle-class radicals, labour patriotism acted
as an essential solvent to hold the party together and a crucial platform for
the post-war catholicity and heterogeneity of the party. As Martin Pugh has
observed of the East End of London – where Labour was effectively two
parties, represented by Lansbury and the radical-socialist tradition in Bow
and Bromley, and the populist-patriotism of Will Thorne and Jack Jones in
West Ham – across Britain, the party displayed a somewhat contradictory
image. Certainly the post-war party was a broad church, but the patriotism
displayed during the war, the securing of union allegiance, and the bespoke
appeal to a broad and varied working-class culture gave credence to the
party as the representative of labour, rather than a vehicle for middle-class
liberal aspirations.

Mathew Worley has noted that 'despite the concerted efforts of Labour's
subcommittees, the party's ability to extend its appeal was neither uniformly
nor quickly achieved. Moreover, potential areas of support were not wholly

realised'.[170] Yet, important breakthroughs had been made, both in terms of
organisation in the constituencies and cultural acceptance, even if they did
not translate into seats. Furthermore, while it is true to say that most of
the advances of the 1920s were wiped away in the defeat of 1931, this defeat
was the result of a particular set of circumstances, rather than a wholesale
rejection of Labour. It did not mean that Labour had ceased to be a national
party any more than 1906 or 1945 signified the wholesale rejection of the
Conservatives. Indeed, Labour began recovering at the local elections of
November 1931; by 1933 it had recovered all of the municipal seats lost in
1931, and within a year of the 1932 'A Million New Members and Power'
campaign, it had recruited one hundred thousand new members.[171] The
crucial initial objections – both economic and cultural – had been overcome,
and although the 1930s were to prove problematic, with core constituencies
alienated – Jews through policy over Palestine, Catholics due to church
schools – these coalitions of support did not collapse.[172]

Henry Pelling wrote in 1953 that 'By the nineteen-twenties [Labour] had
become the party of the Celts and the nonconformists, of the teetotallers
and the pacifists',[173] yet for other historians Labour's weakness in the
interwar period was that it was identified too strongly with organised
labour, and thought of as a 'sectional interest'.[174] So which interpretation
was the more accurate? Did right-wing trade unionists, such as John Ward,
have it right when they painted Labour as a refuge for middle-class liberals
and abstemious, soft-voiced, Nonconformists unrepresentative of the wider
working class? Or were middle-class conservatives right to see the party
as the dangerous vanguard of organised labour? As it turns out, they were
both slightly right, but largely wrong. The Labour Party which emerged
after 1918 was *both* a home to pacifists, teetotallers, Nonconformists, and
middle-class radicals fleeing the Liberals, and a vehicle for socialists,
Fabians, trade unionists, and social democrats. It is this catholicity that

170 Worley, *Labour Inside the Gate*, 44.

171 Although the disaster of 1931 has been overplayed by some, Keith Laybourn has noted
that by 1933 Labour had regained all the municipal seats lost in 1931, and the 'A Million
New Members and Power' campaign of 1932 resulted in one hundred thousand new members
within a year. See K. Laybourn, *Britain on the Breadline: A Social and Political History of
Britain 1918–1939*, Stroud: Sutton Publishing, 1998, 160.

172 Thorpe, *Britain in the 1930s*, 24.

173 A. Reid, 'Henry Pelling', in J. Callaghan, S. Fielding, and S. Ludlam (eds), *Interpreting
the Labour Party: Approaches to Labour Politics and History*, Manchester: Manchester University
Press, 2003, 108.

174 J. Callaghan, 'Ross McKibbin', in J. Callaghan, S. Fielding, and S. Ludlam (eds),
Interpreting the Labour Party: Approaches to Labour Politics and History, Manchester:
Manchester University Press, 2003, 124.

explains the post-war success of Labour, and the First World War – and labour's support for the conflict – had an essential role in enabling this heterogeneity.

As Blatchford himself affirmed in a leading article of May 1915: 'Let us recognise the very obvious fact that one may be an enthusiastic vegetarian, freethinker, spiritualist, meat-eater, teetotaller, moderate drinker, Catholic, Protestant, anti-tobacconist, theatre-goer, footballer, Protectionist, Free Trader, evolutionist, or creationist, and yet remain a sound and loyal Socialist.'[175] In their book on the first Labour government, John Shepherd and Keith Laybourn argued that fear of association with Bolshevism or anti-British sentiment 'was very much in the minds of Labour leaders throughout the early 1920s and beyond, as they endeavoured to demonstrate their party's patriotism, moderation and respectability as suitable candidates for governing Britain and the British Empire'.[176] Keith Laybourn has said of the 1930s: 'Labour's clear hostility towards European fascism, and its support of the Republican side in the Spanish Civil War confirmed it to be a party which was prepared to face up to fascism. It marked it out as a patriotic party, in contrast to the general image it had earned during the 1920s.'[177]

The word *earned* is interesting: on the one hand, the anti-nationalist image was foisted upon Labour by its opponents; on the other, the party did take a very deliberate pacifistic turn in the 1920s. But this was only made viable by the patriotic credentials *earned* during the war. Fortunately, Labour did not need recourse to empty words and hollow sentiments: the record of the movement during the war, when it had been drawn into the government and played an instrumental part in victory, could speak for itself. The empirical fact of labour's support for the war and its crucial role in winning the conflict could not be denied, and allowed the leaders of the 1920s to perform the delicate manoeuvre of pushing for disarmament and decolonisation whilst simultaneously espousing patriotism and their readiness to rule. Indeed, they went on to claim that by 1924 Labour 'had furled the Red Flag and unfurled the Union Jack', yet there was no need to do this; throughout the war and the immediate post-war years, both had been flying together.[178]

In the following chapter the focus changes slightly, away from debates around the war, towards an analysis of the relationship between labour and the state. It discusses the transformation of the British state during the war and the implications of this for the Left, the extent to which the Left acted

[175] *The Clarion*, 7 May 1915.
[176] Shepherd and Laybourn, *Britain's First Labour Government*, 24.
[177] Laybourne, *Britain on the Breadline*, 161.
[178] Shepherd and Laybourn, *Britain's First Labour Government*, 39.

as a safety net or 'second state' for the most vulnerable, and the impact of the war on the doctrinal development of Labour after 1918. In this respect, it argues that the experience of the war was crucial to Labour in vindicating many of its arguments and ensuring a more statist Labour Party developed than might otherwise have been the case.

5

'The experiments are not found wanting' – Labour and the Wartime State

'Thus in the hour of its supreme need does the nation turn to the collectivist experiments urged for so many years by the Labour movement. And the experiments are not found wanting.'

—*Daily Citizen*, 5 August 1914

'[The war] cast its shadow over every domestic hearth. It thrust into the melting pot all our social institutions. It recast all our political parties and associations. It searched every heart and tried every man's mind. It was the parting of our ways, the supreme test of all our ideals and aspirations, and it remains so to this hour.'

—George Wardle, Labour Party Conference, 1917[1]

'Methods of state control which would once have been regarded as intolerable infringements of the rights and liberties both of employers and workmen have been accepted without effective protest even from those bred in the individualist tradition of the last century.'

—Arthur Henderson, January 1919[2]

This chapter is concerned with the growth of the British state during the war, the relationship of the labour movement *vis-à-vis* the state, and the ramifications for the ideology and practice of the Left after the conflict. The expansion and – at least temporary – transformation of the British state during the war has received a great deal of scholarly attention over the past seventy years, yet it is still worth attempting to gauge the true extent of the expansion in the remit, responsibilities, and power of the government.

[1] Report of the Seventeenth Annual Conference of the Labour Party.
[2] Report of the Eighteenth Annual Conference of the Labour Party.

Also worth examination are the debates surrounding the motivations for this expansion (did military necessity march in step with social reform, or was combat efficiency the only concern, and any improvements in welfare incidental?), and the extent to which the enhanced state apparatus was dismantled after 1918. Surprisingly, the co-ordination and operation of the British Left throughout the war is an area which has been largely neglected by historians. This is a significant oversight for, principally through the operations of the War Emergency Workers' National Committee (WNC), the labour and trade union movement fought against the most malign pressures and deprivations of the war upon the civilian population, successfully represented thousands of otherwise powerless people, sought redress of grievance for the voiceless, and helped to ensure that the Britain which emerged from the war was at least a slight improvement on the pre-1914 nation. Finally, it has often been assumed that a larger, more interventionist state was always a long-term goal and aim of the labour movement, and hence that most on the Left would have been pleased by trends in this direction during the conflict. In reality, the first three decades of the twentieth century saw a variety of viewpoints as to how best to theoretically and practically organise the economy and society, and the vision which was put into practice after 1945 was not necessarily destined to dominate. While the experience of the Depression and the Second World War – and the memory of broken promises and failed ambitions after the First – was certainly crucial to the coalescence of the 'spirit of '45', it will be argued here that not enough significance has been attributed to the *experience* of 1914–18 in this development.

The Wartime Growth of the British State

The *Millgate Monthly*, a cultural periodical attached to the Co-operative movement which did not normally advocate a greatly expanded bureaucratic state, still could not help but remark wryly in September 1914 at the sheer speed and alacrity with which the government had moved to interfere in areas previously considered the sacrosanct territory of free market liberalism.[3] What the publishers and readers of the magazine could not have predicted was just how much further the British government would travel from its hitherto accepted role over the following years. If the previous decade had seen the British concept of state provision of welfare radically reformed, then the four years of the war were to see the British state transformed, from the product of Victorian *laissez-faire* liberalism to something containing the seed of the modern welfare state as we understand it today. While previous

---

[3] *Millgate Monthly*, September 1914.

scholarship had tended to underplay this transformation, highlighting the dismantling of much of the wartime changes in the early 1920s, and claiming a lack of continuity between the statist principles of the First and Second World Wars, in her 2001 book *The War Come Home*, Deborah Cohen claims that to fuel their 'war machine[s], the societies of Europe were fundamentally transformed. Belligerent states arrogated unprecedented powers to regulate and coerce. They conscripted labor, rationed commodities, controlled profits, and sent men to die'.[4] This section offers an overview of the expansion of the state during 1914–18 and the debates as to the extent of and motivation for this expansion, and argues that the experience, institutional changes, and ideological changes of the First World War were central to the continuance and development of statism until 1945.

Almost from the outset the British government began to expand into areas previously untouched by the state. Lloyd George may have spoken of 'business as usual' in order to reassure banks and businesses, but, as David French has argued, the actions of the government 'made nonsense of this slogan'.[5] From 4 August onwards the government pledged credit to underwrite the entire financial system and interfered in the markets on a massive scale: the Stock Exchange closed on 31 July and remained so until 4 January 1915, and for the first time governmental controls were imposed on the domestic money market.[6] If Liberals of an earlier generation would have been horrified at the deviation from Gladstonian non-intervention represented by Britain's entry into the war, they would have been left distraught at this heresy against economic orthodoxy. The railways were commandeered on 4 August, mines and other industries soon followed, and as early as February 1915 the government began to buy up wheat.[7] Jose Harris has pointed out that in 1914, unique amongst developed nations, Britain had no tariffs to protect its agriculture; yet from this *laissez-faire* beginning fully eighty-five per cent of the British food supply was under control of the Ministry of Food by the end of the war.[8] In addition to foodstuffs, the government concerned itself with the drinking habits of its citizens: chief constables were given the power to close pubs and alter opening hours in August 1914, and while the Cabinet baulked at full-scale

[4] D. Cohen, *The War Come Home: Disabled Veterans in Britain and Germany, 1918–1939*, Oakland: University of California Press, 2001, 188.

[5] D. French, 'The Rise and Fall of Business as Usual', in K. Burk (ed.), *War and the State*, London: Allen and Unwin, 1982, 19.

[6] K. Burk, 'The Treasury: From Impotence to Power', in Burk (ed.), *War and the State*, London: Allen and Unwin, 1982, 84–87.

[7] French, 'Business as Usual', 20.

[8] J. Harris, 'Ministry of Food', in Burk (ed.), *War and the State*, London: Allen and Unwin, 1982, 135–36.

nationalisation of the liquor trade, it introduced taxes and controls to curb alcohol consumption which would have been impossible before the war, and which set the basis for restrictions that were to last over ninety years.[9]

By early 1915 it was clear that 'business as usual' would not win the war. The shell scandal of May of that year – in which it was revealed that up to a third of British shells were 'duds' that failed to explode – made this even more apparent, plainly exposing the shortcomings of the economic and military organisation of the country.[10] In response, the Ministry of Munitions – one of the most dynamic and far-reaching government departments of the war – was established under the leadership of Lloyd George in May 1915. By 1917 the efficiency and health of the thousands of munitions workers had become a top priority for the government: numerous reports were compiled on the subject, and over six hundred firms appointed supervisors whose sole duty was to promote the welfare of their workers.[11] Sick pay at one pound a week was introduced in the summer of 1916, and a per capita grant to cover the hospitalisation of munition workers suffering from jaundice was issued in March 1917.[12] Both miners and farmworkers benefited from state intervention into their industries, farm labourers in particular, and their importance to the war effort was recognised with the introduction of a minimum wage for agriculture in 1917, a year after it had been introduced for munitions workers.

The war created an acute concern for the well-being of the working classes who provided the bulk of the troops and labour required to win the conflict; an oft-quoted statistic claimed that whilst nine British soldiers died every hour in 1915, more than twelve babies perished in the same time period.[13] In this new environment even traditionally Conservative newspapers like *The Times* and *Daily Telegraph* lambasted previous governments for failing to tackle malnutrition and infant mortality. From 1915 the Board of Education began to finance childcare classes for mothers; the Midwives Act was amended in 1916 to improve mortality rates in childbirth; and the Milk and Dairies Consolidation Act was introduced in 1915.[14] Jay Winter has gone as far as to say that Britain came close 'to the setting up of an embryonic

---

[9] J. Turner, 'State Purchase of the Liquor Trade in the First World War', *Historical Journal* 23 (1980): 589–615.

[10] I. Bet-El, *Conscripts*, Stroud: The History Press, 1999, 7.

[11] Working Class Movement Library (WCML), War (First World War and Before) Folder, Pamphlet: 'British Workers and the War', by Christopher Addison MP, 1917.

[12] N. Whiteside, 'Industrial Welfare and Labour Regulation in Britain at the Time of the First World War', *International Review of Social History* 25 (1980): 313.

[13] N. Whiteside, 'The British Population at War', in J. Turner (ed.), *Britain and the First World War*, London: Unwin Hyman, 1988, 87.

[14] P. Thane, *Foundations of the Welfare State*, London: Longman, 1986, 126.

national health service during the First World War'.[15] In a similar vein, 'captains of industry' began to proclaim the necessity and desirability of public ownership of the electricity supply,[16] and by 1917–18 the majority of workers, perhaps as many as eighty or ninety per cent, were involved in war-related work.[17] By the end of the conflict even the most conservative were questioning the shibboleths of the free market. Winston Churchill asserted his belief that prices 'will have to be fixed so as to secure to the poorest people in this country who are engaged in fighting this War as comrades with us, the power of buying a certain modicum of food';[18] he would also argue in December 1918 for continued railway nationalisation. Meanwhile, Lord Carson claimed in February 1918 that Britain would be beaten by Germany if it 'refuse[d] to learn the lesson that in modern commerce, as in war, the power of organized combinations pursuing a steady policy will speedily drive out of the field the unregulated competition of individual enterprise'.[19]

Many on the Left were naturally exasperated that it had taken the bloodiest conflict Britain had known to create a clamour in the mainstream press for some of the simple, humane reforms they had been proposing for years; that it had been necessary to wait for 'the war [to create] the political conditions necessary for the implementation of ideas formulated in the pre-1914 period'.[20] In 1914 a cartoon in the *Railway Review*, captioned 'Home Defence', depicted barricades marked as 'State Control of Railways', 'National Relief of Unemployment', 'National Control of Food Prices', 'National Shipping Insurance', and 'National Relief of Distress' protecting 'John Bull's Home'. A John Bull figure, complete with rifle and bayonet, mopped his brow, while a Britannia figure stood atop the barricades. The caption had John Bull saying to a railway worker: 'There! Now I think we have fixed up something to help us defend the old home!', to which the worker replied: 'Yes, but how much better to have permanently incorporated them in strengthening our defences, instead of falling back upon them in an emergency! What can be done in time of war can be done in time of peace.' This is an early example of a common feature in the cartoons of

[15] J.M. Winter, *The Great War and the British People*, London: Palgrave Macmillan, 2003, 172.

[16] P. Abrams, 'The Failure of Social Reform: 1918–1920', *Past & Present* 24 (1963): 48–49.

[17] J.M. Winter, 'Public Health and the Political Economy of War, 1914–18', *History Workshop Journal* 26 (1988): 165.

[18] A. Marwick, *The Deluge: British Society and the First World War*, London: Palgrave Macmillan, 2006, 218.

[19] P.B. Johnson, *Land Fit for Heroes*, Chicago: University of Chicago Press, 1968, 384 and 149.

[20] Winter, *The Great War and the British People*, 193.

Figure 3. 'Home Defence', *Railway Review*, 11 September 1914.
Working Class Movement Library.

the *Railway Review*: John Bull pictured as a sympathetic character, allied
with a figure representing labour, sometimes against a German figure
but more often against a figure representing employers. An article in the
Annual Reports of the Amalgamated Society of Papermakers, headlined
'The Duty of the State', proclaimed in October 1914: 'If these men are, as
it were, duty bound to fight on behalf of the State, equally the State owes
a duty to these men in return, and they have a perfect right to receive
at the hands of the State a reasonable and assured recompense'.[21] The
Railway Review published by the National Union of Railwaymen (NUR)
concurred: 'If men have a duty to perform in the common interest of the
State', it argued, 'equally the state owes a duty to those of its citizens who

[21] Modern Records Centre (MRC), MSS.39/50/A/4/1/2 – Amalgamated Society of
Papermakers Annual Reports, October 1914.

are prepared – and readily prepared – to make sacrifices in its defence and for the maintenance of its honour.'[22]

The Ministry of Pensions was created in 1916 to oversee the increasing vast provision to bereaved families: initially mainly for widows, by the end of the war parents were the main recipients.[23] According to Susan Pedersen, the allowance system cost almost half a billion pounds, or almost as much as the amount paid to the soldiers themselves: 'By the Armistice', wrote Pedersen, 'allowances were absorbing some 120 million pounds per year, a figure roughly comparable to two-thirds of the total annual expenditure of the central government in the pre-war years.'[24] Similarly, it became difficult (at least in the short term), for the government to dodge responsibility for the poor and unsanitary housing of its citizens. At the outbreak of the war the Housing (No. 2) Act 1914 empowered the Local Government Board and the Board of Agriculture to spend up to four million pounds on new houses, and although this spending failed to materialise, by 1915 all three political parties accepted that when building began again it would be on the basis of some sort of public control.[25] The Ministry of Munitions itself became a major builder of houses, spending over £4.3 million on hostels, cottages, and houses between 1915 and 1918.[26] In October 1916, the *Daily Chronicle* announced the first 'state farm' for ex-servicemen: a 2,363-acre estate near Hull had been taken over by the government, and was to be settled by former soldiers for paid agricultural training.[27] Such schemes to resettle ex-servicemen on the land may well have had their origin in the land-reform tradition amongst some of the older Lib-Labs – and amongst the Liberal recruits to Labour – but ultimately proved unsuccessful. The fortunes of agriculture continued to decline after the war, and those veterans who did secure smallholdings could be seen to have lost out.[28]

The transformation of the pre-war state caused no little resentment, both during the war and subsequently. In her book *Conscripts*, Ilana Bet-El describes the 'conceptual shift from free will to a printed summons' that

[22] *Railway Review*, 11 September 1914.

[23] Thane, *Foundations of the Welfare State*, 120.

[24] S. Pedersen, 'Gender, Welfare and Citizenship in Britain during the Great War', *The American Historical Review* 95 (1990): 985.

[25] Labour History Archive Study Centre (LHASC), WNC.13/7/1 – Workmen's National Housing Council leaflet, 'HOUSING AND THE WAR'.

[26] Winter, *The Great War and the British People*, 243.

[27] *Daily Chronicle*, 23 October 1916.

[28] Martin Purdy has described the fate of Westfield War Memorial Village in Lancashire, which was announced with great fanfare but wound up by 1921, due to limited support from philanthropy and private enterprise. M. Purdy, 'Westfield War Memorial Village', paper given at Institute for Historical Research's Anglo-American Conference, 4 July 2014.

conscription involved, and the establishment of an unsettling bureaucratic process.[29] 'In theory', writes Bet-El, 'an individual's conscription was a form of trade in which he gave himself as a soldier, and in return the state became responsible for every aspect of his existence'.[30] While Adrian Gregory and others have disputed this picture of individual agency subsumed into an unresponsive, bureaucratic state, there is no doubt that the immediate post-war period featured something of a backlash against the state, not only politically and economically, but also culturally. In terms of aesthetics, for example, Catherine Moriarty has described the controversy surrounding the decision to have identical headstones on war graves, and how head sculptor Eric Gill – later to become a sympathiser of the British Union of Fascists – questioned the uniformity of cemeteries and the role of the state.[31]

There was further controversy around the expansion of the tax system. As Martin Daunton has noted, income tax was conceded as a principle in Britain much earlier than in other countries, to fight the previous 'Great War' a hundred years earlier, and the United Kingdom was able to raise money for warfare and welfare with considerably less strain than other countries – indeed, taxation played a larger part in financing the war effort in Britain than in any other nation.[32] The tax system expanded during the war to incorporate many new tax payers and the standard rate increased; many working-class wage earners were drawn into the tax system for the first time after the lowering of the exemption level in September 1915 from £160 to £130, which caused some resentment. Richard Whiting has recounted that 'a Scottish miner agreed about the injustice of paying income tax but not "when the very existence of the country is at stake, whilst we are fighting for our very existence as a nation"'.[33] George Barnes – Glasgow Gorbals MP and former Minister for Pensions – later recalled that 'there was a great deal of intelligent heckling at the meetings with the [trade union] lodges and even then it could be noted that though the tax was loyally accepted there was a strong undercurrent of opposition to it'.[34] Miners' leader Herbert Smith thought that more direct taxation would result in workers taking a

[29] Bet-El, *Conscripts*, 65 and 84.

[30] Ibid., 137.

[31] C. Moriarty, '"Though in Picture Only" Portrait Photography and the Commemoration of the First World War', in G. Braybon (ed.), *Evidence, History and the Great War: Historians and the Impact of 1914–18*, London: Berghahn Books, 2003, 32–33.

[32] M.J. Daunton, 'Payment and Participation: Welfare and State-Formation in Britain 1900–1951', *Past & Present* 150 (1996): 172–73. See also B. Waites, *A Class Society at War*, London: Berg, 1987, 105.

[33] R.C. Whiting, 'Taxation and the Working Class, 1915–24', *The Historical Journal* 33 (1990): 902.

[34] Ibid., 901–02.

more active interest in their relationship with the state, and that trade union unemployment funds would appear less attractive, and it does indeed seem that this was the case: despite some resentment, the increased tax burden brought people closer to the state.[35]

Noelle Whiteside stridently held that these were not developments in state socialism as such, but were driven instead by scientific concerns for efficiency that gave little thought to the welfare of citizens. For Whiteside, the growth of industrial welfare was a malevolent development designed to place constraints on organised labour.[36] She argued that as the war went on, support for increased state involvement began to wane, claiming that 'in its purest form, scientific management could not be reconciled with free collective bargaining over working conditions', and that in the end, 'it was tacitly acknowledged that welfare at the workplace was best determined by negotiation between employers and unions through joint industrial councils'.[37] Chris Wrigley concurred with this view, arguing that the Ministry of Munitions promoted welfare in order to hold labour in place: there was a high degree of worker mobility due to the labour shortage, and good pay and conditions were needed to keep men. It was American-inspired efficient paternalism, rather than state 'socialism'.[38] Indeed, it could have been that employers feared that, in the words of Arthur Henderson to Lloyd George, the 'only safeguard against control of workmen is control by the State'.[39]

Whatever the motivations behind the transformation of the British state during the war, the changes were to prove temporary in most cases. Asquith had set up the first Reconstruction Committee on 18 March 1916 with a remit including the conversion of munitions factories for civilian purposes and maintaining central control of the railways; Lloyd George established his own in February 1917, and labour men were well-represented on both of these boards.[40] Christopher Addison's February 1918 memorandum on Reconstruction Finance stipulated seven tasks to be tackled immediately upon the outbreak of peace, even 'at considerable cost'. These included housing, road and railway repair, land purchase, financing of essential industries, extending unemployment insurance, strengthening healthcare provision, and guaranteeing credit.[41] For Neville Chamberlain: 'Every legitimate effort

---

[35] Ibid., 896.

[36] Whiteside, 'Industrial Welfare', 307.

[37] Ibid., 322 and 326.

[38] C.J. Wrigley, 'The Ministry of Munitions: An Innovatory Department', in Burk (ed.), *War and the State*, London: Allen and Unwin, 1982, 50.

[39] J.M. Winter, 'Arthur Henderson, the Russian Revolution, and the Reconstruction of the Labour Party', *Historical Journal* 15 (1972): 763.

[40] Johnson, *Land Fit for Heroes*, 10–12 and 36.

[41] Ibid., 108.

should be made to prevent unemployment and its accompanying demorali-
sation [after the war]. It was far better to run the risk of manufacturing
commodities which would not be required, and to resolve them into their
elements later, than to have multitudes in receipt of unemployment benefit.'[42]
Yet the Coalition Government would ultimately reject pressure from Labour
and the unions for post-war investment in construction and other industries
to combat unemployment, and there was no lasting overhaul of economic
orthodoxy. Many Asquithian Liberals joined the Coalition in rejecting
most of the statism of the war years, and as Pat Thane has observed, 'the
Poor Law's unscathed survival of the war ... and the fate of health reform'
indicated the limited extent of change.[43] Yet, as Chris Wrigley has argued,
whilst many of the changes of the war were immediately reversed, this did
not mean they had been for naught:

> The experience ... left a lasting impression on people's thinking, and
> not just on that of politicians and civil servants. After the First World
> War many industrialists, bankers, politicians and trade unionists became
> disillusioned with free market competition at home and abroad and
> favoured cooperation in industry, mergers and large-scale organisation.
> The Ministry of Munitions could be eulogised as an example of what
> could be achieved.[44]

The vast curtailment of public expenditure and the return to the gold
standard in 1925 suggested that no lessons had been learned from the war
– and the war did not introduce Keynesian ideas to Labour or anyone else.
The breaks with the past, both in terms of symbolism and actual policy,
cannot be ignored. In areas such as agriculture there was a clear break with
laissez-faire; although the Corn Production Act was repealed in 1921, farmers
both expected and continued to call for state intervention. The notion
took hold that working-class housing was a responsibility of the state; in
response to the Sankey Report, the government conceded the principle of
nationalisation in some areas; and limited protectionism was introduced in
the shape of the 1920 Dye-Stuffs Act and the following year's Safeguarding
of Industries Act.[45]

Geoffrey Field described a great expansion of social services that took
place during and after the Second World War, including 'controlling rents,
providing nurseries, paying numerous types of allowances, and even fixing
the calorific intake of different occupational groups under the rationing

---

[42] Quoted in Ibid., 280.

[43] Thane, *Origins of the Welfare State*, 132.

[44] Wrigley, 'Ministry of Munitions', 52.

[45] Johnson, *Land Fit for Heroes*, 419, 455, and 464. It should be noted that the Sankey
Report and the government's response did not necessarily help the miners a great deal.

system'. Yet all of these occurred to a certain degree during and after the 1914–18 conflict, and while much was removed in the interwar years, the principle had been conceded, and the mistakes made and lessons learned from the 1918–39 period meant that establishing the wartime state, and the welfare state which followed, was made all the easier, and executed all the more promptly.[46] In terms of the legal and institutional changes, and precedents which were set, the First World War deserves prominence as a time when the British attitude towards the state was transformed. This section has argued that the expansion and contraction of the British state during the war was not for naught: both in terms of the economic and policy changes which remained, and the ideological break with the past, the growth of the state during the First World War gave great encouragement to the Left and set the groundwork for 1939–45 and beyond. The next section considers how labour attempted to create a safety net, or 'second state' for British workers during the war.

Labour and the Workers during the War

The apparatus of the British state – of which Labour formed a part for most of the conflict – expanded and evolved during the First World War, yet the activities of the labour movement *outside* of Parliament in this period are of tremendous significance in the history of the British Left. This section will relate the activities of the labour movement to further the interests of its members, and argue that the WNC provided almost a 'second state' or safety net for the most vulnerable. It represented workers at the highest levels of government, facilitated communication and propaganda within the labour movement, and pursued redress of grievances over individual injustices. These functions enabled the gathering of information, the building of activist bases on the ground, and the attraction of new support to the cause.

Unemployment and Child Labour
Unemployment was one of the first concerns for the WNC: almost immediately after war was declared, certain employers began to use the conflict as an excuse to lay off troublesome workers, and some local authorities began to refuse out-of-work relief to men eligible for the army, in strict contravention of Asquith's proclamation on the matter. Letters flooded in about this discrimination, and the Committee successfully lobbied the Local Government Board to proscribe the practice, and had both Asquith and President of the Local Government Board Herbert Samuel further denounce

---

[46] G. Field, 'Social Patriotism and the British Working Class: Appearance and Disappearance of a Tradition', *International Labor and Working-Class History* 42 (1992): 29.

the policy.[47] Expecting great dislocation and misery after the onset of the war, the Left initially looked to combat the threat of high unemployment. The Parliamentary Committee of the TUC made overtures to the Insurance Commissioners to have the government accord financial assistance to unions in the event of large numbers of their members being laid off, and a number of schemes for dealing with expected joblessness were put forward by labour organisations.[48] A further concern was the use of service personnel for civilian labouring work, at the expense of or undercutting local labour. Within a couple of weeks of the outbreak of war, a letter to Dr J.T. Macnamara at the Admiralty told of coaling work being done at Southampton by Royal Navy sailors, despite dockworkers being unemployed, and men at Deptford working twelve-hour shifts despite similar unemployment there.[49] A month later, another letter to the Admiralty complained of discharges at Chatham dockyard when overtime was being worked and new men were being taken on.[50] Ben Tillett asked Middleton to write to the War Office, requesting that whenever work was required to be done for the military, civilians who were usually engaged in such work should be taken on first. Yet despite an initial slackening of trade in some industries, by the end of the year unemployment had shrunk and most industries faced a shortage of labour.

Such was the labour crisis in agriculture – with men leaving farms in droves for the military or better pay elsewhere – that children were often taken out of school and put to work. The WNC pressurised J.A. Pease, President of the Board of Education, to release the records of school attendance in agricultural districts, and sent out five hundred forms to be distributed amongst National Agricultural Labourers' and Rural Workers' Union (NALRU) branches, in order for them to report the use of child labour.[51] Despite the efforts of the Committee, this issue was still proving problematic by the autumn of 1915, and a deputation met with the Home Secretary on 13 October to discuss it. During the meeting Henderson claimed that 1,538 boys and fifty-three girls had been granted exemption from school in rural areas, and 540 and 228 respectively in urban areas. Of these, fifty-four were under twelve years old, about 930 were twelve, and the rest thirteen; 1,394 boys and twenty-five girls were engaged in agricultural work; 121 boys and fourteen girls in factory work; and 300 and 179 respectively in unspecified employment.[52] The Committee's agitation in this area

---

[47] WNC.8/74.

[48] WNC.30/1/7-140 – Unemployment.

[49] WNC.1/3/1 – letter to Dr J.T. Macnamara at the Admiralty, 15 August 1914.

[50] WNC.1/3/3/6 – letter to Macnamara, 15 September 1914.

[51] WNC.1/4/3/49-50 and 67.

[52] WNC.3/7/2/20 – Henderson's speech to delegation on child labour.

was so persuasive – chiming as it did with concerns about the health and well-being of Britain's youth – that a resolution was moved at a meeting of the National Land and Home League (headed by the Conservative Lord Henry Bentinck): 'This meeting regards with grave apprehension the far-reaching effects of the employment of children in agriculture, which must necessarily put them at a disadvantage throughout their lives, and urges the Board of Education to take measures for restricting the exemption of children under 13'.[53] In addition to keeping children in school, the labour movement worked hard to ensure that they were properly fed; the London Labour Emergency Committee issued a leaflet, which advised:

> If you are out of work, not only can your children be fed by the school authorities on the school days (Monday to Friday), but they can also be fed by them on Saturday and Sunday. You ought not to allow your children to go hungry, and if you are unable to feed them, tell the children to ask the Teachers for BREAKFAST AND DINNER ON SATURDAY AND SUNDAY (as well as the other days of the week), and if necessary see the Teacher yourself.[54]

The high demand for agricultural labour led the military to send men to work on the land, and in August 1915 the Committee received complaints from Norfolk farmworkers alleging that local farmers had been employing soldiers at a lower rate despite agricultural workers being registered at the labour exchange.[55] Later in the war the WNC facilitated petitions to the Secretary of Agriculture complaining of undercutting by soldiers:

> We the undersigned Farm Workers beg most respectfully to inform you that owing to the large number of soldiers now working on the land in this District we are unable to obtain work consequently our wives children and other dependants have to go short of food and other necessaries which we consider most unjust as these soldiers receive pay for and clothing as soldiers and should not be allowed to rob civilians of their living.[56]

There were incidences of this kind around the country but they were usually only temporary: in this case, Bob Walker of NALRU reported a few weeks later that the soldiers had left and the men were reported to be back at work.[57] Eventually, the 1917 pamphlet 'Conscription Enters the Workplace' was able

---

53 WNC.3/7/4/12.
54 WNC.26/1/2.
55 WNC.1/5/2/1-WNC.1/5/2/4.
56 WNC.1/4/9/9 – to the Secretary Board of Agriculture, 18 April 1917.
57 WNC.1/4/7/10 – R.B. Walker to Mackley, 4 May 1917. P.E. Dewey found that whilst there was resentment at the higher wages paid to soldiers – who earned the equivalent of a skilled farm hand – soldiers were usually employed because voluntary labour could not be found, and the establishment of a minimum wage corrected the pay imbalance. See

to proudly claim that: 'As a result of pressure from the Labour Party, Mr. Forster, on behalf of the War Office, has now stated that, in future, when it is found necessary to lend military working parties, the pay of the men shall be based on the current local rates for similar civilian work.'[58] The issue of soldiers employed in agriculture further highlights the WNC's two-way function as a means of airing grievances whilst collecting information and building up an activist base on the ground: former Independent Labour Party (ILP) chairman W.C. Anderson noted to Walker that the information about labour conditions which came in from displaced farmworkers would be useful for Labour during the passage of the Corn Production Bill.[59]

Food and Fuel

Another key concern of the Committee was to stabilise food prices for the poor. As early as October 1914, the WNC was pushing for the commandeering of homegrown wheat to 'interfere with unpatriotic profiteering by British farmers and merchants'.[60] The end of 1914 saw the publication of the pamphlet 'The Workers and the War: A Programme for Labour', point eight of which called for 'The encouragement and development of home-grown food supplies by the national organisation of Agriculture, accompanied by drastic reductions of freight charges for all produce, in the interests of the whole people'. Further attacks were made upon free-market orthodoxy with the call in point nine for 'Protection of the people against exorbitant prices, especially in regard to food, by the enactment of maxima and the commandeering of supplies by the nation wherever advisable'.[61] In November 1916 the WNC established a Food Prices Sub-Committee, incorporating a broad spectrum of the British Left, from trade unionists such as W.C. Anderson, Alfred Bellamy, Fred Bramley, and Ben Tillett, to ILPers and BSPers such as Ramsay MacDonald and Henry Hyndman, the Co-operative Wholesale Society's Bob Williams, and members of the Women's Labour League in Susan Lawrence and Marion Philips. This committee immediately sent out a survey to all local labour organisations requesting information on the prices of various food stuffs.[62]

In 1917 the Committee published a 'Memorandum on the National Food Supply', and distributed thousands of copies nationwide, encouraging

---

P.E. Dewey, 'Government Provision of Farm Labour in England and Wales, 1914–18', *Agricultural History Review* 27 (1979): 110–12.

[58] WNC.5/2/4/6 i – Pamphlet: 'Conscription Enters the Workshop'.

[59] WNC.1/4/9/13 W.C. Anderson to R. Walker.

[60] WNC.1/4/1.i – J.A. Seddon to President of Board of Agriculture, 12 October 1914.

[61] WNC.24/1/1 – The Workers and the War. A Programme for Labour, 1914.

[62] WNC.9/2/47.ii – template of covering letter sent out with food prices information form.

the setting up of Food Vigilance Committees by local leftist organisations, hundreds of which were eventually established. By May of that
year the intensification of the U-boat campaign resulted in a previously
untenable food situation reaching crisis point. The Committee demanded
the purchase of all imported foodstuffs, the commandeering of all
home-grown products, commandeering of ships, control of supply and
regulation, and the fixing of the price of bread and flour for the rest of
the war and six months afterwards.[63] They wrote to Lord Devonport, the
hapless Food Controller, urging him to consider at least some of their ideas
for assuaging the crisis, whether it be the registration of customers, the
adoption of a scheme for sugar rationing, a Food Rationing Committee to
be set up by the Ministry of Food, or controlling the supply and fixing the
price of flour substitutes.[64] A cartoon in *The Co-operative News* of January
1918 depicted a mass of people outside of a shop marked 'Competitive
System', trying to gain entry while a policeman attempted to keep order.
In the caption John Bull speaks to a Co-operator: 'This sort of thing is
undignified and degrading. What do you do?' To which the Co-operator
replies: 'Our system of equal distribution is the only method of dealing
with this crisis.' John Bull responds: 'You seem to be in close touch with
the people. We must solicit your help.'

Dozens of food conferences were held in cities and towns across Britain,
and they were largely successful, rallying the local labour movements
(the efficacy of these conferences in bringing together different groups
in various localities is discussed in the Chapter 6) and raising over one
hundred pounds for the coffers of the WNC. Perhaps their greatest
feature, however, was in allowing labour to take the lead on a vital issue
and demonstrating the relevance of the Left to ordinary people hitherto
untouched by the movement. In the words of the convener of the Bradford
Conference: 'The most pleasing feature of the conference was the hearty
support given by the clergy of the city, in fact one of the Church of
England parsons stated the resolution [calling for state control of the food
supply] did not go far enough for him, so that I think you will agree
things are moving.'[65]

In June 1917, at the height of the food crisis, the WNC learned of a plan
to sterilise and sell meat infected with tuberculosis, and sent the following
strongly worded resolution to the Prime Minister:

> this Committee learns with amazement that the Local Government
> Board has sent to local authorities the suggestion that they should sterilise

[63] WNC.5/1/1/5-20.
[64] WNC.10/2/18 – letter to Lord Devonport, 14 May 1917.
[65] WNC.4/4/10 – letter from Bradford Trades and Labour Council, 16 February 1915.

and offer for sale the purpose of human consumption the meat of cattle affected with tuberculosis and that such meat should be disposed of at a low price to the poor. The Committee protests strongly against such a policy both on the ground of public health and class distinction, and urges that permission to sell such meat should be at once withdrawn.[66]

A report came in from Dundee immediately after the start of the war that the local Labour Representation Committee had been informed that two wholesale firms were trying to corner the sugar supply in Dundee, and called for the government to take action against this behaviour, adding that the names of the firms involved could be forwarded if requested.[67] Middleton replied requesting the names be sent to the Board of Trade, and stating that 'What they require is specific information of the kind you have. It is useless for us to send forward complaints of a general character.'[68]

A letter from the Retford and District Trade and Labour Council carried the resolution that: 'This Trade Council does emphatically protest against the proposed representation of Labour on the Food Control Committee (one in twelve) and contend that as Labour represents the greater portion of the population, it is entitled to at the least half the representatives on such Committees.'[69] The Middlesbrough Co-operative Society complained to Middleton that they had no representation on Middlesbrough Food Control Committee and other committees in the Middlesbrough district. Middleton wrote to the Food Controller – now Labour MP John Clynes – to press him on the matter. Clynes responded that co-operators were proportionately represented on the appropriate committees, and that in any case the appointment of members to Food Control Committees was the responsibility of local authorities. This disappointment anticipated the problem of trade unions and left-wing groups under later Labour governments, who would find out that they faced much the same problems with their own people in power as they had done under Liberals and Conservatives.[70]

This focus on the price of food was to win the movement praise – and from some unlikely quarters. The *Yorkshire Post* noted in December 1916:

This week the Workers' War Emergency Committee, an important auxiliary of the Labour Party, has adopted a series of agricultural resolutions, asking the Government to take over 'at least four million acres of the land at present abandoned to grass or fallow'; the land now devoted

[66] WNC.9/2/89 – letter to David Lloyd George, 22 June 1917.
[67] WNC.11/54 – letter from William Westwood J.P. of Dundee LRC, 17 August 1914.
[68] WNC.11/55 – letter to William Westwood, 20 August 1914.
[69] WNC.10/3/20 – letter from Retford and District Trade and Labour Council, 17 August 1917.
[70] WNC.7/2/135i – letter from J.R. Clynes, 13 May 1918.

to private parks is to be included; implements to be furnished by the Government, and a 'civilian body of mobile labour' organised 'including German prisoners.'[71]

Similarly, the *Sheffield Daily Telegraph* was full of praise for WNC action on high food prices and army allowances.[72] In a May 1917 article entitled 'The Real Danger', the *Pall Mall Gazette* praised the Miners' Federation for their resolutions on food control: 'It is time the Government used the powers they possess to stamp out this trafficking with the food of the people, this wicked exploitation of the war. The profiteer, when discovered, should be prosecuted, and, on conviction, should be sentenced to the imprisonment he so richly deserves.'[73] The *Evening News* excoriated the deeply unpopular Devonport, asking: 'If he has completely misled patriotic and intelligent Labour leaders, is it any wonder that … the nation as a whole has failed to realise the seriousness of the situation?'[74] Finally, the *Daily Mail* praised the work of the Committee, claiming that the 'manifesto issued by the Workers' National Committee shows the effect of Lord Devonport's failure to make the country understand the food position'.[75] Although the cost of food was to remain a significant issue throughout the war, the Left had a great deal of success in this area through Food Vigilance Committees, food councils, and eventually the introduction of rationing and the Corn Production Act. Noting the desirability of the state subsidising farmers to increase production, Sidney Webb wrote to the Secretary of the Rural Advisory Committee in July 1918: '[The Corn Production Act] does nothing to raise the price of food to the consumer. Whatever protection and assurance is thereby afforded to the farmer comes out of the Exchequer, not out of the pockets of the consumers. Its burden falls, therefore, on the tax-payers, roughly in proportion to their means, instead of upon the consumers in proportion to their mouths.'[76]

Further to the increasingly precarious food supply, the price and distribution of coal became a major issue as the war wore on. In 1915 the Coal Prices Limitation Act had fixed the pit head price of coal to a maximum of four shillings above the price generally prevailing before the war, yet by July 1916 the Coal Controller had authorised South Wales coal owners to make a further increase of two shillings six pence (apparently due to the increased wages being paid to miners), so that the maximum pit head price was six shillings six pence per ton above the pre-war prices. Significantly, these

---

71 *Yorkshire Post*, 6 December 1916.
72 *Sheffield Daily Telegraph*, December 1916.
73 *Pall Mall Gazette*, 18 May 1917.
74 *Evening News*, 12 May 1917.
75 *Daily Mail*, 12 May 1917.
76 WNC.1/4/11/1 – Sidney Webb to Secretary of Rural Advisory Committee, 2 July 1918.

restrictions only applied to coal sold at the pit top, and made no allowance for the cost of coal to individual customers. Middleton warned the Prime Minister in 1916 that:

> The concession so readily granted to the South Wales owners will be followed by demands from the owners in other coalfields with the inevitable result that consumers will be faced during the coming winter, and probably earlier, with considerably enhanced retail prices, for it cannot be assumed for a moment that coal merchants will be content to pass on the increased cost without an increased percentage of profit added thereto.[77]

During the winter of 1916–17 the WNC urged the establishment of municipal coal distribution, but the proposal did not find favour.[78] In a rather sarcastically worded letter to E.J. Hollands of the Cowes Trades Council, Middleton warned: 'The presence of Lord Rhondda, who, of course, was formerly Mr. D.A. Thomas, the South Wales Coal Magnate, at the Head of the Local Government Board, is, I think, a pretty firm guarantee that the Coal Trade will not be municipalized just yet.'[79] On the same day, he complained to Robert Brown of the Dartmouth Ratepayers Association: 'The several Governments which have been in office during the War have steadily refused to fix retail coal prices despite the pressure that has been brought to bear repeatedly by the Workers' National Committee and its kindred local organisations.'[80]

Pensions

Soon after the first casualties of the war began returning to Britain, a campaign developed to ensure adequate pensions for wounded and disabled men. A resolution of the Clydebank and District Trades' and Labour Council called upon the government to 'establish adequate pensions for disabled soldiers and sailors, and strongly protests against any attempt to introduce charitable offerings, thus relieving the Government of their duty and humiliating the men who have responded to their country's call'.[81] In September 1916 Middleton wrote to D. Rogers of the Llanelly Labour Association, assuring him that every effort was being made to co-ordinate the various Pensions Authorities, and that the party leadership was very anxious to secure reform for all the existing anomalies.[82]

[77] WNC.3/10/24.i – letter to Asquith, 25 July 1916.
[78] WNC.3/10/1-2.
[79] WNC.3/10/10a – letter to E.J. Hollands, 31 May 1917.
[80] WNC.3/10/12 – Middleton to Robert Brown, 31 May 1917.
[81] WNC.24/1/94i – Resolution of the Clydebank and District Trades' and Labour Council, 16 February 1916.
[82] WNC.24/1/218 – letter to D. Rogers, 11 September 1916.

In addition to agitating for more generous pensions across the board, the Committee also dealt with a great deal of case work on this issue. For example, a County Durham woman, Mrs Gardiner, had a son killed in France; as her husband was in work, the War Office offered a one-off gratuity rather than a pension. Mrs Gardiner insisted that since her husband – a colliery chargeman earning four shillings a day – was sixty years old, he could not be expected to make up the loss of the fifteen shillings a week the son had provided to the household.[83] This obtuseness in withholding pensions from relatives who – while not technically dependent on the deceased were still heavily reliant upon them – was fairly common. Middleton wrote in the case of Mrs Gardiner, 'I am not very hopeful of any change [to this practice] being made in the War Office decision but will do what I can'.[84] Eventually, however, the War Office decided that 'a pension could not be awarded in view of [her] means of support'.[85] A case of active connivance to reduce disablement pensions was reported by Tom Sullivan of the Lanarkshire Miners' Union. Sullivan told of the case of Sergeant Andrew Stoddart who, after nineteenth months in the field, was wounded on 6 December 1916, and had his left leg amputated. Early in January 1917 his wife received a letter informing her that he had been demoted to corporal as of 6 December 1916, and so her allowance would be reduced. Nor had he received any pay since being hospitalised. Sullivan alleged: 'Now you will see the harshness of this case, as their sole object seems to be the fixing of a lower pension as Private instead of the Serjeant's [sic] rank. Trusting you will give your assistance and if possible get justice done.'[86] After Middleton called for an explanation, the War Office claimed that Stoddart had only been 'appointed Acting Sergeant on August 18th; reverted to Corporal November 13th'.[87] Finally, labour activists in Wolverhampton brought to light the case of a soldier discharged after twelve months with a tuberculosis ulceration of the neck – it was confirmed by two doctors that it was almost certainly caused by service in the army. However, it was discovered that he had spent six of those twelve months in Wormwood Scrubs, so despite the protest of the Labour members, the sub-committee (of the Local War Pensions Committee) refused to recommend him for a pension, on the grounds of 'character'.[88]

[83] WNC.2/5/2/1 Letter from W.H. Johnson of the Durham Miner's Association to Middleton, 9 October 1916.

[84] WNC.2/5/2/2 – Middleton to Johnson.

[85] WNC.2/5/2/3.

[86] WNC.2/5/4/2 – letter from Tom Sullivan of Lanarkshire Miners' County Union, 8 January 1917.

[87] WNC.2/5/4/3 – letter to Middleton from Ministry of Pensions, 30 April 1917.

[88] WNC.2/5/8/1 – letter from Wolverhampton WEW Vigilance Committee, 15 May 1917.

Profiteering and Exploitation

One of the more surprising functions of the WNC was its role as a conduit for people to inform on cynical and illegal practices which were either to the detriment of working people, or the war effort, or both. A letter from Liverpool activist Fred Hoey in August 1916 relayed a scandalous report from the Warehouse Workers' Union. The Union alleged that 1,450 cases of Canadian corned beef had been docked in Liverpool around the time of the outbreak of war, stored for two years, and then returned to Canada so that they could be sold to the government at a higher price. An outraged Hoey suggested that a question should be asked in the Commons on the matter.[89] The Newcastle Fabian Society reported in October 1915 that a large number of firms owning merchant ships had sold vessels at greatly inflated prices and made huge profits which could escape taxation due to the transaction being designated as 'realisation of capital' rather than profit. This resulted in a massive loss to national income, as vessels and even whole fleets had been sold at a profit of over one hundred per cent. 'It is hoped', the letter continued 'that the Committee will use its influence to prevent this profit, which has been paid by the poorer classes in this country (in the shape of increased food prices) escaping taxation'.[90] Examples such as these clearly suggest that while the war raged on, organised labour at the grassroots level remained hawk-eyed about profiteering and undermining of the war effort.

Of particular concern for the WNC and local labour bodies was the awarding and completion of government contracts. As early as November 1914 the Committee asked the government to 'make public the names and addresses of the contractors who are supplying material in the form of food, clothing, huts, etc., etc., to His Majesty's forces'.[91] Army and navy contracts had been published prior to the war, but this ceased upon outbreak; due to WNC pressure, the practice was resumed by the army in January 1915, but the navy continued to obfuscate.[92] Within the first few months of the war the Committee began to receive reports of firms producing shoddy materiel and short-changing the government. A letter from H. Bassford of the Ilkeston and District Hosiery Union dated 14 December 1914 reported that: 'There is, I am told by one of the workmen, a firm in our Trade that is robbing the Government on Contracts. There is no doubt about it. I think the firm could, if care was exercised, be caught at the work. It is a firm that has always and is now fighting us [the union].'[93] A further letter added that:

[89] WNC.3/4/4/1 – letter from Fred Hoey, 27 August 1916.
[90] WNC.3/5/1/11 – letter from Newcastle-upon-Tyne Fabian Society, 6 October 1915.
[91] WNC.6/2/3/2.
[92] WNC.6/2/29/3 – letter to T.E. Jenkins of Swansea Labour Association, 13 January 1915.
[93] WNC.6/2/15/2 – letter from H. Bassford, 15 December 1914.

'The firm is not only robbing the Government but are [...] working females until 9. O. Clock at night for about 10/- per week.'[94] Middleton wrote to Sir George Gibb, Director of Contracts at the War Office, to report Bassford's claim that water was being added to the hose to make them the required weight.[95] The Trimmers' Union, Scourers' Union, the Dyers' Society, and the Auxiliary Workers' Union all supported Bassford's claim, and Gibb met with a deputation from the Committee, including Henderson, Anderson, Middleton, and MacDonald, to discuss the matter early in the new year.[96] In February of 1915 the authorities reported back that an investigation had taken place and no water had been found, but Middleton warned the War Office that the unions concerned were not satisfied with this outcome.[97] 'With respect to your communication of February 18th', Middleton wrote, 'I enclose herewith a communication I have received from my correspondent and shall be glad to have your observations on its contents as the allegation so flatly contradicts the opinions of the Department ... I am bound to say that it appears a little unreasonable to suppose that men working in the hosiery factories have imagined the process of which they complain.'[98] He then advised the Contracts Department that if they desired to avoid a scandal it was necessary to undertake a 'frank enquiry' into the matter as 'the organised trades in Leicester were not prepared to allow the matter to rest as it is a present', and that, furthermore, he proposed to secure more publicity of the issue in the *Daily Citizen* and other newspapers.[99] The obtuseness of the state over this issue suggests an absurd situation in which the military was less concerned with the quality of their hosiery than were the men employed to make it, and that the government may even have been complicit in its own deception – an impression confirmed by Middleton:

> On Wednesday, March 3rd, 1915, I had a conversation with an employer in the hosiery finishing department, and in reply to my questions he said: 'Yes, we all water Government hosiery. I have to add water on the instructions of the manufacturers to bring them all to the required weight. We all do it, and the Government knows we do it ... I know it's a fraud, I know it's dishonest, but it's done throughout the trade; and as I know the Government are aware of it my conscience does not prick me, but it's wrong all the same.'[100]

94 WNC.6/2/15/3 – letter from H. Bassford, 19 December 1914.
95 WNC.6/2/16/3 – letter to Sir George Gibb, 23 December 1914
96 WNC.6/2/16/9.
97 WNC.6/2/16/18 – letter from Assistant Director Army Contracts, 18 February 1915.
98 WNC.6/2/16/36 – response to Assistant Director Army Contracts, 15 March 1915.
99 WNC.6/2/16/35 – letter to W. Kilbourne, 15 March 1915, in which he quotes his earlier advice to the Contracts Department.
100 WNC.6/2/16/38.

The hosiery dispute was not the only controversy involving government contracts. An article in *The Clarion* in January 1915 alleged that 'the timber merchants rushed up the price for timber immediately they heard that the troops were to be sheltered in wooden huts, the increase being 37½ per cent above pre-war rates'.[101] Similarly, in a letter to the editor of the *Daily Citizen* which was passed on to Middleton, Timothy Smith – a Labour councillor in Colchester and President of the Local Branch of the Workers' Union – decried the poor standard of army boots being produced, and attached a sample of the shoddy stuffing which lined the shoes. Middleton took up the issue, sending the stuffing on to the War Office.[102] The military tried to dodge the issue, claiming that the boots must have been purchased locally in the enlistment rush which followed the creation of the New Armies.[103] Somewhat bemused by this apparent lack of concern about the quality of the troops' footwear, Middleton replied that 'While … there is a probability that the boots were accepted in an emergency that explanation is surely hardly sufficient to meet the case. Would it not appear desirable for the delinquent contractor to be found and properly dealt with?'[104] Yet the War Office did not share this concern, responding that 'it is regretted it is now impossible to trace the source from which the boots were obtained'.[105] Overall, WNC reports of profiteering and misuse of government contracts tended to come to naught; the government made only perfunctory attempts to follow up and investigate the claims, and indeed seemed rather inconvenienced by the allegations.

The changed atmosphere of the war did not just result in greater scrutiny of firms short-changing the government, but also of members of the government who appeared to be benefiting from the conflict. By no means was this scrutiny confined to the Left. A letter was published in the *Morning Post*, no less, by a Mr F.G. Banbury, who claimed that he had received a circular from 'Mitchelson, Ltd', a company which listed its partners as A. Mitchelson, John Hambly, and the Rt. Hon. Lord Rhondda. This circular had advertised an investment in a company which paid a dividend in ordinary shares in 1915 of fifteen per cent, with an additional distribution of fifty per cent out of accumulated profits. The profits for 1916 were forecast to be in the region of one hundred thousand pounds, and there was to be a dividend of twenty-five per cent, free of income tax, already declared for that year. One of the main sources of profits for this company was everyday

---

[101] *The Clarion*, 8 January 1915.
[102] WNC.6/2/35.
[103] WNC.6/2/35/10 – letter from the War Office, February 1915.
[104] WNC.6/2/35/11 – letter to War Office, 17 February 1915.
[105] WNC.6/2/35/13 – letter from War Office, 20 February 1915.

necessities such as margarine and soap. Banbury noted that ministers were supposed to relinquish directorships of companies, and Rhondda had not done so.[106] The fact that the *Morning Post* had taken this line, along with the condemnation across all media of the malnourishment and unfitness of British recruits, and the praise given to the WNC by organs such as *The Times* and the *Daily Mail*, shows how iconoclastic the war had been. If some of the more over-zealous labour patriots were to venture into a territory of jingoism and sinister ultra-nationalism, then one must not forgot that many on the Right also found a new and short-lived enthusiasm for some economic planning and equality of sacrifice.

Housing

Given the parlous state of working-class housing before August 1914, and the cessation of virtually all house building during the war, the provision of homes for the workers became an even more pressing issue.[107] After being informed via Ben Tillett of delays in house building projects in Swansea, W.C. Anderson asked Walter Long, President of the Local Government Board, whether he would publish a list of housing schemes that had been sanctioned since the outbreak of the war, and those which had been refused. Long responded:

> Speaking generally, the Department have since March last been forced, owing to the restrictions on expenditure, to take the line that loans for housing and other purposes cannot be sanctioned at the present time. An exception has been made in the case of munition areas where further accommodation is urgently required for the workers, and in some half-dozen cases terms have been arranged under which housing schemes will, I am glad to say, shortly be put in hand.[108]

Before the war, most of the working class had lived in privately rented accommodation, and as Ken Weller has noted, distraints for rent in arrears were a depressingly common feature of Edwardian England, with sixteen thousand seizures in 1908 in the North London borough of Islington alone.[109] The War Rents League created a pamphlet, 'Rent Raising Made Illegal', which explained the implications of the War Rents Restriction Act. It advised that increases in rents were not legal and tenants should refuse

---

[106] WNC.9/2/141 – clipping of letter sent to the *Morning Post* by F.G. Banbury (undated).
[107] In some areas, long-term undersupply of housing reached crisis point during the war. See B. White, 'Wigwams and Resort Towns: The Housing Crisis in First World War Devon', in N. Mansfield and C. Horner (eds), *The Great War: Localities and Regional Identities*, Newcastle: Cambridge Scholars Publishing, 2014, 97–118.
[108] WNC.13/7/22/1-2.
[109] Weller, *Don't Be a Soldier!*, 16.

to pay more than pre-war rents; tenants could not be ejected for refusing to pay increases; any increases paid since 25 November 1915 should be deducted from future rent; landlords were not permitted to alter terms of tenancy in any way unfavourable to tenants; increases were only permitted for improvements or structural alterations or for increases in rates; and landlords were obliged to give tenants notice in writing of intentions to raise rent four weeks in advance.[110] Leaflets were distributed to various trade councils, from Abertillery to Sunderland, advising of changes to the law and warning people not to pay excess rents, and the campaign to publicise changes in the law brought in queries and requests from the general public, such as the following from Mrs Westwood of Warrington:

To The Secretary,

Having seen your letters in the *Daily Citizen* I am writing to ask you if my land-lord can take my doors off and turn me out. I owe him a month's rent and as my month's pay has not come I asked him to take 5d a week until it was paid up and he said that would not do for him he asked me for my wing paper and because I would not give it to him he told me he would take the doors off before the night was out and he came everyday last week for rent. Can he stand to turn me out my husband is at the front and I have two children would you kindly give me a little advice. Yours truly Mrs Westwood.[111]

In response, Middleton forwarded the details of the case to a supporter in Warrington and assured Mrs Westwood that under the Courts (Emergency Powers) Act she could not be turned out. Similarly, in a letter to another concerned correspondent he gave assurance that: 'Your landlord cannot distrain or terminate the occupancy of your house without an order from the Court and you will have an opportunity of stating your case to the magistrate and of showing that your arrears are due to the intervention of the war.' He enclosed further particulars relating to the Act and added that 'if you have any difficulty whatever I shall be glad if you will communicate further with us'.[112]

As with the food supply and undercutting in agriculture, the WNC did not merely agitate on behalf of tenants; the rent issue was used as a means of collecting information to bolster Labour's position on the matter in Parliament. Middleton advised Asquith in October 1915 that the WNC

[110] WCML Pamphlet Collection, World War One, Box 2: 'Rent-Raising Made Illegal. The War Rents Restriction Act Explained to Tenants', by Dan Rider (Honorary Secretary of the War Rents League).
[111] WNC.15/4/20 – letter from Mrs Westwood, 14 October 1914.
[112] WNC.27/1/7 – letter to Mr Foulis, 11 January 1915.

was collecting data on rents – amongst other things – that would then be used in official speeches.[113] Given that prosecutions for breaches of the Rent Restrictions Act were very rare, these actions by the WNC were important in reassuring people of their rights under the law, preventing abuses by landlords, and giving poor working-class tenants the novel feeling that the force of the law and the authority of the state could be used to their advantage.

Apprentices

Another area of concern for the Committee was the question of apprenticeships. There was some uncertainty about whether or not the period in which an apprentice was serving with the forces was to be considered part of the apprenticeship. The Amalgamated Society of Carpenters and Joiners, the Shipwrights and Ship Constructers Society, and the Amalgamated Society of Engineers (ASE) reported back that there was no general established practice on this issue. The House Painters and Decorators claimed that they would be considered full members of the Society at the scheduled end of their apprenticeship but whether or not they received full rates would depend on the state of the trade at the time.[114] Perhaps the most candid response came from the Boilermakers and Iron and Steel Shipbuilders:

> The employers in our trade, in many cases, made certain promises to the lads – which, perhaps, don't count for much. It will depend on trade conditions at the end of the war ... We, however, as a Society, have decided to recognise the merits of such lads, and give them some credit for the time they have been away.[115]

Another problem arising out of apprentices serving with the colours was brought to the Committee's attention by Charles Dukes of the Lancashire and Cheshire Federation of Trades and Labour Councils. According to Dukes, if a young man – working as a general labourer or unskilled machine tender and earning sixteen to eighteen shillings a week – were to enlist, his parents or dependents would be able to recover from the government any sum over the cost of his maintenance – assumed to be around five to six shillings a week. In contrast, the parents of an apprentice could not claim the same remuneration 'yet the youth is sacrificing the best years of his apprenticeship & will suffer a greater loss when he returns to his Trade'. Dukes suggested that a flat rate be introduced whereby the parents or guardians of

---

[113] WNC.27/3/2 – letter to Asquith, 18 October 1915.
[114] WNC.2/4/1/1-4.
[115] WNC.2/4/1/5.

an apprentice would benefit to the same extent as those of children earning a full wage.[116] Middleton assured Dukes that George Barnes had suggested such a scheme, but with no success.[117]

Aliens

Letters also arrived from various labour bodies around the country describing the persecution and ill treatment of enemy aliens within Britain. A Hungarian named Oskar Beck of St Pancras had been working with the General Federation of Trade Unions until he was interned; Middleton wrote to the Under Secretary for Home Affairs, the Labour MP William Brace, to try and secure his exemption. In this he was unsuccessful, and Beck was interned on the Isle of Man, although Brace advised that since he was disabled, having only one arm, he might be exchanged for a medically unfit British subject in Germany.[118] Wilhelm Floerke, who had been driven from Germany due to his protests against the autocracy of the regime, and held a professorship at Glasgow University, found himself interned, and the WNC fought vainly on his behalf.[119] Similarly, a Mr Edit Heumann, the Honorary Treasurer of the National Union of Clerks District Council, and Honorary Secretary of the Fulham branch, was to be deported until WNC intervention secured his exemption.[120] A Mr Doviack of Liverpool wished to Anglicize his name; he spoke to Wright Robinson of the local ILP, who put him in touch with Middleton, who then in turn contacted Labour Counsel H.H. Slesser – who had himself changed his name from Schloesser – who advised on the appropriate legal procedures to change his name from Doviack to Denton.[121]

WNC Casework

One of the most important functions of the Committee during the war was its representation of ordinary, otherwise powerless people. There were numerous cases of the WNC and the labour movement aiding and supporting individuals in addition to their agitation on behalf of working people as a whole, and this representation went some way to convincing people of the necessity and viability of trade unions and the Labour Party. G.A. Robinson of the NUR said to Walker of NALRU of his meeting with non-unionised agricultural workers in 1917:

[116] WNC.2/4/2/3 – letter from Charles Dukes, 28 September 1915.
[117] WNC.2/4/2/4.
[118] WNC.2/3/2/10-20.
[119] WNC.2/3/6.
[120] WNC.2/3/7/1-6.
[121] WNC.2/3/5/7.

I told them in very plain words that a Branch of the Union had been in existence over a year and they had only just found out that it could be of assistance to them ... May I suggest to you that it is at a time like the present that there is an excellent chance of building up your [union] by showing the men that real interest is taken in their complaints which in this case are certainly just and require redress.[122]

H.H. Elvin, General Secretary of the National Union of Clerks, told Middleton of his experience, walking down the Strand, where by the Gladstone memorial a recruiting meeting was taking place one Wednesday afternoon. The recruiting officer claimed that:

It was no good for any young fellow of military age stating that he suffered, for example, from rheumatism, because on receiving any excuse of this sort, they immediately got into touch with the Commissioners, and found out from his Society what his health record was. So he warned any would-be recruits not to attempt any excuse of that sort. He also added that every individual of military age had to enlist. If he did not do so voluntarily, he would be compelled to do so; that he had until November 30th to come in, and if by then he had not done so, he would be compelled, and the letter 'C' would be on his coat collar so that everybody would know he had been forced to enlist and he was not a volunteer.[123]

Elvin wanted to know whether someone was liable to be prosecuted under the Defence of the Realm Act (DORA) if they questioned these assertions. Middleton asked Arthur Peters, secretary of the Joint Labour Recruiting Campaign Committee, who passed on the letter to Lord Derby.[124] The introduction of conscription was to provide many more individual cases for the attention of the WNC. Elvin wrote in March 1916 of the Wigan Coal and Iron Company starring single men for work although there were married men in the same office who could do the same work: 'The married men are trade unionists and the single men referred to are non-unionists and remained in with the Company while their fellow clerks were out on strike at the end of last year.' After a strike at the Ardeer factory of Nobel's Explosive Company in June 1915, one of the most active men, a clerk name D. Scullion, found himself called up in March 1916. 'I am convinced', wrote Elvin, 'that the action of the Company, through their official at Ardeer is to punish Scullion for the part he took in the strike last June and I think

[122] WNC.1/4/9/4i – letter to Walker from G.A. Mitchell, treasurer, Sutton Bridge Branch NUR, 20 April 1917.
[123] WNC.8/8/8/8 – letter from H.H. Elvin, 29 October 1915.
[124] WNC.8/8/815 – letter from Arthur Peters, 1 November 1915.

you will see from the above that there is a very strong case in favour of this contention.'[125]

Another controversy was that of Private Charles Keen, of Tottenham. Keen had been awarded non-combatant service by the Middlesex Appeal Tribunal, but this was ignored and he was trained in several combats skills before being transferred to France to await deployment at the front.[126] After WNC pressure on this matter, Keen was transferred to a non-combatant unit, although the War Office did argue:

> It appears that during the four months that Private Keen was in the Reserve Battalion he never informed his Company Officer or Company Sergt. Major that he had been granted a certificate of exemption from combatant service, notwithstanding the fact that he had ample opportunity of so doing, but on the contrary was trained in bomb throwing, bayonet fighting and fired the musketry course without making any protest. In these circumstances Private Keen is largely to blame for the position in which he has been placed.[127]

However, the brother of Private Keen was not content with this explanation, and wrote that:

> After my brother received his certificate of exemption from combatant service, he was called up to report himself for service, which he did. He was sent to Mill Hill and medically examined and passed for General Service. The Colonel of the Regiment was explaining to him what he was to do, to which my brother replied that he quite understood; on which the Colonel remarked that he was a very tame conscientious objector and asked my brother if he knew which the Colonel would sooner kill a conscientious objector or a German. My brother replied that he could not kill anyone. The Colonel said he would sooner kill a conscientious objector. So you see they were fully aware of my brother's exemption and deliberately intended to ignore it. My brother told me that he protested to his officers against his training which they ignored, so he wrote to his Trade Union Secretary for advice and he advised him to write to the Guildhall Tribunal which he did, and they told him they would communicate with his Commanding Officer and he naturally felt quite satisfied. If the Commanding Officer did not receive it, who did? When I asked my brother what was the idea of training him as a rifleman he said he thought the military thought he might give way. My personal opinion is that he ought to have refused to touch a rifle but he felt secure while he held a certificate.[128]

[125] WNC.17/3/1/2 – letter from H.H. Elvin, 3 March 1916.
[126] WNC.17/3/10/5 – question to be put to the Secretary of State for War by W.C. Anderson.
[127] WNC.17/3/10/11 – reply, 26 November 1916.
[128] WNC.17/3/10/15 – reply from brother of Keen, 29 November 1916.

A typical example of WNC activism and government intransigence was the case of Private Forrest. Forrest and his brother owned a tomato farm of some eight hundred acres; his brother's labour alone could not gather the harvest, and so a considerable amount of tomatoes risked being left to ruin. Middleton wrote to the War Office requesting a month's furlough, but this was not granted as Forrest was a Category A man and could not be spared for agricultural work.[129] Another case was that of Robert Sharpe of Walworth, who was passed as unfit to serve, but was then called to be re-examined, and had a policeman call at his house, who only failed to arrest him as he was sick in bed. Middleton was informed of this case by his local trades council, and he wrote directly to the War Office on Sharpe's behalf.[130] The War Office responded apologetically: 'I am afraid there was some mistake on the part of the Recruiting Officer; Mr Sharpe was apparently not liable for military service'.[131] Successful casework such as this shows us that people were not helpless in the face of the juggernaut of the state, and that the WNC could be an effective ally. A great many of the individuals who contacted the Committee had no prior association with the labour movement; and many of the millions of extra votes Labour gained in 1918 may have owed something to this activism.

The Committee also played an active role in attempts to secure compassionate leave for servicemen who had lost family members in the conflict. Robert Smillie brought up the case of Andrew McAnulty of Lanarkshire. McAnulty had lost one son dead of wounds, another son had lost half of his right foot at Ypres, and his son-in-law had been killed, with the result that his daughter and her three small children were back living with him. He had one son left in the army, not yet eighteen, who had been a coal miner and member of the union since he left school. Smillie paid testament to him: 'Mr Andrew McAnulty is a member of our Miners Executive Committee in Lanarkshire and has been a life-long worker in the Socialist Movement. He is a close friend of mine and he is breaking his heart to secure a brief holiday for his boy.'[132]

The Committee's frustrating dealings with the War Office and Ministry of Pensions extended to attempts to restore separation allowances to men executed for cowardice and desertion. This was an issue which particularly aroused Middleton's temper. He wrote to Minister of Pensions John Hodge: 'In view of the extraordinary conditions of modern warfare, and the fact that men are being taken from all sorts of the most unsuitable conditions, and

---

[129] WNC.17/3/27/16 – letter to Private Forrest, 22 September 1917.

[130] WNC.17/3/21/2 – letter from Robert Sharpe of Walworth, February 1917.

[131] WNC.17/3/21/8 – letter from War Office, 24 March 1917.

[132] WNC.2/5/13-14 – Smillie to Middleton, 31 September 1917.

that thoughtful men who have experienced the life at the Front feel most strongly on this subject, may I venture to hope that you may give this subject your own personal thought?'[133]

Early on in the war the contempt of the Committee was aroused by the Home Office announcement considering surveillance of 'the soldiers and sailors [sic] wives while their husbands are serving with the Colours'. Middleton wrote to Reginald McKenna: 'Very strong expressions were voiced, and I was instructed to ask if you would receive a deputation of the women members of this Committee on the subject.'[134] He received a reply assuring him that the police were merely acting on the request of military authorities, and that he should direct his ire at the War Office.[135] Arthur Henderson met with Harold Baker from the War Office and McKenna to discuss the matter, and after condemnation of the practice both publically and in Parliament, the surveillance was abruptly dropped.[136] There may be a certain symbolic value to the defeat of surveillance and the idea that separation allowances should only go to 'deserving' candidates: as with the transformation from charitable donations towards centralised state provision, the war helped burnish the principle that the recipients of welfare should be determined by their need, rather than their morality. By the end of the war such surveillance would have been out of the question, as would the idea that the claims of ex-servicemen and their dependents upon state welfare might be determined by their 'respectability'.

A final vignette from the vast amounts of casework dealt with by the WNC demonstrates how the Committee combated injustice unrelated to the war – and gave a taste of the task ahead in the post-war world. The Committee was informed by the Gravesend, Northfleet and Perry Street Trades and Labour Council of a boy:

> Thomas William Young, aged 12, [who] was recently brought before the Justices at Northfleet, [charged] with stealing three pennyworth of apples from an orchard while under probation for stealing one pennyworth of bottled lemonade. The boy was convicted and sent to an Industrial school for 4 years. The boy's father is a munition worker, and was unable to leave his employment to attend at the court on behalf of his son. Important evidence as to the conduct of home influence given by the Probation Officer, and which apparently influenced the Court, was subsequently shown to be inaccurate, the magistrates refusing to hear one word in defence of the boy. A similar case came before the same Bench at

---

133 WNC.2/5/17/4i – letter from Middleton to Hodge, 6 November 1917.
134 WNC.13/4/2/2 – letter to Reginald McKenna at Home Office, 10 November 1914.
135 WNC.13/4/2/4 – reply from McKenna, 12 November 1914.
136 WNC.13/4/2/8 – letter from Harold Baker at the War Office, 24 November 1914.

a subsequent Court, and upon evidence being given by the father of the boy concerned the charge was dismissed.[137]

After his first letter to the Home Office was ignored, Middleton wrote again, this time receiving a reply from Sir John Simon himself, who regretted that 'despite all the circumstances of this case, I am not able to find any grounds for interfering with the Order'.[138] Despite the WNC's failure, the episode nonetheless demonstrates the importance of having the Committee as an interlocutor between ordinary people and the very highest levels of power.

These are just a few of the many individual cases dealt with by Middleton and the Committee. In some instances they were successful; in many more their efforts failed. Nonetheless a great deal of time and effort was expended on these cases, especially by Middleton. It has been noted above that he was a vehement critic of the war, and many of his friends were conscientious objectors who were persecuted and imprisoned by the British state he worked so closely alongside. Yet he laboured tirelessly throughout the war, falling ill several times over the course of the conflict, and finally suffering a nervous breakdown in February 1918 that kept him from his post for much of that spring. He was not only instrumental in the Committee's successful agitation on various issues, from food to fuel, pensions to employment, but also personally responded to thousands of letters from ordinary Britons, very often not connected with the labour movement, seeking assistance and redress of grievances. Perhaps surprisingly, it was usually women who wrote in, and this was not necessarily due to male absence on account of the war; letters more often regarded sons than husbands, which suggests that though fathers had remained at home, it was mothers who took the initiative to make contact. The success of the WNC and the labour movement during the war was therefore tripartite: as a lobbying organisation protecting the workers against the worst excesses of the war, as a conduit for information across the broad spectrum of the Left, and as friend in high places for those most in need of one. Many of Middleton's humble correspondents, particularly distressed housewives and mothers, soon to be enfranchised, likely would not soon forget the effort the WNC had made on their behalf, even if it was unsuccessful. For these reasons the WNC and labour's wartime activity deserve a great deal more attention than they have received.[139]

---

[137] WNC.13/4/17/2 – letter to from Middleton to Sir John Simon at the Home Office, 24 September 1915.

[138] WNC.13/4/17/11 – reply from Sir John Simon.

[139] In this respect the WNC was not unique: Michael Roper has noted that it was usually mothers who wrote to their sons at the front, not fathers. See M. Roper, 'Maternal Relations:

This section has shown the true extent of labour movement activity on the home front during the First World War, and argued that these experiences were crucial to the Left's ability to formulate policy and attract support in the post-war world. The final section considers how the growth of the state, and the Left's wartime experience of forming a 'second state' for the poorest and most vulnerable, altered the relationship between the British labour movement and the state during the war years and afterwards.

The Impact of the War on the Relationship between the British Left and the State

This section considers how the growth of the state and the activities of the WNC affected the position of the labour movement *vis-à-vis* the state. It is clear that a certain type of labour movement emerged after 1918, and while the tendency of this movement towards a centrist, bureaucratic state has been overemphasised, and is itself the subject of some debate, it is fair to say that the Labour Party emerged from the war with a particular vision for the state that would eventually be realised from 1945. Yet before and immediately after the war there were a variety of visions on offer for the fledging labour movement. It is the purpose of this third section to question why the practical, Fabian-driven vision of the state took precedent within the labour movement after 1918, rather than any of the alternatives, such as syndicalism, guild socialism, or an idealistic, less mechanical means of organising the economy and society.

The early socialists of the decades immediately preceding the First World War were wary of the state: as Stephen Yeo has argued, both William Morris and Thomas Kirkup were anti-statist, and Morris in particular had concerns about 'practical men' who would warp their vision of socialism – emotional, parochial, and ingrained in English traditions (imagined or otherwise) – and turn it into something bureaucratic, impersonal, and centralised.[140] Syndicalism, for a brief period, seemed to offer an alternative. Bob Holton claimed that the Edwardian syndicalists explicitly considered their movement not to be a continental import, but rather a continuation of 'the anti-state traditions of William Morris and the Socialist League, combined with elements of an autonomous socialist

---

Moral Manliness and Emotional Survival in Letters Home during the First World War', in S. Dudink et al. (eds), *Masculinities in Politics and War*, Manchester: Manchester University Press, 2004, 300.

[140] S. Yeo, 'Socialism, the State, and Some Oppositional Englishness', in R. Colls and P. Dodd (eds), *Englishness: Politics and Culture 1880–1920*, London: Croom Helm, 1986, 330 and 347–59.

counterculture available within the Clarion movement'.[141] The influential
radical Thomas Mann, who had been a state socialist prior to his exile in
Australia for most of the first decade of the twentieth century, returned
a convinced syndicalist, and stood for the General Secretaryship of the
ASE in 1913.[142] Mann failed to win election, securing only 8,771 out of the
34,507 votes cast – an indication that one should not overstate the influence
of syndicalist ideas in the British labour movement at this time. Yet this
does not mean that a political or constitutional approach was strongly
favoured before the war: an attempt to establish an ASE political fund
to support the Labour Party was defeated by 17,324 votes to 15,336 in 1913.
Further, at the annual general meeting of the NUR the following year
the syndicalist Charles Watkins was able to secure unanimous support
for a resolution criticising railway nationalisation as then proposed by the
Labour Party: 'This Congress expresses the opinion that nationalisation of
public services, such as the Post Office, is not necessarily advantageous to
the employees and the working classes unless accompanied by a steadily
increasing domestic control, both by employees and the representatives of
the working classes in the House of Commons.'[143] Thus, while Holton
overstated the significance of and support for syndicalism in the pre-war
era, his assertion that 'it was the war itself … which finally halted the
development of syndicalism' contains a seed of truth, in that the war did
determine the path of the labour movement after 1918.[144] Bill Schwarz
and Martin Durham have noted of Ben Tillett's description of Parliament
as a 'rich man's Duma' that: 'Even though the speech was delivered in a
moment of defeat Tillett's tone and critique were consistent with much that
he had been saying in previous years. Coercion, repression and militarism
were all that could be expected from the state.'[145]

There were a variety of opinions on the government amongst the British
Left, but the general position was one of distrust, and that the state was more
likely to present a problem than a solution. In this sense, we can see how far
the conflict changed the discourse prevalent before 1914, and how instrumental it was in defining the type of Labour Party which emerged in 1918.
Yet the war did not have a uniform effect on the British Left. G.D.H. Cole,
the guild socialist, wrote in the *ASE Monthly Journal* of April 1915:

---

[141] B. Holton, *British Syndicalism 1900–1914*, London: Pluto Press, 1976, 35.

[142] Ibid., 53.

[143] Ibid., 153 and 166.

[144] Ibid., 134.

[145] B. Schwarz and M. Durham, '"A Safe and Sane Labourism": Socialism and the State,
1910–24', in M. Langan and B. Schwarz, *Crises in the British State 1880–1930*, London:
Hutchinson, 1985.

The doctrine of Guild Socialism, of which the central idea is the democratic control of industry by the workers in partnership with the State, is being forced more and more to the front by the unanswerable logic of events. Let the Trade Unions once become conscious of the true nature of the demand behind the Labour unrest and it will not be long before our industrial system is radically transformed in the interests of the workers. If, on the other hand, the unions fail to realise their responsibilities and to rise to their opportunity the period of depression after the war will merely serve as the capitalists' chance to fix yet more firmly upon society the shackles of the immoral and demoralising wage system under which we live.[146]

Discussing the philosophies of labour thinkers such as Cole in this period, Jose Harris has argued that 'the idealist frame of reference became even more powerful and all-encompassing in the period *after* the First World War, when for a time at least the earlier traditions of positivism and empiricism virtually faded out of large areas of the vocabulary of social science'.[147] This is supported by the assertions of prominent Labour recruits of the after-war period, such as Josiah Wedgwood, who spoke out against the increasing Fabianism of the party, arguing that 'Real Socialism puts freedom above ease and utility. Better to be a man, with God and a crust, rather than a well-greased cog in the food factory'.[148] Harris did not try to overstate the influence of the 'idealist' strain of the post-war Labour Party, but for a short period it did hold some influence and, crucially, was particularly influential upon provincial Nonconformists who had previously been libertarian individualists (such as Wedgwood and many other formerly Liberal recruits).[149] Perhaps what can be said for the war is that it transformed the state from an embodiment of malevolent force to a potential force for good. In the words of Steve Meredith and Philip Catney, 'This debate was not just a mechanistic one based upon the most efficient way to achieve social justice, but one that focussed on the nature of democracy and the place of man in the social system'.[150]

The introduction of a comprehensive welfare state was not something clamoured for by a majority of the population in the pre-war years. As Henry Pelling noted, 'the mass of working people were hostile or indifferent

---

[146] ASE, *Monthly Journal and Report*, April 1915.

[147] J. Harris, 'Political Thought and the Welfare State 1870–1940: An Intellectual Framework for British Social Policy', *Past & Present* 135 (1992): 123.

[148] Quoted in Clare Griffiths, *Labour and the Countryside: The Politics of Rural Britain 1918–1939*, Oxford: Oxford University Press, 2007, 270.

[149] Harris, 'Political Thought and the Welfare State', 138–39.

[150] S. Meredith and P. Catney, 'New Labour and Associative Democracy: Old Debates in New Times?', *British Politics* 2 (2007): 347–71.

to state welfare at least until *after* measures such as old age pensions and national insurance were introduced',[151] and many working-class organisations opposed state welfare not merely out of opposition to the state, but rather from a position of working-class mutual support and independence.[152] In 1890 the *Cotton Factory Times* argued: 'We sincerely believe that is what the German Emperor is aiming at: When people look to the state and receive from it almost everything they get, they will become the strongest supporters of those from whom they obtain their privileges.'[153] There is no little irony, of course, that it was the German Emperor's servile state which created many of those privileges for Britons in the years 1914–18. Nor was suspicion of a centralised, bureaucratic state confined to the radical Nonconformist strand of the movement: Hyndman and others in *Justice* did not merely mistrust the state for its persecution of socialists and trade unionists, but felt – before the war, at least – that a centralized bureaucracy would be dangerous even in a socialist society.[154] In terms of trade unions, the long-established craft societies could boast hefty welfare and strike funds – £750,000 in the case of the Boilermakers and £2.5 million in the case of the ASE – and were therefore disinclined towards state welfare; why should time-served skilled men pay for the misfortunes of the unskilled when they had their own funds to fall back on?[155]

In contrast, the unskilled unions were warmer on state welfare, given that they were less able to provide for their own members, and their own people were more likely to slip into destitution in the first instance, while the rank and file were usually unimpressed by abstractions relating to the 'servile state' and more likely to place trust in the state rather than union activity.[156] An example of this was the Workers' Union, one of the most significant of the new general labourers' unions. Although it had its origins in the syndicalist sentiment stoked by Tom Mann, by the time of the war – of which it was decidedly supportive – it was led by statist parliamentarians and labour patriots in Charles Duncan and John Beard.[157] Beard went as far as to welcome the Munitions Acts – decried by most trade unionists, even the patriots, for the restrictions it placed on workers' rights – and to urge

---

[151] Quoted in P. Thane, 'The Working Class and State "Welfare" in Britain, 1880–1914', *Historical Journal* 27 (1984): 877.

[152] Ibid., 880.

[153] Ibid., 885.

[154] Ibid., 883.

[155] A. Reid, 'The Impact of the First World War on British Workers', in R. Wall and J. Winter (eds), *The Upheaval of War*, Cambridge: Cambridge University Press, 1988, 227–28.

[156] Thane, 'Working Class and State Welfare', 884 and 886.

[157] R. Hyman, *The Workers' Union*, Oxford: Clarendon Press, 1971, 37.

workers to adopt a conciliatory stance with employers.[158] Overall, fear of the servile state was not a dominant concern of most workers. As Pat Thane has concluded, resentment of state intrusion was not strong enough to provoke widespread opposition to the state before 1914, and 'only a highly politicized minority of liberals and socialists thought with any precision about the desirable extent and nature of state action'.[159]

One of the first effects of the war was to ameliorate a great deal of union antipathy towards state interference.[160] For some of the general unions such as the NUR, the change was welcome and long overdue. The *Railway Review* triumphantly claimed within weeks of the outbreak:

> Everywhere the State has asserted its power. The State seizes the railways and not a word is uttered in protest. The State takes over flour mills, fixes prices, commandeers horses and motor-cars, nay, in some cases, even controls the food supply, not merely for military purposes, but for the general welfare, and no one says them nay. It is a wonderful change. Why in many of those cases should it ever lose its hold?[161]

The *Railway Review* welcomed a speech by Andrew Bonar Law praising the government-controlled railway system with a cartoon depicting 'private ownership' being blasted off the plinth of 'British Railways' by a shell. A shocked John Bull was knocked to the seat of his trousers by the impact. The caption read: 'Another idol shattered. One of the shocks the War has given John Bull'.[162]

Before long organisations as diverse as the largely middle-class National Union of Clerks and the ILPers of the *Bradford Pioneer* were joining the railwaymen in calling for the nationalisation of wheat, banks, and shipping.[163] In May 1915 *The Clerk* saluted the decasualisation of dock work that followed the formation of the Liverpool dock battalions:

> Another part of the organisation of industry which the country has had to take in hand, there has now been formed a battalion of dockers, uniformed and guaranteed a regular minimum weekly wage, with more wages if there is more than the minimum work to do. For the docker's wife the change must be immense – instead of never knowing whether plenty or starvation will be the lot of the family a couple of days hence, she can now reckon on having, at the worst, the minimum of 35s. a week, with her husband's clothes provided. The officers of the battalion are the officials of the Union,

---

[158] Ibid., 82.
[159] Thane, 'Working Class and State Welfare', 899.
[160] *Boilermaker's Reports*, April 1915.
[161] *Railway Review*, 21 August 1914.
[162] *Railway Review*, 19 January 1917.
[163] *The Clerk*, February 1915; *Bradford Pioneer*, 11 September 1914.

ANOTHER IDOL SHATTERED,
One of the shocks the War has given John Bull.

Figure 4. 'Another Idol Shattered', *Railway Review*, 19 January 1917.
Working Class Movement Library.

and *every member of the battalion must be a member of the Union*. If he lapses his membership of his Union he is at once 'fired' and loses the guarantee of regular employment.[164]

By August of 1916 the Boilermakers' were marvelling at unemployment reaching the lowest level recorded, yet criticised the government for not taking over shipping with the same haste as it had taken control of the railways; they alleged that merchant vessels were changing hands for five hundred or one thousand per cent of their real value; unacceptable profiteering which could

---

[164] *The Clerk*, May 1915. Emphasis in the original. See also K. Grieves, 'The Liverpool Dock Battalion: Military Intervention in the Mersey Docks, 1915–1918', *Transactions of the Historic Society of Lancashire and Cheshire* 131 (1982): 139–58.

have been avoided had the government taken a more proactive stance.[165] The following month the Boilermakers' pressed for the state to expand further, calling for a Minister of Industry to 'sort Health, Housing Agriculture and Food Supply, the control of Shipping, National storehouses, and Complete national ownership of war munitions, ships, railways, mines, etc'.[166]

What is notable about the Boilermakers' enthusiasm for greater state intervention and control of industry is that it was a long-established craft union with considerable strike and welfare funds and a healthy interest in remaining free of state interference. Skilled unions such as the Boilermakers' and the ASE, and left-wing socialist newspapers such as the *Bradford Pioneer*, had usually been particularly averse to statism pre-1914, but the war changed this. Even the passage of the Munitions Act, which was to cause a great deal of resentment on many shop floors, was greeted in the Boilermakers' journal as 'our latest national confession that uncontrolled private enterprise and production for profit has hopelessly failed us, as it always has done when our need was greatest'.[167] In an editorial of May 1917, ASE General Secretary Robert Young responded to a letter criticising 'tub thumpers' in Hyde Park, arguing that:

> The theories of 'tub thumpers' in Hyde Park and elsewhere, are fast becoming realities, and some of us expect that even their ideals, in spite of the horrible calamity of war, will be brought considerably nearer as a result of the war. Railway nationalisation, liquor control, early closing, minimum wages, women's suffrage, and other 'silly, shallow stuff' advocated by 'tub thumpers' are now openly accepted, not merely as possible, but actually practicable and essential to the country's moral, political, and economic welfare now and after the war.[168]

Similarly, an editorial in *The Clerk* of December 1916 admitted that the National Union of Clerks had achieved more in the past two years through arbitration than it could have expected to do without it, that a minimum wage was both practical and desirable, and that there may have been something in what was once called the 'servile state' after all.[169] General Secretary of the Boilermakers John Hill warned that the government's new responsibility in industry 'will not end with the war', and that while 'we have good reasons for misgivings against too much interference with customs, which have much to recommend them, even in war time, we might as well try and stop the ocean with a broom as fight against Government control

---

[165] *Boilermaker's Reports*, August 1916.
[166] Ibid., September 1916.
[167] *Boilermakers' Reports*, August 1915.
[168] ASE, *Monthly Journal and Report*, May 1917.
[169] *The Clerk*, December 1916.

of industry, the fixing of interest on capital, and the awarding of wages for labour'. He ended on a positive note, however, reflecting a change in opinion precipitated by the war:

> The mistake we make is to look upon the Government as a power which will always be biased against labour, as it certainly is and has been. We forget that Labour appoints the Government. Personally, I welcome the entrance of the Government into our common everyday life. When the Government awards us less in wages for our labour than our district delegates consider fair and reasonable, we shall begin to realise the need for our own class in Parliament in numbers sufficient to give us a majority in the Government.[170]

The anti-war William Leech had written in analogous terms in March 1915 that:

> The British Junkers and Jingoes are welcome to make what use they like of their own discovery that the application of Socialist principles makes war easier to conduct. If the result is to be an addition to the advocates of Socialism of all the military-minded people it should give no cause for alarm. The nation which adopts Socialism with a view to strengthening militarism and aggressive Imperialism [as he claimed the Germans had effectively done] is welcome to do so, and we will promise it our full support in the work of getting for it a sound economic constitution and leave the rest to fate and the future with the utmost confidence.[171]

Overall, the mainstream of trade union opinion had grown notably warmer towards public ownership and the state by the end of the war. A cartoon in the *Railway Review* – organ of the admittedly statist NUR – depicted a group of workers, a businessmen, and the state. The caption read: 'For you, sir we would willingly work and die, but there is always likely to be strife and trouble whilst *he* [the state] comes in between!'[172] In an editorial entitled 'Collective Responsibility is Individual Responsibility', Robert Young highlighted how the war had changed attitudes:

> The collective responsibilities of the nation become also the responsibilities of each individual in the nation. We are no longer interested and anxious onlookers hoping for a successful end to the war. We become active participants in the struggle through sheer force of economic circumstances. The economic needs of the nation must be met by the voluntary abstinences of each in the interests of all. If in this we fail, compulsion becomes necessary.

[170] *Boilermakers' Reports*, November 1916.
[171] *Bradford Pioneer*, 12 March 1915.
[172] *Railway Review*, 30 July 1915.

Of the close co-operation of the trade union movement and the coalition during the conflict, he stated:

> I am thoroughly convinced that the interests of the workers would have been more seriously jeopardised if the Trade Union officials had refused to consult with the various government officials in relation to the many trade problems which the war has caused ... The Labour Party in Parliament cannot be separated from the Labour Party in the country. It is mainly Trade Unionist. The Trade Unionists of the country have made their influence felt in the industrial arrangements made. Why should their representatives not make their influence felt in the government of the country by assisting the nation to cope with the greatest crisis in its history?[173]

Heralding the appointment of Henderson to the Pensions' Board, the *Railway Review* solemnly claimed that:

> One by one the old shibboleths are going. Sugar, rent, coal, meat, and wheat have all come under Government control by instalments. Now a more vigorous and wholesale policy is indicated. It is not before time. Even now it is too late to have the effects which such a policy would have had if it had been undertaken in the early days of the war as urged by the party, and I am entitled to claim for it a far-seeing policy in this matter for which the country ought to be grateful.[174]

Similarly, an editorial by NUR chairman George Wardle in the *Railway Review* of December 1916 noted that:

> The war has changed all social values ... if we were asked to mention the main change we should hesitatingly select the deliberate alteration of the status of the individual and the growing recognition of the value of the collective and corporate effort of the people as whole. If the individualism of the past is not dead, it is dying. It has been stricken in a vital part. War has shattered its illusory philosophy and destroyed its false thesis. It has proved a broken reed, a wornout fetish, and a creed from which the life has departed.[175]

Alastair Reid has claimed that:

> There was a general tendency for organised labour to drop its pre-war separation of 'economic' and 'political' issues. Thus the unions most centrally involved in the war effort began very rapidly to raise non-industrial issues when they made demands on the government (perhaps most marked in the case of house rents), there was a slowly growing acceptance among all trade unionists that the election of Members of Parliament could have a

---

[173] ASE, *Monthly Journal and Report*, February 1917.
[174] *Railway Review*, 24 November 1916.
[175] Ibid., 29 December 1916.

direct effect on industrial conditions, and there was a marked increase in trade union support for the permanent nationalisation of key industries, above all coal mining and railways.[176]

This concurs with the view of the *Railway Review* from October 1917: that because of the increasing numbers of men being employed by the state, 'a quarrel between a body of wage workers and an employer is not now a personal affair in which none other is presumed to have interest. Such a quarrel promptly attracts the attention of the controllers of the State and State machinery is set at work to settle the difficulty'.[177] Fear of the state did not end with the war, however: by January 1917 the *Bradford Pioneer* was carrying articles claiming that the 'state slavery' introduced during the war was anathema to true socialism, and asking whether trade unions would be 'tricked' by the 'sham' proposals of representation and conciliation being put forward by the government.[178] Even Ramsay MacDonald argued in 1917 that:

> The war has given a new significance to some of the later movements within Trade Unionism and Socialism, especially to that known as the Guild movement ... no doubt should be left regarding the fact that the guild must play a characteristic part in the Socialist industrial State. It is required to guard against the deadly evil of over-centralisation in a political servile state, of a community the material comforts of which will stifle spiritual spontaneity, of a working class deprived of the stimulus of freedom by legal arrangements of a mechanical nature.[179]

Guild theorist G.D.H. Cole felt that the enhanced state sheltered capitalists from pressure and created official machinery designed to control the unions.[180] In September of that year, in an article entitled 'The Trade Unionists' Cross Road', the Shop Assistants' J.J. Mallon argued that nationalisation was a false panacea, and that robust trade unions, aided by the conciliation framework recommended by the Whitley Committees, would secure better results:

> Would the happiness and satisfaction of men necessarily be augmented by such a transference [of ownership]? Private ownership is bad enough, but it is now seen to have some compensations: to be pliable, to reflect and diffuse whatever kindliness may reside in the 'owner', to allow for human weaknesses and alternations, in short, to be in many ways preferable to

---

[176] Reid, 'The Impact of the First World War', 228.

[177] *Railway Review*, 5 October 1917.

[178] *Bradford Pioneer*, 19 and 26 January 1917.

[179] J.M. Winter, *Socialism and the Challenge of War*, London: Routledge Kegan Paul, 130.

[180] M. Pugh, *Speak for Britain! A New History of the Labour Party*, London: Vintage, 2011, 110. Guild socialism advocated workers' control of the economy through de-centralised trade-specific guilds.

the rigid 'government by regulation' which at present is imposed on us from Whitehall.[181]

However, despite remaining reservations and scepticism amongst some on the Left, it was not the case, as Winter had it, that 'after three years of war, the state was seen to be a very different and far more dangerous creature by even a moderate socialist like MacDonald'; on the contrary, despite the awfulness of the war and the imposition of conscription, most of the labour movement viewed the *state* with a great deal more sympathy; the *government* was another matter.[182] The orthodox Marxists of the Plebs' League – vehemently anti-war, decidedly undemocratic, and unapologetically out of touch with mainstream working-class opinion – were even more critical of the wartime state than the ILPers. In an article entitled 'Will Socialism Survive the War?', H. Wynn-Cuthbert argued that state socialism – 'respectable, modern, evolutionary, revisionist Socialism' – had:

> Damped the revolutionary ardour of the workers of Europe, and in the present great crisis is leading them forth, flag in hand, to the trenches and the cannon's mouth in defence of 'their' country. But we will see to it that Reformism, if it is not destroyed in the war, is 'scotched' very soon after by the organized Proletariat. We must make it perfectly clear that the workers of the world have no more to do with the 'State' than they have with the transmigration of souls. The fetish of the State must go the way of the fetish of Royalty.

He concluded by predicting that 'Socialism will survive the war, but the movement will be far more revolutionary in character'.[183] In a period not known for foresight and prescience, Wynn-Cuthbert rather distinguished himself: not only did he greatly misjudge the temper of the 'workers of Europe'; within a few years of the Armistice it had become clear that it was through the machinery of the state that socialist ambitions would be realised. The extent to which there were any viable alternatives is debatable, and post-war experiences such as the General Strike, the failure of hard-Left movements, and unhappy experiences of minority government must not be discounted, but nor must the significance of the First World War in determining this route for Labour.

This chapter has analysed the growth of the British state during the war and its subsequent contraction; it has detailed how far Labour was drawn into the British state during the war, what it did to protect working-class interests; and noted how this affected the relationship between the labour

---

[181] *The Clerk*, September 1917.
[182] Winter, *Socialism and the Challenge of War*, 131.
[183] *Plebs*, December 1914.

movement and the state. Whilst it cannot be said that the First World War permanently changed British political economy or the role of the state – the developments of the 1920s and 1930s are proof of that – this does not mean that the changes of 1914–18 should be disregarded. On the contrary, I concur with Chris Wrigley in arguing that the experience of the First World War made an enhanced state politically practical and ideologically palatable. Further, many of the results of state expansion during the war, such as rent control, housing provision, and minimum wages – whilst uneven in application and of limited duration – made a significant difference to the lives of many people. Since many of the changes brought about by the Second World War had their genesis in the First, the latter deserves greater recognition as a break in British attitudes towards the state.

Furthermore, we have seen here how the British Left was not handicapped as an agitating, representative movement, despite being drawn into government and declaring a political and industrial truce. Nor did wartime patriotism and support for the prosecution of the conflict neutralise the labour movement as a force for social justice. Indeed, largely through the auspices of the WNC, the full breadth of the Left – incorporating socialists, trade unionists, labourites, suffragettes, and co-operators – was able to fight against the worst effects of the war.

Finally, this chapter has argued that the growth of the state during the war, and the closer relationship between the labour movement and the state, led to the development of a bureaucratic labourism based on a central redistributive state.[184] By no means did the war remove all suspicion of the state, and even in the early 1920s the model of state bureaucracy aspired towards was more devolved and involved greater workers' control than that which emerged in the 1940s.[185] Yet, given the evidence of the positive view of the state taken by various unions, and their desire for greater state intervention, it is impossible to concur with John Turner's assertion that the war witnessed greater *hostility* between trade unions and the state.[186] Further, it was not simply the case that, as Winter had it, 'when the time came in 1917 for the reconstruction of the Labour Party as a national organisation committed to socialist objectives, it would be to Sidney Webb and his ideas that the party leaders would turn', for this suggests merely

[184] The theory of 'labourism' held that the British Left fatally diluted itself and compromised with capitalism, to the detriment of its ability to affect real change. See J. Saville, 'Labourism and the Labour Government', *Socialist Register* 4 (1967): 43–71; G. Elliott, *Labourism and the English Genius: The Strange Death of Labour England*, London: Verso, 1993.

[185] A. Thorpe, 'The Industrial Meaning of "Gradualism": The Labour Party and Industry, 1918–1931', *Journal of British Studies* 35 (1996): 91.

[186] See J. Turner, *British Politics and the Great War: Coalition and Conflict, 1915–1918*, New Haven: Yale University Press, 1992.

the filling of an intellectual void by the predominant theory of the hour, rather than the experience of the war providing an ideology which embraced community, patriotism, and a benevolent view of the state.[187] A.M. McBriar, in his book on Fabianism, claimed that 'The Fabians supplied a doctrine which could enable a churchwarden, or an English trade unionist, to call himself a Socialist', and that 'Fabianism permitted Englishmen to swallow these [statist, anti-*laissez-faire*] pills without too much of a shock to their constitution'.[188] Yet, far more than any germane theory of political economy, it was *the war* which made socialism acceptable to the parson, the private, the housewife, and the labourer; and the war which laid the practical and ideological groundwork for the subsequent success of the Labour Party. Ultimately, the experience of the war directly led the post-war Labour Party and trade union movement to adopt and accept a more statist programme than might otherwise have been the case.

The next and final chapter will address one of the more troubling political questions of the First World War: how did the disparate strands of the labour movement remain intact despite the tremendous centrifugal pressures occasioned by the conflict? It will discuss the interaction between the Co-operative, the trade unions, the Parliamentary Labour Party, various women's groups, and sundry socialist societies during and after the conflict. Once again, we shall see the importance of labour patriotism and the WNC in this development.

---

[187] Winter, *Socialism and the Challenge of War*, 6.
[188] A.M. McBriar, *Fabian Socialism and English Politics 1884–1918*, Cambridge: Cambridge University Press, 1966, 348.

6

'The greatest democratic force British politics have known' – Labour Cohesion and the War

'A trade unionist who is only a trade unionist is a barbarian.'

—R.B. Suthers, *The Clarion*, March 1915[1]

'The three great Movements – Industrial – Political – and Co-operative – will be linked up so as to become the greatest Democratic Force that ever British politics have known.'

—Jim Middleton to Bob Williams, October 1917[2]

This final chapter is concerned with the continued cohesion of the labour movement during and after the war. Given that the conflict divided the Liberal party to the extent that it was excluded from office for almost a century, why did it not have the same effect on Labour, a far more recent political creation, and one facing apparent existential ideological conflicts over nationalism and internationalism? British labour emerged stronger, more united, and with a new sense of purpose. The idea that the Liberals merely 'lost' their position, allowing Labour to become the main opposition to the Conservatives by default, is unsatisfactory; and the question of how Labour was able – institutionally and ideologically – not merely to survive the war intact, but to actively prosper, has not received enough attention. This chapter takes a broad view of all of the various organisations which could be said to compose the British Left at the time of the war: the Labour Party itself; the roughly one thousand trade unions in different groups and associations; various women's groups which, while not necessarily sympathetic with all of Labour's policies, sometimes co-operated on franchise reform; the three-million strong Co-operative movement, consisting of the

---

[1] *The Clarion*, 12 March 1915.
[2] WNC.8/1/19 – letter to Williams, 11 October 1917.

Co-operative Wholesale Society (CWS) and the Co-operative Union; and the socialist societies such as the British Socialist party (BSP), the Fabian Society, and the Independent Labour Party (ILP). Finally, the war created great impetus for an ultra-patriotic secession from the labour movement, or even a nationalistic coup within labour. The failure of this movement will also be examined. The selection of trade unions here deliberately eschews groups such as miners or cotton operatives, and includes both skilled craft and general labourers' unions, the overtly patriotic and those more sceptical of the war.

Sixty years ago, in his analysis of the adolescence of the Labour Party, J.H. Reid claimed that before the war, Labour was 'in danger of losing the support of both militant socialists and dissatisfied trade unionists', and that the outbreak of the war was in some ways a blessing in disguise, providing as it did a 'period of grace'.[3] While the intervening years have not produced reasons to suspect Professor Reid of overstating the precariousness of the party's situation pre-1914, there is a compelling argument that, far from merely providing breathing space to deal with institutional and ideological dilemmas, the war was actually instrumental in assuaging these issues. The pre-war labour movement was a loose alliance consisting of hundreds of trade unions (themselves very often divided according to trade, skill, and association), sundry socialist societies with varying levels of membership, some women's groups, the Labour Party itself (a federal, dissolved structure), and the Co-operative movement. Yet instead the war produced in 1918 a Labour Party that was structurally and institutionally reformed and in possession of – if not a fully formed ideology embraced by all quarters – then at least an agreed programme on which to campaign.

This chapter argues that the labour movement in general and the Labour Party in particular was able to survive the war and prosper intact because of institutional and structural co-operation – particularly through the auspices of the War Emergency Workers' National Committee (WNC), which acted as a crucial adhesive – and due to the broad spectrum of support for the war on the Left. Labour patriotism encompassed socialists, trade unionists, co-operators, and women as well as ultra-patriots, and allowed the Left to turn the war to its advantage in constructing a national party to fight for power, and an inclusive message on which to fight.

---

[3] J.H. Reid, *Origins of the British Labour Party*, Minneapolis: University of Minnesota Press, 1955, 204. Quoted in C.L. Mowat, 'Ramsay Macdonald and the Labour Party', in A. Briggs and J. Saville (eds), *Essays in Labour History 1886–1923*, London: Macmillan, 1971, 140.

The Trade Unions and the Labour Party

A vital condition for the relative cohesion of the labour movement that emerged after 1918 was the failure of the war to cut across different sections of the movement. There was no easy dichotomy with right-wing trade unionists at one extreme and middle-class radicals on the other; instead, disagreement occurred within different unions and socialist societies. There were some casualties of patriotic versus pacifistic clashes; some local trade councils (such as Birmingham and Sheffield) were divided by the war, and some unions (such as the National Union of Railwaymen (NUR)) used their own patriotism as a means of criticising craft societies such as Amalgamated Society of Locomotive Engineers and Firemen (ASLEF). A *Railway Review* cartoon of September 1916 attacked the non-unionised workman, presented being fed the war bonus that the unionised men had worked for. The caption read: 'How long before you come off that stool, and do something for yourself? Or are you waiting to be knocked off?' A further cartoon in November of that year – which depicted the NUR as a tank, another example of the parallels drawn between the war and the trade union crusade at home – claimed that the securing of the war bonus had proved 'the superiority of unified organisation'.

An editorial in the *Railway Review* of August 1917 claimed: 'The action of the Associated Society can fairly be described as a policy of frightfulness, and the adoption of the doctrine that in things paramount might is right ... The threatened strike is not against the railway companies, against aggression, nor against the owning section of the community, but at this time is against the State.'[4] Nor was it only over strike action that the two great railway unions disagreed; in April of the same year the NUR fought and won a libel case against ASLEF over charges of incompetence and dishonesty regarding war bonuses.[5] A cartoon in the NUR's *Railway Review*, captioned 'Not the time and place', showed a train driver (or, 'the sectionalist on the footplate' in the language of the cartoon), attempting to catch the elusive 'rabbit' of an eight-hour day, wondering: 'If only I can catch him all to myself.' Meanwhile, John Bull calls out to him 'Hi! What about me and the war?' This cartoon is significant not merely for its criticism of ASLEF, but also for its use of patriotism as a means to attack the craft union.[6]

The division between skilled and unskilled unions was initially given new significance by the war due to the 'dilution' of unskilled men and women into positions previously reserved for craft men, and the alleged 'poaching' of

---

[4] *Railway Review*, 24 August 1917.
[5] *Railway Review*, 27 April 1917.
[6] *Railway Review*, 21 August 1917.

NOT THE TIME AND PLACE.

THE SECTIONALIST OF THE FOOTPLATE: "Now if I can only catch him
all to myself!"

Figure 5. 'Not the Time and Place', *Railway Review*, 21 August 1917.
Working Class Movement Library.

skilled men by general unions. In this respect the arriviste Workers' Union
was the greatest troublemaker; it alone opposed the restoration of pre-war
practices that the craft unions insisted on, and it was felt to be 'poaching'
men from industry and agriculture who should more properly have joined
a sectional union instead.[7] Despite this, the Workers' Union rejoined the
TUC in 1917, and the Congress of that year – held at Blackpool in October
and lauded as the 'biggest on record' in the journal of the Boilermakers'
Union – saw over seventy resolutions agreed, including ambitious calls
for a conscription on wealth, education for all children under sixteen, and
pensions for all over fifty.[8] A resolution calling for an international peace

[7] R. Hyman, *The Workers' Union*, Oxford: Clarendon Press, 1971, 117 and 122.
[8] Report of the Forty-Ninth Annual Gathering of the Trades Union Congress; *Boiler-makers' Reports*, October 1917.

conference was passed by over three million votes, causing the editor of the journal to proclaim:

> At Blackpool, under some influence which we cannot explain, we all seemed to realise that the forces dividing us were not within our movement but without, and we had the joyful experience of our extreme right and extreme left, men such as Smillie and Thorne, moving and seconding the same resolution. It was good business. We began right ... In our search for a settlement amongst the nations, we first laid the foundations of clear understanding and unity of purpose amongst ourselves at home.[9]

The spirit of inter-union co-operation generally took precedence over the sporadic fractiousness described earlier. As a leader in the *Railway Review* of October 1915 had it, 'Neither trade unionists nor nations in these strenuous days find it profitable to emulate Daniel by standing alone. That way disaster lies.'[10] As early as March 1915 *The Post* was calling for a new industrial strategy for the post-war world: 'The present should be a time of stock-taking, careful revision, and overhauling. The defects in methods and organisation should be remedied. Old forms and traditions should be scrapped for up-to-date methods and new ideas. Amalgamation or federation with other unions in allied or similar industries should be the first consideration.'[11] Nor was the spirit of amalgamation and co-operation confined to patriotic unskilled unions; also in March 1915, the editor of the Amalgamated Society of Engineers' journal called for the combination with the Boilermakers and Ironfounders.[12] Despite disagreements over support for and the prosecution of the war, these fault lines existed within – rather than between – different unions, and economic pressures engendered by the conflict saw to it that the war was a time of amalgamation and co-operation for the union movement. Gilbert Smith claimed in the Annual Report of the General Federation of Trade Unions:

> If in normal times the advice to all unions that have not already done so to join the GFTU has been sound, it is ten times more so now, in the stormy times which face the Labour movement in all its forms in the near future. There has never yet been a great war which was not followed by a period of specially severe internal strain, social, economic and political. I make no prophecies, but so far as I have been able to ascertain there is no shrewd Trade Union leader who does not anticipate troublous [*sic*] times. Men are at a premium now, but capital will be at a premium when the war is over, and heavy rates of interest and heavy taxation will be added to

[9] *Boilermakers' Reports*, October 1917.
[10] *Railway Review*, 29 October 1915.
[11] *The Post*, 26 March 1915.
[12] ASE, *Monthly Journal and Report*, March 1916.

the burdens the productive worker has to bear. Unemployment, lock-outs, strikes against reductions of wages are some of the troubles that may be reasonably anticipated. Now is the time to prepare. Now is the time for Trade Unions to strengthen themselves against the perils of the immediate future. It is all very well to do this by building up reserve funds, it is much better to do so by strengthening the organisation.[13]

As the trade union movement remained intact and increased substantially despite the poaching issue and skilled/unskilled tensions, attention turned towards building closer links between the unions and the Labour Party. Symptomatic of the wider behaviour of 'new' unions, the Workers' Union continued to support the Labour Party – although some leaders had flirted with the ultra-patriotic National Democratic Party (NDP) – yet even unskilled unions had trouble persuading their members to back Labour financially.[14] A cartoon in the *Railway Review* entitled 'Our Little Inconsistencies' asked: 'Why does this member of the NUR treat with contempt the "non" who shelters himself behind the worn-out rag of "objection" – and shelter himself behind the same worn-out rag when asked to pay into the political fund?'[15] Similarly, an editorial in the same paper of August 1917 lamented that: 'Seven-eighths of the members are so careless and indifferent that they fail to find the supplies [money for the political fund]. We are convinced that it is not so much a desire to avoid their share of supply, but that they suffer from mass indifference which can be removed by an extension of knowledge of the political fund.'[16] Creating greater harmony between the trade unions and the Labour Party would prove a trickier proposition even than trade union unity. R.B. Suthers predicted in *The Clarion*: 'These ... problems confront the trade unionist, and they will require all the skill and energy and patience he can evoke if he is to find a satisfactory solution – a solution that will be a real aid to the building up of a sane and civilised State. A trade unionist who is only a trade unionist is a barbarian.'[17]

The formation of a trade union-only party had previously been mooted, and the right-wing union leader Havelock Wilson persisted in agitating for its creation, convinced as he was that Labour was contaminated by middle-class pacifists. This idea was rejected by the TUC of September 1916, by 3.8 million to 567,000 votes.[18] But this motion did not end the debate, and

13 Quoted in *The Post*, 21 May 1915.
14 Hyman, *The Workers' Union*, 155.
15 *Railway Review*, 11 May 1917.
16 Ibid., 31 August 1917.
17 *The Clarion*, 12 March 1915.
18 Report of the Forty-Eighth Annual Gathering of the Trades Union Congress.

OUR LITTLE INCONSISTENCIES.

Figure 6. 'Our Little Inconsistencies', *Railway Review*, 11 May 1917.
Working Class Movement Library.

many individual unions continued to have ballots on the issue of whether the unions should go it alone: the Amalgamated Society of Papermakers, for example, reported in October 1918 that 570 of its members had voted for a purely trade union party, ninety-seven against, with three spoiled ballot papers. 'It is therefore very evident', the report continued, 'that so far as our members are concerned, the majority do not agree with the recently altered constitution of the Labour Party, by which any individual may become a member providing he signs the constitution and pays his contribution.'[19]

Yet if some unionists felt that trade unions did not possess enough clout within Labour, some feared the opposite. An editorial in *The Clerk* of January 1917 noted that the lay press and the general public were often confused when the tone of debates and resolutions at conferences was not reflected in the votes. The reason for this, he explained, was that:

> The Socialist societies, Trades Councils, and local Labour Parties send a large number of delegates, but carry only few votes, their financial contribution to the party funds being small and their members to a great extent already represented by one or other of the Trade Unions. They are, however, the effective representation of the active workers in the constituencies – the advanced social and political thinkers who are building up the moral force behind the party; and they are inevitably the critics of the Executive and of the Parliamentary groups, and the advocates of an uncompromising policy … The Trade Unions, on the other hand, generally content themselves with a smaller representation in numbers than they are entitled to have, secure of their influence in the card vote, when the 'money talks'. Their delegates, in the main, represent the silent voter, the passenger carried by the party, who pays for his share in its direction through the Political Fund of his Union; and their attitude is naturally a closer reflection of the views and feelings of the average man in the street and in the workshop. Hence on so many questions the rebels take the lead in debate, secure the most applause, and are, after all, borne down in the division by the 'damned, compact majority' of miners, cotton operatives, and metal workers. Bearing these facts in mind, we shall be wise not altogether to ignore the spirit shown in the debates, but to judge the party chiefly on the votes cast.[20]

Similarly, in a report on the Labour conference in Manchester of January 1917, J.W. Ormanroyd of the *Bradford Pioneer*, complained:

> Anyone listening to the debate, and trying to forecast the vote by the reception of the men and the speeches would have thought that the Labour Party would have to leave the Government. But he would have been wrong, for as most of you will be aware the Coalitionists won by a thumping majority … The votes cast at the conference did not represent either the delegates or the people who sent them and the system of block

[19] Modern Records Centre (MRC), MSS.39/40/A/4/1/2 – Amalgamated Society of Papermakers Annual Reports, October 1918.
[20] *The Clerk*, January 1917.

voting will have to be dealt with before the real voice of labour can find its expression.[21]

A.M. McBriar wrote that 'at the price of increased trade union control over the party organisation, the Labour Party had accepted Fabianism as its doctrinal basis'.[22] Certainly, after December 1918 the Parliamentary Labour Party (PLP) was dominated by unionists: most of the fifty-seven Labour MPs were trade union candidates, and fully twenty-five of them were from the Miners' Federation.[23] Thus the overall trend during the war was for greater co-operation within the union movement, and between the unions and the Labour Party; union membership itself increased by fifty per cent during the war, and the number of unions affiliated to the party doubled.[24]

Labour and Women's Organisations

The relationship between the labour movement and women's groups had been uneasy before the war. Whilst some labour figures such as Keir Hardie were prominent suffragists and women's rights' campaigners, many on the Left felt that votes for women was a distraction from the demand for a full adult franchise, that gender issues were a lesser part of the class struggle, and that women's groups were dominated by rich ladies of Tory inclination. By 1912 the relationship between Labour and the Women's Suffrage and Political Union (WSPU) had fractured: Labour candidates were opposed at elections; and speakers, particular Snowden, MacDonald, and even Keir Hardie, were frequently jeered by suffragettes.[25] During the by-election of that year, triggered by George Lansbury's resignation, the local Labour Party secretary refused to send voter lists to suffragettes – who had cars to collect voters – and suffragettes refused to lend their cars to the Labour Party.[26] Though the war did little to enlighten some of the more reactionary men of the labour movement, it did bring women's organisations, the trade unions, and the Labour Party closer together, both structurally and culturally.

---

[21] *Bradford Pioneer*, 2 February 1917.

[22] McBriar, *Fabian Socialism*, 345.

[23] A. Marwick, *The Deluge: British Society and the First World War*, Palgrave Macmillan, 2006, 305.

[24] R. Barker, 'Political Myth: Ramsay MacDonald and the Labour Party', *History* 61 (1976): 47.

[25] W. Ugolini, '"We Must Stand by Our Own Bairnes": ILP Men and Suffrage Militancy, 1905–1914', *Labour History Review* 2 (2002): 162.

[26] J. Bush, *Behind the Lines: East London Labour 1914–1919*, London: Merlin Press, 1984, 28–29.

Although some women's organisations – including the WSPU – supported the war, and others such as the East London Federation of Suffragettes opposed it, the efforts of the labour movement to protect the poorest and most vulnerable from the worst effects of the conflict undermined patriotic/pacifistic divisions. Barely a month after the declaration of war, Jim Middleton received a letter from Sylvia Pankhurst: 'As the East London Federation of the Suffragettes is a working women's organisation, we have come to the conclusion that it would be useful for us to apply to you to ask if we may have representation on the War Emergency Workers National Committee.'[27] Though Sylvia Pankhurst opposed the war, the establishment of the WNC as an umbrella organisation for all labour groups led even those who vigorously opposed the conflict to seek representation. The WNC itself made a particular effort to ensure that women were adequately represented on both its own sub-committees and regional organisations; early on, it was agreed that the proposed local Citizen Committees should include representatives not only of male trade unions but also of Co-operative societies and women's groups.[28] An informal conference was held at the TUC offices on 22 March 1915, called by Sylvia Pankhurst, Julia Scurr, Ben Tillett, and George Lansbury, and the following resolution passed:

> this conference representative of the various phases of the organised women's movement invites the War Emergency: Workers' National Committee to convene a National Conference of delegates from the Women's Trade Unions, Socialist, Labour, Suffragists, and other Societies for the purposes of discussing the proposals put forward by the Government for the employment of women in the present war emergency and recommends that representatives of Trade Unions affected by the Government's proposals be invited to co-operate.[29]

This new spirit of inclusion did not extend to all aspects of the WNC's and the Labour Party's actions; a letter from the Standing Joint Committee of Industrial Women's Organisations arrived on 14 September 1916, protesting against the actions of the Joint Labour after the War Committee in placing no women on three out of the four Advisory Committees which they had recently appointed.[30]

A key source of tension *vis-à-vis* women and the labour movement was the issue of female workers undercutting wage levels. H. Ludlow Crofts of

---

[27] Labour History Archive and Study Centre (LHASC), WNC.9/1/21 – letter from Sylvia Pankhurst, 10 September 1914.

[28] WNC.3/6/1/3.

[29] WNC.20/1/1/45 – War Service for Women.

[30] WNC.8/4/16 – letter from Standing Joint Committee of Industrial Women's Organisations, 14 September 1916.

the Ilford and District Trades and Labour Council wrote to the Secretary of the CWS on 24 April 1915, on the topic of women typists replacing men. He claimed that there was a great danger of a permanent lowering of wages and conditions if men were replaced by women at lower rates: 'Seeing that special efforts are being made throughout the Labour movement to endeavour to secure the same pay for women who replace men as such men received, it is thought that the Co-operative Wholesale should be one of the first to recognise this'. Furthermore, claimed Crofts, 'delegates from the NUR told the meeting that where women were replacing men on the Railways during the War, they were in every case to receive equal payment to what the men replaced received, and therefore, my Council think that in only asking what a Capitalist organisation accepts, the C.W.S. are only asked to do what is fair and just'.[31] In 1915 the WNC appealed to women taking men's jobs to join the relevant trade union and demand equal wages and equal conditions: 'Women cannot more truly express their love of their country than by helping to secure justice and well-being for man and woman alike.' This was signed by scores of women from local labour societies, women's groups, academics, and trade unions.[32]

The issue of the surveillance of soldiers' and sailors' wives while their husbands were serving with the colours caused a great deal of offence amongst the labour movement, as has been seen. 'Very strong expressions were voiced', Middleton wrote to Home Secretary Reginald McKenna, 'and I was instructed to ask if you would receive a deputation of the women members of this Committee on the subject.'[33] Similarly, there were protests at the idea that there would be a glut of 'war babies' born due to an increase in sexual activity; allegations which the Women's Subcommittee described as 'offensive', while nevertheless stressing the need for the WNC to improve the condition not only of the children of servicemen, but of unmarried mothers and their babies in general. They also called for a change in English law that would legitimise babies if parents subsequently married, as existed in Scotland; for the Public Health Authorities to set up adequate numbers of Mother and Baby Clinics, as established by a few municipalities already, including on a large scale in Bradford; that the Notification of Births Act be made compulsory; and that sufficient numbers of qualified health visitors be appointed by each Public Health Authority.[34] In a letter to Mary Macarthur of the Women's Trade Union

[31] WNC.7/2/48 – letter from H. Ludlow Crofts of the Ilford and District T&LC to Sec of CWS, 24 Apr 1915.

[32] WNC.32/4 – Women's Signatures.

[33] WNC.13/4/2/2 – letter to Reginald McKenna at Home Office, 10 November 1914.

[34] WNC.30/4/4 – Memorandum on War Babies, 2 June 1915.

League on 23 July 1915, Middleton stated that the 'WNC is very anxious that full advantage should be taken of the new Notification of Births Act'; he also suggested agitating for the adoption of the Act's provisions by local authorities, and ensuring the representation of working women upon committees that may be set up by local authorities.[35]

Gillian Scott has highlighted an enduring body of opinion within the labour movement over issues such as birth control and family allowance payments which reflected a masculine culture in which 'women's issues' were subordinate to matters of class and economics. For Scott, the war served to enthrone this body of thought: suffrage and women's incorporation into the Labour and Co-operative parties undermined commitments to married women's rights and connections to wider feminist and socialist ideals: '[Women's Co-operative] Guild leaders followed priorities set by the Labour Party, rather than by their membership; as they did so, they tacitly laid to rest the critical analysis of sexual relations in the private sphere, alongside the willingness to recognize the gendered character of the working-class [sic], which had been such outstanding hallmarks of the earlier, pioneering phase of its history.'[36] There is little to challenge this in terms of the post-war labour movement, yet one has to ask how much of an appetite there was amongst working-class women to challenge prevalent gender roles, and whether or not the radicalism of post-war women's movements may have manifested itself in other ways. As Mathew Worley has argued: 'Though some women referred to their being sidelined or ignored within the party, most Labour women did not seem to perceive their role as inferior, but as their shared contribution to broader party activity', and 'the home was exactly where a large proportion of working-class women were located in the early twentieth century'.[37]

The suffrage issue attracted new prominence during the war, and also served to join women's movements – including those of Liberal or Conservative disposition – to work with the WNC and Labour, if only on this one issue. Writing to Sylvia Pankhurst in December 1915, Middleton argued:

> Personally, I hold very strongly that no move should be made at present to renew the public aspect of the Suffrage agitation. Such action would, I think be very premature, and would have exactly the contrary effect that we all desire. I hope it will be possible to have a useful debate on the subject at the Labour Party Conference, and I am also anxious that the Workers'

---

[35] WNC.30/4/4 – Memo on War Babies, 2 June 1915.

[36] G. Scott, *Feminism and the Politics of Working Women: The Women's Co-operative Guild, 1880s to the Second World War*, London: UCL Press, 1998, 152.

[37] M. Worley, *Labour Inside the Gate: A History of the British Labour Party between the Wars*, London: I.B. Tauris, 2005, 62.

National Committee upon a suitable opportunity arising will give a lead to a united movement to forward the women's cause, but I do feel most strongly at the present moment the public mind is far too much centred on war matters to concern itself very much about Suffrage. Women have an exceedingly strong case which will be recognised by considerable sections of the public as being much more convincing than was the case prior to the war, but if by any false move public irritation is aroused it will be rendered extraordinarily difficult for us to regain our position.[38]

By 1916 Middleton had grown less circumspect. He sent letters to Ben Turner and John Clynes on 7 June 1916 calling for a resolution on women's suffrage to be adopted at the TUC in September. He received a reply from Clynes informing him that the Gasworkers' and General Labourers' Union had already prepared resolutions ahead of the Congress.[39] As Joint Secretary – along with K.D. Courtney – of the National Council for Adult Suffrage, Middleton dispatched the following circular in October of that year:

> The men prevented from enlisting and retained in the munition shops, in the mines, on the railways, in the fields and in other branches of industry, are serving their country as truly as those who fight, while the help of women – apart from their first service to the State as mothers – has been called for, and thousands have answered the call … Even many of the foremost opponents of women's suffrage now admit that the services rendered by women during the war have won them the right, so long denied, to exercise a voice in national affairs … In a word, the war has revealed to many what some sections of society recognised in peace time: that the strength of the nation lies in its men and women and not in the material property they may or may not possess – that full-grown life itself, not inanimate bricks and mortar, is the only basis for the Government of a great nation.[40]

As with other issues, the voluminous correspondence between Middleton and various women's and suffrage groups across the country had their own significance in binding these groups to each other and to the labour movement. Information passed from peripheries to the centre and vice versa about possible speakers and supporters, mooted policies, and local grandees, such as the following letter from Pankhurst in March 1915: 'The Wimbledon WSPU Secretary, Mrs R. Lamartine Yates … is very anxious to be summoned to the Conference. Mrs Lamartine Yates is a great power in

[38] WNC.29/5/2 – letter to Sylvia Pankhurst, 13 December 1915.

[39] WNC.29/5/53-4 – letters to Ben Turner and Clynes, 7 June 1916; WNC.29/5/55 – reply from Clynes, 8 June 1916.

[40] WNC.29/5/43 – NATIONAL COUNCIL FOR ADULT SUFFRAGE circular 6 October 1916.

her district and on the Mayor's Committee, and the Union has many good working members. I think you will be well advised to invite them; they are practically an independent society.'[41]

Perhaps the most significant congress for joining female pressure groups and different labour organisations together was the grand Women's Conference held at Caxton Hall on 16 April 1915. This asked for safeguards that women's war service be recognised by the government: 'In the event of the Board of Trade making difficulties about guaranteeing these safeguards, may we hear what steps the WNC and the trades unions whom it represents will take to secure effective protection for women workers from sweating and underpayment, without penalising their entry into the various trades for which their war service is required?'[42] The extensive list of representatives demonstrates just how wide-ranging and inclusive the conference was, suggesting that the war brought closer association between disparate groups. George Lansbury represented the Poplar trades council; Leslie Boyne the Gasworkers and General Labourers; Sylvia Pankhurst the East London Federation of Suffragettes; Barbara Ayrton Gould, Mary Neal, John Scurr, and Therese Muir Mackenzie the United Suffragists; Marion Holmes the Women Writers Suffragists; Susan Lawrence the London County Council; Lillian Harris the Women's Co-operative Guild; Ethel Weaver the National Federation of Women Workers; L.A. Dawson the Fabian Women's Group; A.M. Florence the Association of Women Clerks and Secretaries; Mary Macarthur the Women's Trade Union League; Margaret Hicks the National Women's Council; Grace Neal the Domestic Workers Union; Winfred Mayo the Actress Franchise League; and Middleton himself representing the WNC.[43]

Ultimately, the war brought women's groups closer to, and further integrated them into, the labour movement. Specifically female concerns were nevertheless still forced to take a secondary position to class issues, and, in the words of Worley, 'What Labour often failed to do – along with other political parties and organisations – was to appreciate that women comprised multiple identities: housewives, workers, mothers, consumers, wives, lovers, Catholics, and so on'.[44] Issues related to birth control, maternal

[41] WNC.32/5/22 – letter from E.S. Pankhurst to Middleton, 29 March 1915.

[42] WNC.32/5/65 – letter from Women's Freedom League, 17 May 1915.

[43] WNC.32/5 – Women's Conference, Caxton Hall. Of the women mentioned here, probably the most significant were Susan Lawrence and Mary Macarthur. Lawrence was a Labour member of the London County Council and was elected for East Ham North in 1923. See Bellamy and Saville, *Dictionary of Labour Biography III*, London: Macmillan, 2002. Macarthur had founded the National Federation of Women Workers in 1906. See Bellamy and Saville, *Dictionary of Labour Biography II*, London: Macmillan, 2002.

[44] Worley, *Labour Inside the Gate*, 62.

healthcare, and welfare benefits were to cause tensions within the movement in the interwar period, yet overall alliances forged in the war held during the interwar period, and were vital in channelling newly enfranchised women towards Labour.

The Co-operative Movement and Labour

Of all the various trade unions, socialist societies, women's groups, and sundry organisations which could loosely be said to compose the 'Edwardian Left', the Co-operative movement had the most ambiguous relationship with the Labour Party. With a membership of around three million at the start of the war – which grew by more than a million during the conflict, reaching 4,131,000 in 1919 – the group was a potentially mighty ally, if it could be persuaded to seek political representation and fight with Labour in Parliament.[45] Yet the prospects of a political alliance did not look promising. Although the 1907 Co-operative Congress voted in favour of direct political representation, apathy and opposition amongst the local societies killed the initiative. Subsequently, the Congress at Aberdeen in 1913 decided for neutrality, and on 4 August 1914 Secretary Whitehead of the Co-operative Union wrote to Arthur Henderson, explaining his refusal to send a representative to the meeting of the Peace Emergency Committee (soon to be the WNC): 'I regret to say that owing to a resolution passed by our last Congress, the Union cannot accede to your wishes in sending a delegate to the meeting.'[46] The war was to change all this. Firstly, the Co-operative movement soon overcame its previous neutrality and joined with the WNC; secondly, the movement was persuaded that it needed political representation; and finally, bonds were formed during the war which ensured that in the post-war world the Co-operative movement and Labour would be closely allied.

The main issue which drew the WNC and the Co-operative together was the supply of food. Middleton wrote again to Whitehead on 6 August 1914, calling for two nominees to the WNC: 'In addition to the accounts of the Government's proposals respecting the national food supply, the work in which we are to be engaged will be of immense importance to all working-class households'.[47] This time the response was favourable: 'We have a Congress Resolution debarring us from taking certain steps; but I

---

[45] R. Rhodes, *An Arsenal for Labour: The Royal Arsenal Co-operative Society and Politics 1896–1996*, Manchester: Holyoake Books, 1998, 26.

[46] WNC.4/1/10 – letter to Henderson from A. Whitehead, Secretary of the Co-operative Union Ltd, 4 August 1914.

[47] WNC.7/2/11 – Letter to A. Whitehead of Co-operative Union Ltd., 6 August 1914.

am of the opinion that this resolution should not debar us at the time of this national crisis'.[48] At the start of 1917 the Parliamentary Committee of the Co-operative Congress sent a deputation to the Food Controller, Lord Devonport, featuring: S. Galbraith and A. Varley (CWS), W.T. Charter (Co-operative Union), J. Bardner (Scottish Co-operative Wholesale Society), W. Openshaw (CWS), E. Ross (Scottish Co-operative Wholesale Society), and H.J. May (Secretary), along with several representatives of the WNC.[49] Arguing that the Co-operative's experience of equitably distributing food made their principles ideal for the war, H.M. Hyndman wrote to the *Morning Post* in June 1917:

> There can be no more important post in the country, at the present moment and for at least two or three years to come, than that of Food Controller; I do not wonder that the Government finds very great difficulty in filling it ... The great Co-operative Societies, with their 3,000,000 members and 11,000,000 customers, can, as I believe, furnish a thoroughly-experienced man possessing all these qualifications.

Specifically, he suggested Bob Williams, secretary of the CWS.[50]

In addition to stimulating collaboration at the highest levels of organisations through the WNC, the food supply issue brought together different groups at a regional level. There was a highly successful northeast food conference at Newcastle with 610 delegates representing 265 different organisations. These included 158 trade unions, forty-five co-operatives, nine women's co-operative guilds, eighteen branches of the ILP, thirteen workmen's clubs, nine local Labour parties, six trade and labour councils, four branches of the Women's Labour League, four friendly societies, and the Church Labour Committee.[51] A West of Scotland conference of Co-operative, trade union, women's, and socialist organisations was held at the Co-operative Hall, Glasgow, under the auspices of the Scottish Co-operative Wholesale Society on 20 February 1915, 'for purposes of reduction of Food and Fuel Prices, as recommended by the Workers' National Committee'. Robert Stewart of the Scottish Co-operative Wholesale Society presided, with miners' leader Robert Smillie also on the platform.[52] Similarly, Rachael Vorberg-Rugh has highlighted the significance of the 1916 Bolton Food Protest Meeting. The Co-operative, BSP, trade council, and Labour Party were all represented, and were addressed by

[48] WNC.7/2/2i – Reply from Whitehead to Middleton, 7 August 1914.
[49] WNC.29/6/16 – Deputation to Lord Devonport, 1 January 1917.
[50] WNC.9/2/62 – letter from Hyndman to *Morning Post*, 5 June 1917.
[51] WNC.5/1/1/51 – *Newcastle Chronicle*, 12 May 1917.
[52] WNC.4/7/21i – Flyer: West of Scotland Conference of Co-operative, Trade Union, Industrial Women's, and Socialist Organisations.

Bob Williams, who had been sent by the WNC. Vorberg-Rugh has noted that the meeting did not address the national Co-operative programme, but instead concentrated on Bolton and local issues.[53]

These food conferences show in microcosm how the ILP, trade unions, and the Co-operative started to coalesce at a local level. An important role of the WNC, and Middleton in particular, was co-ordinating speakers for these various events. Certain well-known male rhetoricians, such as Smillie, Barnes, and Tillett, were highly sought after, but so were female lecturers such as Margaret Bondfield, Mary Macarthur, and Susan Lawrence; in fact, roughly half of the scores of local food conferences requested female speakers.[54] Besides the connections, motivation, and goodwill engendered by these conferences, they were a useful source of income: by February 1915 thirty-five pounds had been raised and conferences were contributing four or five pounds on average to the WNC coffers.[55] The regional food conferences thus had a similar significance to closer organisational and ideological co-operation at the centre; in terms of organisation, camaraderie, fundraising, and even recruitment. Amongst the dozens of letters of feedback hailing these councils as a resounding success came an enquiry from J.W. Blenkey of the Stockton Trades Council as to the fees and process involved in affiliating to Labour, information which Middleton was happy to supply.[56] The labour and Co-operative movements also found a great deal of common ground on the issue of direct/indirect taxation. In November 1914 Henderson appealed to Lloyd George to lessen indirect taxes on the working classes and lower the threshold on income tax;[57] and the budget of 1916 was particularly infuriating for both parties due to the amount of tax that was to be levelled on expenditure, rather than income.[58]

Already by October 1914 the editor of *The Co-operative News* was praising Clynes and advancing the prudence of political representation: 'In his address at Warrington on Saturday last, Mr. J. R. Clynes, M.P., was right in reminding us that if co-operators decide to stay out of Parliament, they will not find private traders ready to follow their example.' The editorial continued by predicting that a 'democratic fusion' of trade unionists and co-operators would be even more important after the

---

[53] R. Vorberg-Rugh, 'The British Co-operative Movement and the Politics of Food in the First World War', paper given at 'The Great War and Localities' Conference, 20 June 2012 at Manchester Metropolitan University.

[54] See WNC.5/1 – Food Conferences.

[55] WNC.4/4/2 – letter to Gibbin of Newcastle, 1 February 1915 and WNC.4/11/16 – letter from S. Higginbotham, 15 February 1915.

[56] WNC.4/13/18 – letter to J.W. Blenkey, Stockton Trades Council, 16 February 1915.

[57] Reported in *The Co-operative News*, 28 November 1914.

[58] *The Co-operative News*, 15 April 1916.

war, and that the movement should co-operate with Labour in fielding candidates.[59] Similarly, at the northern sectional conference of the Women's Co-operative Guild held at the Co-operative hall in Hartlepool on 17 April 1915, there was a great deal of praise for the Labour Party and talk of the need for unity and parliamentary agitation; one woman claimed that if Labour had been around in the time of Robert Owen, they would all have been members of the party.[60]

There was particular praise for the WNC after the government conceded to its pressure on pension rates: 'the announcement that the Government has decided to make a grant to increase the scale of old age pensions to those who are suffering special hardships on account of the high prices of food and other oppressive economic conditions caused by the war, will be especially gratifying to the members of the Workers' War Emergency Committee'.[61] Describing an interview with Hyndman in March 1915, *The Co-operative News* editor declared that:

> His sympathetic attitude towards the Co-operative Movement ... surprised some of us who had been prone to regard him as wholly devoted to Democratic Socialism of the political variety ... 'The War', he declares, 'is galvanising the whole of the working classes, and particularly their leaders, into an activity which did not exist before. Even the co-operators, so long holding aloof from other advanced movements, are moving forward. The various forms of the great Labour movement will tend to coalesce so that they may work together after the Declaration of Peace for the future of the country.'[62]

There was corresponding praise for the Co-operative movement from the WNC and Labour Party: William Brown of the WNC wrote an article in *The Co-operative News* of January 1915 entitled 'Co-Operation As the Only Hope. Endorsement by Representatives of Working and Middle-Class People.' Brown argued that the WNC 'has shown how co-operators and trade unionists have much in common. The latter have helped the former in getting rid of anti-co-operative methods on relief committees; the former have assisted the latter in showing standard rates of employment'.[63] Links between the two movements were also strengthened by the number of unions using the CWS Bank; trade union branch CWS bank accounts grew from nine hundred in 1918 to over eight thousand by 1922, while CWS member

---

[59] Ibid, 24 October 1914.
[60] Ibid., 1 May 1915.
[61] Ibid., 9 September 1916.
[62] Ibid., 6 March 1915.
[63] Ibid., 30 January 1915.

societies declared in 1919 that all CWS employees had to be a member of a trade union recognised by the TUC.[64]

'Do It Now!' urged *The Co-operative News*'s editorial of 9 June 1917, reporting how the Swansea Congress had decided that the time had come to secure direct Co-operative representation in Parliament and on local authorities; and the correspondence columns of the newspaper were full of readers calling for direct representation. Two months later the newspaper claimed that attempts to hamper co-operatives by legislation had led to the Swansea conference and the call for direct representation: 'The blasts of war had blown the sheep's clothing off the profiteering wolves, and they stood revealed, with all their fangs, to the open gaze of the people who, forthwith, began to flock to the co-operative stores.'[65] Five months after the Swansea Congress, an emergency conference was held in October 1917, at which Arthur Henderson spoke:

> I would not insult the Co-operative Movement as a whole by suggesting that it should affiliate even with the Party whose secretary I have the honour to be. What we want is to have you properly organised; and until experience provides us with better means, to have you working with us for the same common cause ... Under the terms of your proposed scheme it permits friendly relations between us. We of the Labour Party have begun to work with the Co-operative Movement.[66]

Needless to say, the war did not witness an entirely amicable fraternity between the labour and Co-operative movements. In June 1916 *The Co-operative News* asked: 'Why is it that the Labour Party in Parliament remain so remarkably silent respecting the wholesale exploitation of the wage-earners they were elected to represent?'[67] The Co-operative Congress of May 1915 still did not have a majority for political fusion, and as late as April 1917, while there were demands for direct Co-operative representation in Parliament, the majority was still against a formal alliance with Labour.[68] The close organisational and ideological interaction between Labour and the Co-operative movement did not yet mean that there was any political understanding between Labour and the proposed new Co-operative party. Indeed, after it became apparent that co-operators would seek separate political representation independent of Labour, press coverage of the party became more circumspect. In the editorial 'Partyism or Co-operation?', *The*

---

[64] J.F. Wilson, A. Webster, and R. Vorberg-Rugh, *Building Co-operation: A Business History of the Co-operative Group, 1863–2013*, Oxford: Oxford University Press, 2013, 186.

[65] *The Co-operative News*, 9 June and 22 September 1917.

[66] Rhodes, *An Arsenal for Labour*, 30.

[67] *The Co-operative News*, 3 June 1916.

[68] Ibid., 21 April 1917.

Co-operative News advocated supporting candidates because they were 'good co-operators', not because they were good Labourists, and the June 1918 edition carried rumours of discord in the Labour Party ranks, claiming that the ILP was not happy with the direction of Labour, the British Workers' League was at odds over many issues, and there was talk of forming a separate trade union party.[69] As Tony Adams has argued, far from being resolved, 'the battle to bring co-operation into closer political alliance with Labour had only entered a new and particularly difficult phase as a result of the 1917 Congress decision'.[70]

In fact, given the decision to found a Co-operative party to compete for parliamentary seats, in September 1917 the Parliamentary Committee of the Co-operative Congress elected to end its affiliation with the WNC.[71] While the movement had been persuaded of the value of political representation, the neutralist sentiment remained strong. Therefore, paradoxically, although the war had brought labour and the Co-operative closer together, and brought the latter into the political arena, it was considered important to put some distance between the two groups. The move came as a great shock and disappointment to Middleton, yet the bonds formed in the war were not so easily dissolved:[72] 'I need not assure you', wrote Henry May as he informed Middleton of the development, 'that this decision was arrived at reluctantly as the Committee are in sympathy with the work with which they have been connected for the past 3 years.'[73] M.A. Gasson of the Co-operative Union also wrote of her regret: 'Personally, I am extremely sorry, because I am certain this Committee has had a greater influence upon the Government, and the country, in calling attention to, and suggesting remedies for many of the evils brought into existence through war conditions than any Committee I know.'[74] CWS Secretary Bob Williams was particularly saddened by the schism, yet felt optimistic for the future:

> However great my regret as regards the personal issue, it is completely eclipsed by that which I feel respecting the severance of the link between our Co-operative movement and the other organisations comprehended in

[69] Ibid., 26 January and 22 June 1918.

[70] T. Adams, 'The Formation of the Co-Operative Party Re-Considered', *International Review of Social History* 32 (1987): 59.

[71] For the founding of the Co-operative Party in 1917, see the entry for Samuel Perry in *Dictionary of Labour Biography XII*. Perry served as the first national secretary for the Co-operative Party and was elected as Member for Kettering in 1923.

[72] WNC.8/1/21 – letter to Mrs Katherine Veals, 11 October 1917.

[73] WNC.8/1/1.i – letter from Henry May of Parliamentary Committee of the Co-operative Congress to Middleton 24 September 1917.

[74] WNC.8/1/8 –letter to Middleton from A. Gasson, of Southern Section of Co-operative Union, 28 September 1917.

the representation upon your Committee. It is nothing short of disastrous that, at a time when all working-class movements should be more closely related in order to face the grave situation created by the war crisis ... this sudden severance should have taken place. I desire to thank very heartily your colleagues for the kindness and courtesy they have always shown to me; to wish them all success in their future labours; and to express the belief that the work they have already accomplished will be found, in future days, to have been of epoch-making importance.[75]

Middleton was of a similar mind, and agreed with Williams that the war had created an indelible bond between Labour and the Co-operative movement:

Our three years' work on the National Committee has been a great endeavour, and has really helped to keep us sane in these mad times. I believe that we have done much more permanent work than we quite realise. The keeping together of our local forces in the constituencies, which after all, from a political point-of-view, has been a great success, will make our task of re-organising the Labour Party much easier than I fear otherwise would have been the case ... I am hoping that the severance will be only temporary, and that in any case, before many months are over, the three great Movements – Industrial – Political – and Co-operative – will be linked up so as to become the greatest Democratic Force that ever British politics have known.[76]

This analysis of the effects of the war on the relationship between the Co-operative movement and the political and industrial branches of the labour movement argued that, *pace* Sidney Pollard, it was the specific circumstances engendered by the war which led to closer co-operation between the two groups. In the words of Tony Adams: 'Long-established and firmly held views [on political neutrality] were undermined by the practical experiences of active co-operators during the war rather than any mass conversion to Labour consequent upon a re-defined ideology'.[77] Although Mary Hilson stressed the importance of the war, she counselled that 'whilst there is evidence from Plymouth to support such a reading, I argue that calls for independent political representation may be read another way, which suggests a developing analysis of society in terms of opposing economic systems and class conflict, and that furthermore this reading indicates a shift in attitudes during this period'.[78] However, the evidence of friendship and

---

[75] WNC.8/1/11.i – letter from B. Williams of Southern Section Co-operative Union, 3 October 1917.

[76] WNC.8/1/19 – letter to Williams, 11 October 1917.

[77] Adams, 'The Formation of the Co-Operative Party', 54.

[78] M. Hilson, 'Consumers and Politics: The Co-operative Movement in Plymouth, 1890–1920', *Labour History Review* 67 (2002): 7–27.

camaraderie between leaders of Labour and the Co-operative, and desire for closer integration despite official policy supports Adams's argument that 'far from being a conservative force, the national leadership of the Co-operative Union made repeated attempts to drag a largely indifferent and often hostile membership into closer alliance with Labour and the trade unions'.[79]

Socialist Societies and the Labour Party

In 1914 the ILP, BSP, and the Fabian Society accounted for only 33,000 out of the 1.6 million members of the Labour Representation Committee. But despite being far less numerically significant than the trade unions, they provided many of the MPs, leaders, and the intellectual and ideological basis of the movement.[80] The Fabians generally supported the war; the BSP split over the conflict, its right wing joining other ultra-patriots to form the Socialist National Defence Committee; while the ILP – though internally divided – remained within Labour, albeit representing a source of criticism and occasional division. The early days of the war saw much greater hostility towards the supposedly pacifistic ILP than 1917 and 1918: describing ILP criticism of the Labour Party's support for the war, an editorial in the *Railway Review* of November 1914 complained: 'I find the tone of superiority and pity for the straying Labour Party much more difficult to stand than any other aspect of the case'.[81] By June of 1916 the exasperation with the ILP had hardened: 'The ILP is totally out a touch with the main currents of Trade Union opinion … It may be, of course, that the Labour Party as present formed can weather the storm, but I confess the prospect is not alluring.'[82] In a broadside against the war which appeared in the *Bradford Pioneer* of October 1915, the ILP's T. Russell Williams lambasted the labour leaders for failing in their first duty, to protect the working classes. He further claimed that a week earlier he had sent a letter to the *Labour Leader*, only to have a key paragraph excised 'for no apparent reason, unless it was fear of misunderstanding with our trade union colleagues. We seem to be unable to measure the value of anything except by material standards. *The unholy influence of the voter colours our thoughts and makes us false to every godlike instinct within us.* We are almost as much afraid of a Labour Party rout as we might be of a German invasion'.[83] Writing in the *Pioneer* of February 1917, the doctrinaire

---

[79] Adams, 'The Formation of the Co-Operative Party', 54.

[80] J.N. Horne, *Labour at War: France and Britain 1914–1918*, Oxford: Clarendon Press, 1991, 24.

[81] *Railway Review*, 13 November 1914.

[82] Ibid., 9 June 1916.

[83] *Bradford Pioneer*, 1 October 1915. Emphasis added.

socialist and pacifist Philip Frankford criticised the 'so-called' Labour Party, and claimed that the ILP, 'to be successful must STAND ALONE. If it makes temporary alliances with non-Socialist bodies, such as we might do here, with radical antimilitarists to overthrow militarism, it MUST BE OF A TEMPORARY NATURE ONLY, AND THIS SOLELY TO OBTAIN ONE OF THE VITAL PRINCIPLES OF SOCIALISM'.[84] Of course, the Labour Party itself did the exact opposite, and made alliances with right-wing trade unionists as well as radical, Liberal pacifists.

Discussing the proposed new Labour Party constitution in November 1917, Fred Jowett of the ILP claimed that:

> In the first place … there is nothing contained in the proposed constitution that commits the party to Socialism. It is true that in the statement concerning the objects of the party 'common ownership of the means of production' is mentioned as the basis for securing the full fruits of their industry 'for producers by hand or by brain'. There is nothing, however, to prevent Co-operators, for instance, who look rather to the gradual extension of voluntary Co-operative activities until the whole field of industry and commerce has been brought within the scope of its operations, from subscribing to this form of declaration … The proposed new constitution treats Socialist organisations exactly on the same footing as Trade Unions, as if all members of Trade Unions were active supporters of the Labour Party, whereas probably not more than fifty per cent support the Labour Party at public elections, and as if, on the other hand, the political strength of Socialist organisations could be exactly measured by the number of their members.[85]

Yet the ILP did not split from Labour over the war. This was partly due to internal divisions over the conflict and to the federalised nature of Labour at the time, but also because there was clearly room in the labour movement for dissent and pacifism. It also helped that the ILP found much to agree with in the type of socialism adopted by the Labour Party in 1918. In the words of Jay Winter, 'to make of the Labour Party a moderate alternative to extra-Parliamentary action or even revolution itself was all the more important, Henderson argued, because so many men "have become habituated to thoughts of violence" during the war'.[86] The *Railway Review* concurred with this in July 1918 when it described the Labour conference that had just been held in London: 'Whatever taint of misplaced Bolshevism existed was shriven in shreds when Mr Henderson had read the translation of Kerensky's

---

[84] Ibid., 23 February 1917.

[85] Ibid., 9 November 1917.

[86] J.M. Winter, 'Arthur Henderson, the Russian Revolution, and the Reconstruction of the Labour Party', *Historical Journal* 15 (1972): 771.

oration. His picture of Russia bleeding white under the dual autocracy
of anarchism and Prussianism conveyed a moral not to be forgotten by
those hearing who desired the truth'.[87] Similarly, Guild Socialists such
as G.D.H. Cole became, in the words of Beatrice Webb, 'willing to work
with the Labour Party in order to get in touch with the Trade Unions', and
this was reciprocated by the party; before the war there had been a certain
'disdain' of intellectuals, but in the post-war atmosphere Cole, Tawney, and
the Webbs were increasingly prominent.[88]

The Rise and Decline of the Ultra-Patriots

Joseph Burgess, one of the founders of the ILP and editor of the *Bradford
Pioneer* until his break with the pacifistic Left over the war, had argued
in his book *Homeland or Empire?* that 'capitalism is national ... socialism
is international'.[89] Yet the motivations of much of the British Left at this
time were national, and very often parochial; this led to labour support
for the war and an electoral boost for Labour after 1918. There was a very
real risk, however, that an ultra-nationalistic socialism could develop, and
Joseph Burgess was one of many on the Left who swiftly abandoned previous
internationalist and pacifistic positions for an altogether different ideology.
The correspondence column of *The Clarion* of the 22 October 1915 contained
a missive signed with the pen name 'British Nationalist':

> I agree with Mr Blatchford that 'Socialism now covers so many ideas
> which I hate that I wince when I call myself a Socialist. After the war
> we shall have to find a new name.' I suggest the words 'Nationalism' and
> 'Nationalist.' ... 'Nationalism' can easily cover 'Nationalisation', which is
> Socialism, and the corrupted word 'Socialism' can be left to the discredited
> rump ... All respect to Messrs. Will Thorne, Will Crooks, Ben Tillett,
> G.H. Roberts, John Hodge, and their like, who are men of big brains
> as well as loyalty of heart and sense. But the time has come to repudiate
> slackers and shockers, and leave them to their own rubbish-heaps.

The 'Our Point of View' column – usually written by *The Clarion* deputy
editor Alex Thompson – took as its title 'The Nation's Re-Birth':

> There is so much that we might do after the war. We shall then be able to
> show that in the time of danger our nationalistic principles were embraced
> by all parties as the only means of saving the nation. We can show that
> in the reorganisation of labour, in the revival of industry on an essential

[87] *Railway Review*, 5 July 1918.
[88] J.M. Winter, *Socialism and the Challenge of War*, London: Routledge and Kegan Paul,
1974, 140 and 272.
[89] Quoted in *Plebs*, December 1915.

basis of production for use, in the scientific distribution of wealth for the avoidance of wholesale bankruptcy, our principles must necessarily hold the field. If we oppose the nation, we shall be shamed and execrated as much as the Germans. If we prove ourselves nationalists now, if we help loyally to ensure the enemy's defeat, the future is ours ... That is why we venture to claim – perhaps with excessive conceit of its capabilities – that the survival of the *Clarion*, the steadfast champion of Socialistic Nationalism expressed in the phrase 'Britain for the British', may be of some use after the war to save some Socialist influence from the threatened *debacle*.[90]

These ideas reached their logical linguistic conclusion in a call by Burgess at the end of 1915 for 'A National Socialist Party'. In this declaration he stated that he had finally resigned his membership of the ILP – despite his being a founding member – and felt that:

> The time is right for a new departure. All existing British Socialist papers have been paralysed by a futile Internationalism. For another generation at least the Socialist of all nations would be well-advised to concentrate on achieving Socialism in their own boundaries. I would be delighted to cooperate with Socialists who accept that view in an attempt to establish a National Socialist Party with the emphasis on the 'National'.[91]

Jay Winter has written that 'It may not have been a complete accident ... that Oswald Mosley, the Fascist leader, emerged not from the Conservative, but rather from the Labour Party', but this reflects a rather sanitised view of the early labour movement.[92] If Britons at the time of the First World War had an entirely different conception of 'race', ethnicity, nations, and nationalism than we do today, then labour people – intellectuals as much as workers – were little different. Biological racism, eugenics, and Social Darwinism undermined any true internationalism as we would understand it today and anti-Semitic sentiment was commonplace across the political spectrum. A letter to Arthur Henderson in late 1916 conveyed a resolution unanimously adopted at a meeting of the WNC on 30 November 1916, 'that this War Emergency Workers' National Committee, having regard to the serious *moral*, social, industrial, and economic considerations in any

---

[90] *The Clarion*, 22 October 1915.

[91] Ibid., 3 December 1915.

[92] Winter, *Socialism and the Challenge of War*, 50. In fact, Mosley formed the New Party with six ex-Labour MPs and one Ulster Unionist. See R. Thurlow, *The Secret State: British Internal Security in the Twentieth Century*, Oxford: Blackwell, 1994, 180; P.M. Coupland, '"Left-Wing Fascism" in Theory and Practice', in N. Copsey and D. Renton (eds), *British Fascism, the Labour Movement and the State*, London: Palgrave Macmillan, 2005; D. Howell, *Mosley and British Politics 1918–32*, Basingstoke: Palgrave Macmillan, 2015.

introduction of coloured labour into this country, supports the Labour Party
in its emphatic protest against such introduction'.[93] Towards the end of
the war *The Co-operative News* complained of 'A catering company, largely
controlled by Jewish financiers, with depots in London and the provinces,
return[ing] a profit of 25 per cent on its year's working.'[94] Given that there was
momentum for a nationalistic, statist, patriotic, and economically populist
doctrine on both Left and Right towards the end of the war, why was the
advent of a popular British fascist movement delayed until over a decade
after the conflict? Why, given the popularity of prominent labour patriots
and the expulsion of labour peacemakers from the PLP in the immediate
post-war period, was the ultra-patriotic Labour right unable either to take
control of the party, or to establish themselves an as independent force in
politics?

In *The Clerk* of September 1916, Mr O. Prevost outlined what he saw as
the folly of the British Left:

> Thousands of workers in this country have declined to support the
> movement because of its short-sighted policy in permitting … unpatriotic
> sentiments to be expressed. Such workers have rightly argued thus: 'What
> is the use of Socialists telling us to socialise the means whereby we live,
> if the Socialists want to cut down the Navy and Army, and thus leave us
> inadequately protected against foreign aggression?'

The British Workers' League (BWL), he continued:

> Has been formed to combat this sort of thing and to create a sane, practical
> organisation to stimulate real patriotism (not Jingoism, or Chauvinism, or
> Pan-Germanism) among all sections of the community, thus compelling
> the State to guarantee every citizen the right to live (not merely exist), to
> protect the British workers from the unfair competition of cheap labour
> and cheap markets, whether at home or abroad, and to establish on a
> democratic basis defences adequate to the Empire's safety.

He concluded by lampooning the ILP and *Herald* pacifists' 'Tolstoyan
ethics of passive-resistance, meekness, humility, and brotherly love', and
proclaiming: 'I believe in Internationalism in so far as I would like to see
the workers of the world unite in order to free themselves from exploitation
by the ruling classes; but such an Internationalism is only possible by the
proper organisation of its constituent nations, and that organisation is only
possible through nationalism'.[95]

The 'Manifesto' of the BWL appeared in *The Clarion* in the same year.

[93] WNC.3/12/1 – letter to Arthur Henderson, 2 December 1916. Emphasis added.
[94] *The Co-operative News*, 29 June 1918.
[95] *The Clerk*, September 1916.

Signed by the Council of the BWL, including Vice Presidents Charles Duncan, John Hodge, James O'Grady, Charles Stanton, Stephen Walsh, and H.G. Wells, Chairman Alex Thompson, and Honorary Secretary Victor Fisher, it outlined the following: 'Competition and private profiteering have led to waste, inefficiency, and fraud. The nation has only been saved from destruction in so far as it has depended on patriotic national solidarity.' The BWL did not show any great hostility towards the Labour Party at first, due to the crossover in personnel and cross-fertilisation of ideas, particularly with the sizeable patriotic labour strand within the mainstream of the movement. The BWL was imperially minded and supported free trade within the empire, yet was still strongly socialist, anti-*laissez-faire*, and opposed a return to free importation, particularly of German goods.[96] The first BWL conference was held in London on 28 March 1917, and the resolutions passed included calls for a standardised living wage, the exploitation of empire resources for all, financial support for motherhood, the nationalisation of the railways, and welcoming the fall of the Tsar.[97]

The Conservative Lord Alfred Milner certainly saw the potential value of the secession of patriotic trade unionists from the main body of the labour movement. 'I need not point out', he wrote to Lord Willoughby de Broke in October 1915, 'what an advantage it would be if any considerable section of the working class could, without giving up their special class aspirations, nevertheless be induced to look at national questions in a broader and less exclusively class spirit'.[98] Milner, along with fellow Tory Arthur Steel-Maitland, met with labour patriots Victor Fisher and Charles Stanton on at least one occasion, and Alex Thompson claimed of Milner that he had 'never read so much of any man's writing that I agree with so whole heartedly'.[99] J.A. Seddon of the BWL wrote in *The Co-operative News* of the 'New Spirit' that would develop in post-war Britain, with greater co-operation between labour and capital.[100] With the advent of the National Alliance of Employers and Employed in 1917, it seemed possible that a break-away faction of right-wing trade unionists could result in a serious schism within the labour movement, yet although the Parliamentary Committee of the TUC twice considered involvement with the National Alliance of Employers and Employed, it was twice rejected.[101] But division in the PLP proved

[96] R. Douglas, 'The National Democratic Party and the British Workers' League', *The Historical Journal* 15 (1972): 533–52.

[97] J.O. Stubbs, 'Lord Milner and Patriotic Labour', *The English Historical Review* 87 (1972): 736.

[98] Ibid., 723.

[99] Ibid., 724 and 726.

[100] *The Co-operative News*, 11 November 1916.

[101] Horne, *Labour at War*, 273.

unavoidable. Despite the party deciding to leave the Coalition government in November 1918 in order to present itself to the electorate as an independent, serious contender for power, several politicians refused to cut their ties with the Lloyd George-led ministry, and stood as 'Coalition Labour' candidates in December 1918. The five returned were James Parker at Cannock, George Barnes for Glasgow Gorbals, John Hodge in Manchester Gorton, George Roberts for Norwich, and George Wardle for Stockport.

By the time of the December 1918 general election, the BWL had renamed itself the National Democratic Party, and won nine seats in that poll: Charles Stanton in Aberdare, Eldred Hallas at Birmingham Duddeston, Charles Loseby at Bradford East (defeating anti-war Fred Jowett of the ILP), James Watson in the Don Valley, Clem Edwards at East Ham South, Joseph Green in Leicester East (defeating Ramsay MacDonald), J.A. Seddon in Hanley, Matthew Simm in Wallsend, and Charles Jesson in Walthamstow West. At the same election, Jack Jones was returned in Silvertown as a National Socialist. This may seem quite impressive for a newly formed party, but it should be noted that only one of the successful NDP MPs – Clem Edwards, who defeated Arthur Henderson – had Conservative opposition. Furthermore, Jack Jones almost immediately took the Labour Party whip, and four years later stood for re-election in 1922 as a Labour candidate, while all the MPs elected under the auspices of the NDP in 1918 were defeated.[102]

Clearly this populist mixture of imperialism, protection, public works, mass employment, patriotism, and the expansion of the state was attractive to some workers. Why then did these seeds of far-Right sentiment meet with so little success within the labour movement? Perhaps one reason is that Labour was able to *absorb*, rather than expel this sentiment, until Mosley left over what he saw as the fiscal timidity of the second MacDonald ministry. Yet another important factor is that it did seem as though the post-war Labour movement – whilst able to accommodate all manner of former Liberals and radicals and present a decidedly pacifistic, internationalist face over Ireland and India – was still able to honestly reflect and represent the sensible, patriotic, socially conservative values of most working-class Britons. In this respect, we can see the significance of labour support for the war in averting the possible development of a very sinister strand of politics in Britain after 1918.

We have seen how the WNC utilised food supply, the cost of living, women's suffrage, and other issues as a means of binding the movement closer together, and how various leftist groups appreciated the importance of

---

[102] Douglas, 'The NDP and the BWL', 542. See entry for Clem Edwards in Bellamy and Saville, *Dictionary of Labour Biography III*.

the Committee to ensuring labour cohesion. In 1917 the party changed the method of election to its Executive. Under the previous federal structure, this had been delegated to local organisations; now it would be decided at annual conferences. Furthermore, no organisation was able to nominate more than one candidate unless its membership was over half a million; the marginalised ILP tried to reverse this in 1918 but failed.[103] Yet, as ILP influence declined, Fabian influence grew, and while the trade unions' position was further augmented, the establishment of local parties and the future fielding of candidates across the country prevented excessive union dominance. NUR Chairman George Wardle told the party conference in Manchester on 23 January 1917:

> From the very first the ties which bound the party together were of the loosest possible kind. It has steadily, and, in my opinion, wisely, refused to be bound by any programme, to subscribe to any dogma, or to lay down any creed. It has refused to adopt any mechanical formulas or to submit to any regimentation either of ideas or of policy. It has not, like the German Socialist Party, been drilled into an army or regimented into a bureaucracy based upon Marxist dogma. On the contrary, its strength has been its catholicity, its tolerance, its welcoming of all shades of political and even revolutionary thought, providing that its chief object – the unifying of the workers' political power – was not damaged or hindered thereby.[104]

There has been a great deal of scholarship on the disintegration of the Liberal party after 1916, while not enough work has concentrated on precisely why the labour movement was able to stay united across the war years and beyond. In their essay 'A Safe and Sane Labourism', Bill Schwarz and Martin Durham held that the Labour Party which emerged after 1918 represented both a missed opportunity and a reactive move against Lloyd George and the Coalition. They argued that the expansion of the franchise furthered the division between the constitutional and direct action wings of the labour movement, and that 'out of this double movement – the recomposition of the power bloc and the divide within the labour movement – emerged, in its fully formed state, modern Labour socialism'. Labour wanted to extend into Parliament 'in the exact same terms as before, creating Labour in the image of the Liberals before them'; failed to link democracy with direct action for fear of accusations of Bolshevism; and 'spurned a strategy which could [have] construct[ed] a mass popular democratic movement'.[105]

---

[103] McBriar, *Fabian Socialism and English Politics*, 341.

[104] *Railway Review*, 26 January 1917.

[105] B. Schwarz and M. Durham, '"A Safe and Sane Labourism": Socialism and the State, 1910–24', in M. Langan and B. Schwarz, *Crises in the British State 1880–1930*, London: Hutchinson, 1985, 143.

Furthermore, Schwarz and Durham held that it was 'the prospect of ... cashing in on the growing opposition to the Lloyd George coalition [which] healed the breech between the pro and anti-war factions inside the party',[106] and that 'the constitutionalists in the Labour Party were right in their assessment that to break the caesarism of the Lloyd George coalition required the rotation of parliamentary parties with the Labour Party itself integrated into the dominant structure'.[107] This analysis makes it sound as though labour abandoned a combined parliamentary and extra-parliamentary strategy not for reasons of feasibility and desirability, but due to a myopic desire to depose Lloyd George. This suggests that the Labour Party which emerged after 1918 was formed not so much by the ideological and institutional upheaval of the war, but rather as a reaction against the dominance of Lloyd George.

Schwarz and Durham felt that the most profound divisions within the movement were between syndicalists like Tom Mann and Ben Tillett and statists such as MacDonald and Philip Snowden, but the reconstituting effects of the war made that dichotomy anachronous by 1918. This chapter has argued that the war also brought the unions, women's groups, and socialist societies closer towards the Labour Party. In this sense, it was crucial that support for and opposition to the war were not organised along traditional divisions, but instead cut across them. Tony Adams has argued that the war brought the labour and Co-operative movements closer together, and this is also true for elements of the labour movement. Stuart Ball, Andrew Thorpe, and Matthew Worley concluded in their study of constituency political parties that 'over the inter-war period as a whole, Labour undoubtedly emerged as the most centralised and disciplined of the three parties'.[108] For this Labour could be grateful to the war; labour patriotism provided an issue on which different strands of the Left could agree, the WNC provided the institutional framework for co-operation between different groups, and the war created an environment where a remoulding of the labour movement was possible.

---

[106] Ibid., 137.
[107] Ibid., 143.
[108] S. Ball, A. Thorpe, and M. Worley, 'Researching the Grass Roots: The Records of Constituency Level Political Parties in Five British Counties, 1918–40', *Archives* 29 (2004): 14.

Conclusion

This book has argued that the British Left's reaction to the First World War was characterised by support for Britain during the conflict, and that this patriotism was by no means incompatible with their leftist beliefs. Further, this support for the war effort was instrumental to the growth in support for Labour, the statist development of the labour movement after the war, and the enhanced cohesion of the Left after 1918. In Chapter 1, there is little to challenge Douglas Newton's argument that the commitment of the British Left to internationalism before 1914 was rather artificial. Further, while the chapter did not take issue with most of the arguments outlined in Paul Ward's *Red Flag and Union Jack*, perhaps Ward underestimated the extent to which socialism and patriotism sat together. To quote from Stefan Berger's review, Ward's book is 'still informed by a clear sense of binary opposition between the two concepts'.[1] Chapter 1 aimed to show how the Red Flag and the Union Jack could be one and the same banner. It argued that the events of August 1914 did not represent a great turning point for the Left, but rather demonstrated continuity with pre-war values. Nonetheless, there was an easing of some of the various contradictions of the Left's attitude towards nationalism in this period. No longer did they have to espouse pacifistic internationalism whilst campaigning for the voters of a working class that did not share these instincts; in the climate of 1914–18 they could be unapologetically patriotic, and use that patriotism to indict the government.

Chapter 2 argued that, far from being a minority strand, labour patriotism – whilst equivocal and conditional – defined the Left's response to the First World War. Though most on the Left looked to prevent the coming conflict in the final days of July and early August, after war was declared most

---

[1] S. Berger, 'Review: *Red Flag and Union Jack*', *International Review of Social History* 45 (2000): 190.

promptly reversed their position. John Horne was correct to write of the 'choice of 1914' – the belief that Britain, however imperfect, was preferable to Germany – but he understated the extent to which this choice was forced upon labour elites by a patriotic working class. Scholarship that has sought to downplay left-wing commitment to the war effort, such as Catriona Pennell's *A Kingdom United*, simply cannot be sustained by the evidence of labour patriotism at both elite and subaltern levels. Significantly, support for Britain in the war did not imply support for the government of the day. Rather, support for the war seems to have radicalised many on the Left, to have increased their resentment of the people empowered to run the country, and further committed them to changing Britain after the conflict.

Chapter 3 discussed conscription, wartime strikes, and opposition to the conflict, and found that while the agitation against conscription, shop-floor strikes, and the anti-war movement may not have characterised the Left's response to the war, these experiences were an important part of the left-wing wartime experience. Furthermore, anti-war agitation made a crucial contribution to the type of labour movement which emerged after 1918. While work on opposition to the war from Cyril Pearce to Karen Hunt is to be commended, these portraits of minority movements at a grassroots level should not be allowed to obscure the overall picture of left-wing support for Britain during the war. Indeed, very often these studies, particularly those of Dai Egan and Alison Ronan, actually confirm the minority status of such movements, and their alienation from the wider population.

Chapter 4 argued that support for the war was vital to securing Labour's patriotic credentials, allowing the post-war party to offer a radical face on the questions of Ireland, empire, and disarmament, whilst picking up conservative working-class votes. The experience of the war shocked the Labour leaders into a fresh internationalism, but the patriotism displayed during the war allowed them to win in new places. Keith Laybourn and John Shepherd, amongst others, have showed how accusations of pacifism, Bolshevism, and anti-nationalism were used against Labour in the early 1920s; the party's war record provided a riposte to these attacks. Similarly, Martin Pugh has spoken of the need for Labour to pick up working-class Tory votes, and in this respect too, the war was significant, particularly in areas like the East End of London and West Lancashire. To be sure, by the time of the first minority Labour government of 1924, a great deal remained to be done, and as Labour's record between 1924 and 1939 shows, the party was never simply one general election away from a parliamentary majority during the interwar years. However, several obstacles which had hampered the pre-war Left had been overcome: Labour had its foot in the door, and now needed to build on the progress made between 1914 and 1924; the failures of the interwar years, particularly 1929–31, meant that this progress was slower than it might have been.

Chapter 5 discussed the growth of the state during the war and its retreat after 1918. It concurred with Chris Wrigley in arguing that this expansion broke many existing taboos and free market shibboleths. It also claimed, *pace* John Turner, that the war allowed for a warming of relations between the labour movement and the state. Prior to the war, there had often been a great deal of suspicion of the state, not just of national but also of local government, within labour. During the conflict, the Left was drawn into the running of the state and, through the auspices of the Workers' National Committee, did a great deal to prevent the worst effects of the war from having an impact on the most vulnerable. The growth of the wartime state and labour's role assuaged many of the fears about the state felt by some on the Left. Furthermore, the war made the statist, redistributive policies of Sidney Webb and the Fabians more palatable. It increased the desire of the Left to change the country and demonstrated how, through the mechanism of the state, it might be done.

Finally, Chapter 6 claimed that labour patriotism served to unite, rather than divide, the labour movement. Tony Adams has rightly argued that the war was crucial to drawing together the labour and Co-operative movements, and this was also true of the various groups within the labour movement. The Parliamentary Labour Party, trade unions, socialist societies, and some women's suffrage societies were all brought closer together through the experience of 1914–18. The Workers' National Committee in particular ensured that the war was to have a centripetal effect of the Left, uniting its different components rather than further dividing them. This is notably different from the experience of other nations, such as France and Germany, where the conflict instigated a fracturing of the labour movement and the emergence of competitors to the Left. In Britain, by contrast, labour patriotism allowed for the blending of the social conservatism of the working class with the technocratic thinking of the Fabians, and provided a great deal of ideological latitude within the reformist, constitutional approach to politics espoused after 1918. While certain interests, notably religious and gender concerns, became subordinate to the dominant culture, the structural and ideological agreements of the war years were to remain intact until 1945. A certain kind of labourism emerged in 1918 and was finally crowned in 1945, and would dominate British politics until the 1970s.

This book has many implications for how we understand the relationship between Leftist politics, 'patriotism', and 'nationalism'. As Linda Colley has argued, 'we need to stop confusing patriotism with simple conservatism, or smothering it with damning and dismissive references to chauvinism and jingoism'.[2] William Gillman, a trade unionist and labour activist for almost fifty years, noted in his interview in the Imperial War Museum's collection that he remained a 'Proud Britisher, [who] would take up a rifle now at eighty-six and fight; can't stand people always shouting peace, peace, peace'.[3] The lives and careers of most of the labour patriots are consistent in their critique of militarism and bloodshed from the pre-war to the post-war world. Following the 1922 general election, only six Labour MPs had retained their seats consistently since 1906: Charles Bowerman, John Hodge, John Clynes, Stephen Walsh, Will Thorne, and James O'Grady.[4] While that list would be longer and more diverse if not for the deposition of many critics of the war at the 1918 election, the fact that these men – all of whom played a prominent role in the war effort – were returned at five different elections over sixteen years suggests that their blend of radical patriotism was well-received by their electors.

While Jack Jones may have been elected as a 'National Socialist' in Silvertown in 1918, utilising virulently anti-German language and calls for continued military spending, this did not prevent his being a principled and conscientious constituency MP. When the government introduced a new Aliens Restrictions Bill in April 1919, Jack Jones and Will Thorne were among the Labour members who spoke up against its blatant anti-Semitism.[5] Furthermore, in a debate at the 1923 Conference, on a motion to commit the Parliamentary Labour Party to oppose all military and naval estimates, G. Buchanan, MP and Patternmakers' Union official – who supported the motion – paid tribute to Jones – one of the few who spoke in opposition – claiming 'he was sorry he had a difference of opinion on this matter with Mr. Jack Jones, because he wished to say quite frankly that it would be a good thing if every member of the Labour Party would fight as strenuously on behalf of the working class as Mr. Jack Jones did in the House of Commons'.[6]

Bill Nasson has spoken of how the war in South Africa brought the world forward rapidly; it was good for black Africans in terms of confidence and solidarity, as it was for industrial workers in Europe.[7] The war was significant,

---

[2] L. Colley, *Britons: Forging the Nation 1707–1837*, New Haven: Yale University Press, 1992, 372.

[3] Imperial War Museum, Catalogue No. 9420, William Gillman, interviewed 1986.

[4] Report of the Twenty-Second Annual Conference of the Labour Party: National Agent's Report.

[5] J. Bush, *Behind the Lines. East London Labour 1914–1919*, London: Merlin Press, 1984.

[6] Report of the Twenty-Second Annual Conference of the Labour Party.

[7] B. Nasson, 'British Imperial Africa', paper given at the Institute for Historical Research's Anglo-American Conference, 'The Great War', 3 July 2014.

not for crude mechanical reasons relating to reduced waged differentials or economic homogeneity, but rather for the experience of the war itself: the camaraderie, confidence, and communalism it engendered and the structural and ideology changes it brought about. Krisztina Robert has claimed that pre-1914, women were associated with negative aspects of modernity (sexually transmitted disease, promiscuity, loucheness, and ill-discipline) but that this changed with the war.[8] Deborah Thom concurred: after the war, women were associated with new technologies such as electricity, telegraphy, and aeronautics.[9] This change instituted by the war, the acceptance of modernity, was not confined to gender but touched many aspects of life. The war acted as a midwife for modern Britain and the modern labour movement, and the 'Merrie England' strand within populist socialism came to terms with it. In the words of Peter Mandler: 'A nation that had come to terms with its urbanity had less need to justify its condition, less need of the origin-myth of Merrie England that the culture industry had peddled so successfully in the early nineteenth century.'[10]

According to Alistair Bonnett:

Towards the end of the nineteenth century, those forms of radicalism that claimed to be rooted in the history and the natural rights of the people were being displaced by modernist radicalisms that viewed nostalgia with intense suspicion. It was an awkward moment. But the power of the modernist imagination was, if not overwhelming, the stronger force. Before long the radical nostalgia of William Morris would be treated as a charming contradiction in terms and the convivial socialism of the Clarion movement a whimsical footnote in the story of mainstream socialism.[11]

Yet Bonnett overstated the extent to which nostalgic socialism was banished; rather the Merrie England strain was transferred into patriotism, community spirit, and popluar culture. Frank Trentmann has spoken of 'a general redefinition of fights linking the radical culture of the nineteenth century to that of social democracy in the twentieth, emphasizing rights rooted in work and social membership', and a 'growing emphasis on the social role of the state against the background of ideas stressing the reciprocal ethnical relationship between community and individual', and it seems that this compromise

---

[8] K. Robert, '"Neither Nursing, nor Philanthropy": A Reassessment of Women's Military Employment during the First World War in Britain and on the Western Front', paper given at 'Labour and the First World War' Conference, Anglia Ruskin University, 3 May 2014.

[9] D. Thom, 'Women, War, Socialism and Public Memory', paper given at 'Labour and the First World War' Conference, Anglia Ruskin University, 3 May 2014.

[10] P. Mandler, 'Against "Englishness": English Culture and the Limits to Rural Nostalgia, 1850–1940', *Transactions of the Royal Historical Society* 7 (1997): 160.

[11] Bonnett, *Left in the Past*, 77.

between the different trends within the labour movement was brought about by the war.[12]

George Orwell wrote in the context of the Second World War that 'the Bloomsbury high-brow, with his mechanical snigger, is as out of date as the cavalry colonel'.[13] Yet across Britain in the 1920s, despite the influx of Liberals into the Labour Party, the pacifism and anti-militarism of the period, and the so-called 'aristocratic embrace', there was a Labour Party at the grassroots level which welcomed neither high-brow abstraction nor passive, stoic acceptance of the existing social order. This meant that when Labour's foreign policy turned towards the threat from fascism and began to advocate rearmament, it could do so with credibility, and the wartime fusion of radicalism with patriotism that Orwell described as merely needing to be resurrected, rather than built afresh. The Left which emerged after 1918 was broad-based, catholic, happy with new world, 'patriotic', reformist, and labourist.

[12] F. Trentmann, 'Wealth versus Welfare: The British Left between Free Trade and National Political Economy before the First World War', *Historical Research* 70 (1997): 97.

[13] G. Orwell, *The Lion and the Unicorn: Socialism and the English Genius*, London: Penguin, 1982, 64.

Bibliography

Primary Source Material

Printed Sources
Attlee, C., *Memoirs*
Edwards, G., *From Crow-Scaring to Westminster*
Higdon, T.G., *The Burston Rebellion*
Ward, J., *With the Die-Hards in Siberia*
Graves, R., *Goodbye to All That*
Graham, S., *The Challenges of the Dead*
Gibbs, P., *Realities of War*
Masterman, C.F.G., *England after War*
Roberts, R., *The Classic Slum*
Morel, E.D., *The Horror on the Rhine*
Brittain, V., *Testament of Youth*

Personal Papers
Percy Allot Papers (Modern Records Centre (MRC), University of Warwick)
Ben Tillett Papers (Labour History Archive and Study Centre (LHASC), People's History Museum)
Papers pertaining to Ben Tillett (MRC)
Douglas Houghton Papers (LHASC)
John Ward Papers (LHASC)
Havelock Wilson Papers (MRC)

Institutional Records
Hansard
Papers of the War Emergency: Workers National Committee (LHASC)
Labour Party Annual Reports (LHASC)
Trade Union Congress Annual Reports (LHASC)
Amalgamated Society of Watermen, Lightermen and Bargemen of the River Thames (MRC)

National Union of Teachers War Record (MRC)
National Federation of Construction Unions (MRC)
Amalgamated Society of Papermakers Annual Reports (MRC)
Ship Constructors and Shipwrights Minutes (Working-Class Movement Library (WCML), Salford)
Miners Federation of Great Britain Minutes (WCML)

Assorted Files (all at the Working-Class Movement Library)
War: First World War and Before Folder
War of 1914–1918 British Pamphlets
World War One Folder
WW1 Box 1
WW2 Box 2

Imperial War Museum Interview Collection
9019 Robert Fagg, interviewed 1973–2001
9253 Jack Dorgan, interviewed 1986
11113 Raynor Taylor, interviewed 1990–92
10411 Frederick Orton, interviewed 1988
5868 Anonymous, interviewed 1980
9420 William Gillman, interviewed 1986

Newspapers
ASE's *Monthly Journal and Reports*
Boilermaker's Reports
Bradford Pioneer
The Clarion
Clerks
Co-Partners' Magazine
The Co-operative News
Daily Citizen
Daily Chronicle
Daily Mail
Daily Telegraph
Forward (Glasgow)
Justice
Manchester Guardian
The Millgate Monthly
Plebs
The Post
Railway Review
The Times
The Wheatsheaf

Secondary Literature

Books

Adams, R.J.Q. and Poirier, P.P., *The Conscription Controversy in Great Britain, 1900–18*, London: Macmillan, 1987.

Ashworth, T., *Trench Warfare, 1914–18: The Live and Let Live System*, London: Pan Macmillan, 1980.

August, A., *The British Working Class, 1832–1940*, London: Routledge, 2007.

Baylies, C.A., *History of the Yorkshire Miners 1881–1918*, London: Routledge, 2003.

Beckett, I. and Simpson, K., *A Nation in Arms: A Social Study of the British Army in the First World War*, Manchester: Manchester University Press, 1985.

Belchem, J. (ed.), *Popular Politics, Riot and Labour: Essays in Liverpool History 1790–1940*, Liverpool: Liverpool University Press, 2000.

Belchem, J. and Kirk, N. (eds), *Languages of Labour*, Aldershot: Ashgate, 1997.

Benewick et al. (eds), *Knowledge and Belief in Politics – The Problem of Ideology*, New York: St. Martin's, 1973.

Bet-El, I., *Conscripts. Forgotten Men of the Great War*, Stroud: The History Press, 1999.

Biagini, E. and Reid, A. (eds), *Currents of Radicalism*, Cambridge: Cambridge University Press, 1991.

Billig, M., *Banal Nationalisms*, London: Sage, 1995.

Blackwell, T. and Seabrook, J., *The Revolt Against Change*, Chicago: Vintage, 1993.

Bonnett, A., *Left in the Past: Radicalism and the Politics of Nostalgia*, London: Bloomsbury, 2010.

Bourke, J., *Dismembering the Male: Men's Bodies, Britain, and the Great War*, London: Reaktion, 1996.

——, *An Intimate History of Killing: Face-to-Face Killing in Twentieth-Century Warfare*, London: Basic Books, 1999.

Bragg, B., *The Progressive Patriot*, London: Black Swan, 2007.

Brassley, P. et al. (eds), *The English Countryside between the Wars: Regeneration or Decline?*, London: Boydell and Brewer, 2006.

Braybon, G., *Women Workers in the First World War*, London: Routledge, 2010.

Braybon, G. (ed.), *Evidence, History and the Great War: Historians and the Impact of 1914–18*, Oxford: Berghahn Books, 2003.

Briggs, A. and Saville, J. (eds), *Essays in Labour History, 1886–1923*, London: Macmillan, 1971.

Brodie, M., *The Politics of the Poor: The East End of London, 1885–1914*, Oxford: Clarendon Press, 2004.

Brown, K., *Essays in Anti-Labour History: Responses to the Rise of Labour in Britain*, London: Macmillan, 1974.

Burk, K. (ed.), *War and the State: The Transformation of British Government, 1914–19*, London: Allen and Unwin, 1982.

Burke, P. (ed.), *History and Historians in the Twentieth Century*, Oxford: Oxford University Press, 2002.

Bush, J., *Behind the Lines: East London Labour, 1914–1919*, London: Merlin Press, 1984.

Callahan, K., *Demonstration Culture: European Socialism and the Second International, 1889–1914*, Leicester: Troubadour Publishing, 2010.

Cannadine, D., *Class in Britain*, London: Penguin, 2000.

Carey, J., *The Intellectuals and the Masses: Pride and Prejudice among the Literary Intelligentsia, 1880–1939*, Chicago: Academy Chicago, 2002.

Carsten, F.L., *War against War: British and German Radical Movements in the First World War*, Berkeley: University of California Press, 1982.

Cecil, H. and Liddle, P. (eds), *Facing Armageddon: The First World War Experienced*, London: Pen and Sword, 1996.

Clarke, J., Critcher, C., and Johnson, R. (eds), *Working-Class Culture*, London: Hutchinson, 1979.

Clarke, P.F., *Lancashire and the New Liberalism*, Cambridge: Cambridge University Press, 2007.

Cline, C.A., *Recruits to Labour: The British Labour Party, 1914–1931*, New York: Syracuse University Press, 1963.

Coates, D., *The Labour Party and the Struggle for Socialism*, Cambridge: Cambridge University Press, 1975.

——, *The Context of British Politics*, London: Hutchinson, 1984.

Cohen, D., *The War Come Home: Disabled Veterans in Britain and Germany 1914–1939*, Berkeley: University of California Press, 2001.

Collette, C., *For Labour and for Women: The Women's Labour League, 1906–1918*, Manchester: Manchester University Press, 1989.

Colley, L., *Britons: Forging the Nation 1707–1837*, London: Pimlico, 1992.

Collins, M., *The Likes of Us*, London: Granta, 2005.

Colls, R. and Dodd, P. (eds), *Englishness: Politics and Culture 1880–1920*, London: Routledge, 1987.

Cook, C., *The Age of Alignment*, London: Macmillan, 1975.

Copsey, N. and Renton, D., *British Fascism, the Labour Movement and the State*, London: Palgrave Macmillan, 2005.

Corthorn, P. and Davis, J., *The British Labour Party and the Wider World: Domestic Politics, Internationalism and Foreign Policy*, London: I.B. Tauris, 2007.

Cowling, M., *The Impact of Labour, 1920–24*, Cambridge: Cambridge University Press, 2005.

Cronin, J.E., *Labour and Society in Britain, 1918–1979*, London: Batsford, 1984.

——, *The Politics of State Expansion: War, State and Society in Twentieth-Century Britain*, London: Routledge, 1991.

Crowther, A., *Social Policy in Britain 1914–1939*, London: Macmillan, 1988.

Dallas G. and Gill, D., *The Unknown Army*, London: Verso, 1985.

Davies, A. and Fielding, S. (eds), *Workers' Worlds. Cultures and Communities in Manchester and Salford, 1880–1939*, Manchester: Manchester University Press, 1992.

Davies, S., *Liverpool Labour: Social and Political Influences on the Development of the Labour Party in Liverpool, 1900–1939*, Keele: Keele University Press, 1996.

Davis, R., *Tangled Up in Blue*, London: Ruskin, 2011.

Devine, D. et al. (eds), *Rethinking Class: Culture, Identities and Lifestyle*, London: Frank Cass, 2005.

DeGroot, G.J., *Blighty: British Society in the Era of the Great War*, London: Longman, 1996.

Dudink, S., et al. (eds), *Masculinity in Politics and War: Gendering Modern History*, Manchester: Manchester University Press, 2004.

Dudink, S. et al. (eds), *Representing Masculinity*, New York: Palgrave, 2007.

Duncan, R., *Objectors and Resisters: Opposition to War and Conscription in Scotland, 1914–1918*, Glasgow: Common Print, 2015.

Duncan, R. and McIvor, A., *Militant Workers: Labour and Class Conflict on the Clyde, 1900–1950: Essays in Honour of Harry McShane*, Edinburgh: John Donald, 1992.

Dwork, D., *War is Good for Babies and Other Young Children*, London: Taylor and Francis, 1987.

Dworkin, D., *Class Struggles*, London: Pearson Longman, 2007.

Dyrenfurth, N., *Heroes and Villains: The Rise and Fall of the Early Australian Labor Party*, Melbourne: Australian Scholarly Publishing, 2011.

Eley, G. and Nield, K., *The Future of Class in History: What's Left of the Social?*, Ann Arbor: University of Michigan Press, 2007.

Elliott, G., *Labourism and the English Genius: The Strange Death of Labour England*, London: Verso, 1993.

Fielding, S., *Class and Ethnicity: Irish Catholics in England, 1880–1939*, Buckingham: Open University Press, 1993.

Fielding S. and McHugh, D., *Interpreting the Labour Party: Approaches to Labour Policies and History*, Manchester: Manchester University Press, 2003.

Fuller, J.G., *Troop Moral and Popular Culture in the British and Dominion Armies, 1914–1918*, Oxford: Clarendon Press, 1990.

Fussell, P., *The Great War and Modern Memory*, Oxford: Oxford University Press, 1975.

Gildart, K. and Howell, D. (eds), *Dictionary of Labour Biography Vol. 12*, London: Palgrave, 2005.

Gordon, M.R., *Conflict and Consensus in Labour Foreign Policy, 1914–1965*, Stanford: Stanford University Press, 1969.

Gorman, J., *Images of Labour*, London: Scorpion Press, 1985.

Grainger, J.H., *Patriotisms: Britain 1900–1939*, London: Taylor and Francis, 1986.

Graves, P., *Labour Women in Working-Class Politics, 1918–1939*, Cambridge: Cambridge University Press, 1994.

Gregory, A., *The Silence of Memory: Armistice Day, 1919–1946*, Oxford: Berg, 1995.

——, *The Last Great War*, Cambridge: Cambridge University Press, 2008.

——, *A War of Peoples, 1914–1919*, Oxford: Oxford University Press, 2014.

Grieves, K., *The Politics of Manpower, 1914–18*, Manchester: Manchester University Press, 1988.

Griffiths, C.V.J., *Labour and the Countryside: The Politics of Rural Britain 1918–1939*, Oxford: Oxford University Press, 2007.

Griffiths, T., *The Lancashire Working Classes: 1880–1930*, Oxford: Oxford University Press, 2001.

Groves, R., *The Strange Case of Victor Grayson*, London: Pluto Press, 1975.

Harrison, B., *Peaceable Kingdom: Stability and Change in Modern Britain*, Oxford: Clarendon Press, 1982.

Hinton, J., *The First Shop Stewards Movement*, London: Allen and Unwin, 1973.

Hoggart, R., *Uses of Literacy: Aspects of Working-Class Life*, London: Chatto and Windus, 1957.

Holliday, I. and Ball, S. (eds), *Mass Conservatism: The Conservatives and the Public Since the 1880s*, London: Frank Cass, 2002.

Holton, R. J., *British Syndicalism 1900–1914*, London: Pluto Press, 1976.

Holford, J., *Reshaping Labour: Organisation, Work and Politics – Edinburgh in the Great War and After*, London: Croom Helm, 1988.

Holmes, R., *Tommy. The British Soldier on the Western Front 1914–1918*, London: Harper Perennial, 2005.

Holt, R. (ed.), *Sport and the Working Class in Modern Britain*, Manchester: Manchester University Press, 1990.

Horne, J., *Labour at War: France and Britain, 1914–1918*, Oxford: Oxford University Press, 1991.

Howell, D., *British Workers and the Independent Labour Party 1888–1906*, Manchester: Manchester University Press, 1983.

——, *MacDonald's Party: Labour Identities and Crisis, 1922–1931*, Oxford: Oxford University Press, 2002.

Howkins, A., *Poor Labouring Men: Rural Radicalism in Norfolk, 1870–1923*, London: Routledge Kegan Paul, 1985.

——, *Reshaping Rural England: A Social History 1850–1925*, London: Routledge, 1991.

Hoyle, R.W. (ed.), *Our Hunting Fathers: Field Sports in England after 1850*, Lancaster: Carnegie Publishing, 2007.

Hyman, R., *The Workers' Union*, Oxford: Clarendon Press, 1971.

Hynes, S., *A War Imagined. The First World War and English Culture*, London: Random House, 2011.

James, L., *Mutiny in the British and Commonwealth Forces, 1797–1956*, London: Ashford Buchan and Enright, 1987.

Jeffrey, K., *The British Army and the Crisis of Empire 1918–22*, Manchester: Manchester University Press, 1984.

John, A., *War, Journalism and the Shaping of the Twentieth Century: The Life and Times of Henry W. Nevinson*, London: I.B. Tauris, 2006.

Johnson, P., *Land Fit for Heroes: The Planning of British Reconstruction, 1916–1919*, Chicago: University of Chicago Press, 1968.

Johnson, M., *Militarism and the British Left, 1902–1914*, London: Palgrave Macmillan, 2013.

Jones, S.G., *Workers at Play: A Social and Economic History of Leisure 1918–1939*, London: Routledge and Kegan Paul, 1986.

Joyce, P., *Work, Society and Politics: The Culture of the Factory in Later Victorian England*, Brighton: Harvester Press, 1980.

——, *Visions of the People: Industrial Englander and the Question of Class, 1848–1914*, Cambridge: Cambridge University Press, 1993.

Kenefick, W., *Red Scotland!*, Edinburgh: Edinburgh University Press, 2007.

Kenefick W. and McIvor, A. (eds), *The Roots of Red Clydeside 1910 to 1914? Labour and Industrial Unrest in West Scotland*, Edinburgh: John Donald, 1996.

King, A., *Memorials of the Great War in Britain: The Symbolism and Politics of Remembrance*, Oxford: Berg, 1998.

Kinnear, M., *The Fall of Lloyd George: The Political Crisis of 1922*, London: Macmillan, 1973.

Kushner, T. and Valman, N., *Remembering Cable Street Fascism and Anti-Fascism in British Society*, London: Vallentine Mitchell, 1998.

Langan, M. and Schwarz, B., *Crises in the British State 1880–1930*, London: Hutchinson, 1985.

Lawrence, J., *Electing Our Masters: The Hustings in British Politics from Hogarth to Blair*, Oxford: Oxford University Press, 2009.

Lawrence, J. and Taylor, M., *Party, State and Society*, London: Scolar Press, 1996.

Laybourne, K., *Labour Heartland: The History of the Labour Party in West Yorkshire during the Inter-War Years, 1918–1939*, Bradford: University of Bradford Press, 1987.

——, *Britain on the Breadline: A Social and Political History of Britain 1918–1939*, Stroud: Sutton Publishing, 1998.

Laybourne, K. and Reynolds, J., *Liberalism and the Rise of Labour*, London: Croom Helm, 1984.

Leed, E.L., *No Man's Land: Combat and Identity in World War I*, Cambridge: Cambridge University Press, 1979.

Liddington J. and Norris, J., *One Hand Tied behind Us: The Rise of the Women's Suffrage Movement*, London: Virago, 1985.

Liddle, P., *Home Fires and Foreign Fields: British Social and Military Experience in the First World War*, London: Brassey's Defence Publishing, 1985.

Liebknecht, K., *Militarism and Anti-Militarism*, trans. Alexander Sirnis, intro. Philip S. Foner, New York: Dover, 1972.

Lloyd, D. W., *Pilgrimage and the Commemoration of the Great War in Britain, Australia and Canada, 1919–1939*, Oxford: Berg, 1998.

Lunn, K. and Kushner, T. (eds), *Traditions of Intolerance: Historical Perspectives on Fascism and Race Discourse in Britain*, Manchester: Manchester University Press, 1989.

Macdonald, C.M.M. and McFarland, E.W., *Scotland and the Great War*, East Linton: Tuckwell, 1999.

MacKenzie, J.M., *Imperialism and Popular Culture*, Manchester: Manchester University Press, 1986.

Mansfield, N., *English Farmworkers and Local Patriotism, 1900–1930*, Aldershot: Ashgate, 2001.

——, *Buildings of the Labour Movement*, Swindon: English Heritage, 2013.

Mansfield, N., and Horner, C., *The Great War: Regions and Localities*, Newcastle: Cambridge Scholars Publishing, 2014.

Marriott, J., *The Culture of Labourism: The East End between the Wars*, Edinburgh: Edinburgh University Press, 1994.

Marwick, A., *The Deluge: British Society and the First World War*, London: Penguin, 1965.

Marquand, D., *Ramsay MacDonald*, London: Jonathan Cape, 1977.

McBriar, A.M., *Fabian Socialism and English Politics*, Cambridge: Cambridge University Press, 1962.

McCartney, H., *Citizen Soldiers: The Liverpool Territorials in the First World War*, Cambridge: Cambridge University Press, 2005.

McDermott, J., *British Service Tribunals, 1916–1918*, Manchester: Manchester University Press, 2011.

McKenna, F., *The Railway Workers, 1840–1970*, London: Faber, 1980.

McKibbin, R., *The Evolution of the Labour Party, 1910–1924*, Oxford: Oxford University Press, 1974.

——, *The Ideologies of Class: Social Relations in Britain, 1880–1950*, Oxford: Oxford University Press, 1990.

McLean, I., *The Legend of Red Clydeside*, Edinburgh: John Donald, 1983.

Meeres, F., *Norfolk in the First World War*, Chichester: Phillimore, 2004.

Middlebrook, M., *The First Day on the Somme*, London: Allen Lane, 1975.

Middlemas, K., *Politics in Industrial Society: The Experience of the British System since 1911*, London: Andre Deutsch, 1979.

Middleton, L. (ed.), *Women in the Labour Movement*, London: Croom Helm, 1977.

Minkin, L., *The Contentious Alliance: Trade Unions and the Labour Party*, Edinburgh: Edinburgh University Press, 1992.

Mommsen, W. and Husung, H.-G. (eds), *Development of Trade Unionism in Britain and Germany, 1880–1914*, London: Allen and Unwin, 1985.

Moorhouse, G., *Hell's Foundations*, London: Faber and Faber, 2008.

Mosse, G., *Fallen Soldiers: Reshaping the Memories of the World Wars*, Oxford: Oxford University Press, 1994.

Morgan, K., *Hardie*, Oxford: Oxford University Press, 1967.

Newby, H., *The Deferential Worker: A Study of Farm Workers in East Anglia*, New York: Viking, 1977.

Newton, D., *British Labour, European Socialism, and the Struggle for Peace, 1889–1914*, Oxford: Clarendon Press, 1985.

Offer, A., *The First World War: An Agrarian Interpretation*, Oxford: Clarendon Press, 1989.

Orwell, G., *The Lion and the Unicorn: Socialism and the English Genius*, London: Penguin, 1982.

Oughton, F. and Smyth, V., *Mannock, VC: Ace with One Eye: The Life and Combats of Maj. Edward Mannock, VC*, London: Frederick Muller, 1963.

Paris, M., *Warrior Nation: Images of War in British Popular Culture, 1850–2000*, London: Reaktion, 2000.

Pearce, C., *Comrades in Conscience: The Story of an English Community's Opposition to the Great War*, London: Francis Boutle Publishers, 2001.

Pennell, C., *A Kingdom United: Popular Responses to the Outbreak of the First World War in Britain and Ireland*, Oxford: Oxford University Press, 2012.

Pierson, S., *Marxism and the Origins of British Socialism*, Ithaca: Cornell University Press, 1973.

Pimlott, B. and Cook, C. (eds), *Trade Unions in British Politics*, New York: Longman, 1991.

Porter, R. (ed.), *Myths of the English*, Cambridge: Polity Press, 1992.

Price, R., *An Imperial War and the British Working Class*, London: Routledge, 1972.

Pugh, M., *Speak for Britain! A New History of the Labour Party*, London: Vintage, 2011.

Putkowski, J., *The Kinmel Park Riots 1919*, Hawarden: Flintshire Historical Society, 1989.

Reader, W.J., *At Duty's Call: A Study in Obsolete Patriotism*, Manchester: Manchester University Press, 1988.

Reese, P., *Homecoming Heroes*, London: Leo Cooper, 1992.

Rhodes, R., *The International Co-operative Alliance during War and Peace 1910–1950*, Geneva: ICA Communications Department, 1995.

——, *An Arsenal for Labour: The Royal Arsenal Co-operative Society and Politics 1896–1996*, Manchester: Holyoake Books, 1998.

Richards, H., *The Bloody Circus: The Daily Herald and the Left*, London: Pluto Press, 1997.

Robb, G., *British Culture and the First World War*, London: Palgrave Macmillan, 2002.

Rose, J., *The Intellectual Life of the British Working Classes*, New Haven: Yale University Press, 2001.

Rosen, G., *Serving the People: Co-operative Party History from Fred Perry to Gordon Brown*, London: The Co-operative Party, 2007.

Rothstein, A., *The Soldiers' Strikes of 1919*, London: Macmillan, 1985.

Rubin, G., *War, Law and Labour: The Munitions Acts, State Regulation, and the Unions 1915–1921*, Oxford: Clarendon Press, 1987.

Samuel, R. (ed.), *Patriotism – The Making and Unmaking of British National Identity, Vols 1–3*, London: Routledge, 1989.

Samuel, R., and Stedman Jones, G. (eds), *Culture, Ideology and Politics*, London: Routledge, 1982.

Savage, M., *The Dynamics of Working-Class Politics*, Cambridge: Cambridge University Press, 2009.

Savage M. and Miles, A., *The Remaking of the British Working Class 1840–1940*, London: Routledge, 1994.

Scott, G., *Feminism and the Politics of Working Women: The Women's Co-operative Guild, 1880s to the Second World War*, London: Routledge, 1998.

Seabrook, J., *City Close-Up*, London: Penguin, 1973.

——, *What Went Wrong?*, London: Victor Gollanz, 1978.

Sheffield, G., *Forgotten Victory: The First World War: Myths and Realities*, London: Headline Review, 2002.

Shepherd, J. and Laybourn, K., *Britain's First Labour Government*, London: Palgrave Macmillan, 2006.

Shepherd, J., Wrigley, C., and Davis, J., *The Second Labour Government 1929–1931: A Reappraisal*, Manchester: Manchester University Press, 2011.

Smyth, J.J., *Labour in Glasgow 1896–1936*, Edinburgh: Tuckwell Press, 2000.

Silbey, D., *The British Working Class and Enthusiasm for War, 1914–1916*, London: Frank Cass, 2005.

Spiers, E., *Army and Society*, London: Longman, 1980.

Stedman Jones, G., *Languages of Class: Studies in English Working-Class History 1832–1982*, Cambridge: Cambridge University Press, 1983.

Stevenson, J., *British Society 1914–1945*, London: Penguin, 1984.

Sullivan, D., *Navvyman*, Norwich: Coracle Books, 1983.

Swartz, M., *The Union of Democratic Control in British Politics during the First World War*, Oxford: Clarendon Press, 1971.

Swenarton, *Homes Fit for Heroes: The Politics and Architecture of Early State Housing in Britain*, London: Heinemann, 1981.

Tanner, D., *Political Change and the Labour Party, 1900–1918*, Cambridge: Cambridge University Press, 1990.

Tanner, D., Thane, P., and Tiratsoo, N. (eds), *Labour's First Century*, Cambridge: Cambridge University Press, 2000.

Taplin, E., *The Dockers' Union: A Study of the National Union of Dock Labourers, 1889–1922*, Leicester: Leicester University Press, 1986.

Thane, P., *Foundations of the Welfare State*, London: Longman, 1996.

Thompson, E.P., *The Poverty of Theory and Other Writings*, London: Merlin Press, 1978.

Thorpe, A., *The British General Election of 1931*, Oxford: Clarendon Press, 1991.

——, *Britain in the 1930s: The Deceptive Decade*, Oxford: Blackwell, 1992.

—— (ed.), *The Failure of Political Extremism in Inter-War Britain*, Exeter: University of Exeter Press, 1998.

——, *A History of the Labour Party*, London: Palgrave Macmillan, 2008.

Thurlow, R., *The Secret State: British Internal Security in the Twentieth Century*, Oxford: Blackwell, 1994.

Tilley, J., *Churchill's Favourite Socialist: A Life of A.V. Alexander*, Manchester: Holyoake Books, 1995.

Todman, D., *The Great War: Myth and Reality*, London: Hambledon and London, 2005.

Tolliday, S. and Zeitlin, J. (eds), *Shop Floor Bargaining and the State*, Cambridge: Cambridge University Press, 1985.

Turner, J. (ed.), *Britain and the First World War*, London: Unwin Hyman, 1988.

——, *British Politics and the Great War: Coalition and Conflict, 1915–1918*, New Haven: Yale University Press, 1992.

Van Emden, R. and Humphries, S., *All Quiet on the Home Front: An Oral History of Life in Britain during the First World War*, London: Headline, 2003.

Waites, B.A., *A Class Society at War: England 1914–1918*, Oxford: Berg, 1989.

Wall, R. and Winter, J. (eds), *The Upheaval of War*, Cambridge: Cambridge University Press, 1988.

Waller, P.J., *Democracy and Sectarianism: A Political and Social History of Liverpool, 1868–1939*, Liverpool: Liverpool University Press, 1981.

Ward, P., *Red Flag and Union Jack: Englishness, Patriotism and the British Left, 1881–1924*, London: Boydell, 1998.

Watson, J.S.K., *Fighting Different Wars: Experience, Memory and the First World War in Britain*, Cambridge: Cambridge University Press, 2004.

Weller, K., *'Don't be a Soldier!' The Radical Anti-War Movement in North London 1914–1918*, London: Journeyman Press, 1985.

Weiner, M., *English Culture and the Decline of the Industrial Spirit 1850–1950*, Cambridge: Cambridge University Press, 2004.

Williams, G.A., *When Was Wales?*, London: Penguin, 1985.

Wilson, J.F., Webster, A., and Vorberg-Rugh, R., *Building Co-operation: A Business History of the Co-operative Group, 1863–2013*, Oxford: Oxford University Press, 2013.

Wilson, T., *The Myriad Faces of War*, Cambridge: Polity Press, 1986.

Winter, J., *Socialism and the Challenge of War: Ideas and Politics in Britain, 1912–1918*, London: Routledge Kegan Paul, 1974.

—— (ed.), *The Working Class in Modern British History: Essays in Honour of Henry Pelling*, Cambridge: Cambridge University Press, 1983.

——, *The Great War and the British People*, London: Palgrave Macmillan, 1988.

Winter, J. and Sivan, E. (eds), *War and Remembrance in the Twentieth Century*, Cambridge: Cambridge University Press, 2000.

Wootton, G., *The Politics of Influence: British Ex-Servicemen, Cabinet Decisions, and Cultural Change*, London: Routledge Kegan Paul, 1963.

Worley, M., *Labour Inside the Gate: A History of the British Labour Party between the Wars*, London: I.B. Tauris, 2005.

—— (ed.), *Labour's Grass Roots: Essays on the Activities of Local Labour Parties and Members, 1918–1945*, Aldershot: Ashgate, 2004.

Wrigley, C., *Lloyd George and the British Labour Movement in Peace and War*, Hassocks: The Harvester Press, 1986.

——, *Lloyd George and the Challenge of Labour: The Post-War Coalition 1918–1922*, Hemel Hempstead: Harvester Wheatsheaf, 1990.

Journal Articles

Abrams, P., 'The Failure of Social Reform: 1918–1920', *Past & Present* 24 (1963): 43–63.

Adams, R.J.Q., 'Asquith's Choice: The May Coalition and the Coming of Conscription, 1915', *Journal of British Studies* 25 (1986): 243–63.

Adams, T., 'The Formation of the Co-operative Party Re-Considered', *International Review of Social History* 32 (1987): 48–68.

——, 'Labour and the First World War: Economy, Politics, and the Erosion of Local Peculiarity?', *Journal of Regional and Local Studies* 10 (1990): 23–47.

Anderson, P, 'Origins of the Present Crisis', *New Left Review* 23 (1964): 26–53.

Archer, R., 'Stopping War and Stopping Conscription: Australian Labour's Response to World War I in Comparative Perspective', *Labour History* 106 (2014): 43–67.

Barker, B., 'The Anatomy of Reform', *International Review of Social History* 18 (1973): 1–27.

Barker, R., 'Guild Socialism Revisited?', *Political Quarterly* 46 (1975): 246–54.

——, 'Political Myth: Ramsay MacDonald and the Labour Party', *History* 61 (1976): 46–56.

Beaven, B., 'Challenges to Civic Governance in Post-War England: The Peace Day Disturbances of 1919', *Urban History* 33 (2006): 369–92.

Bean, R., 'Police Unrest, Unionization and the 1919 Strike in Liverpool', *Journal of Contemporary History* 15 (1980): 633–53.

Blewett, N., 'The Franchise in the United Kingdom, 1885–1918', *Past & Present* 32 (1965): 27–56.

Bogacz, T., 'War Neurosis and Cultural Change in England, 1914–22: The Work of the War Office Committee of Enquiry into "Shell-Shock"', *Journal of Contemporary History* 24 (1989): 227–56.

Boughton, J., 'Working Class Conservatism and the Rise of Labour: A Case Study of Birmingham in the 1920s', *The Historian* 59 (1998): 16–20.

Bourke, J., 'Effeminacy, Ethnicity and the End of Trauma: The Sufferings of "Shell-Shocked" Men in Great Britain and Ireland, 1914–39', *Journal of Contemporary History* (1989): 57–69.

Boyce, F., 'Irish Catholicism in Liverpool between the Wars', *Labour History Review* 57 (1992): 17–20.

Brooke, S., 'Identities in Twentieth-Century Britain', *Journal of British Studies* (2001): 151–58.

Bryder, L., 'The First World War: Healthy or Hungry?', *History Workshop Journal* 24 (1987): 141–57.

Byles, J.M., 'Women's Experience of World War One: Suffragists, Pacifists and Poets', *Women's Studies International Forum* 8 (1985): 473–87.

Cannadine, D., 'The Past and the Present in the English Industrial Revolution', *Past & Present* 103 (1986): 131–72.

Clampin, D., '"The War Has Turned Our Lives Upside-Down": The Merit of Commercial Advertising in Documenting the Cultural History of the British Home Front in the Second World War', *Visual Resources* 24 (2008): 145–58.

Clarke, P.F., 'Electoral Sociology of Modern Britain', *History* 57 (1972): 31–55.

——, 'The Progressive Movement in England', *Transactions of the Royal Historical Society* 24 (1974): 159–81.

Cline, P.K., 'Reopening the Case of the Lloyd George Coalition and the Postwar Economic Transition 1918–1919', *Journal of British Studies* 10 (1970): 162–75.

Colls, R., 'The Constitution of the English', *History Workshop Journal* 46 (1998): 97–128.

Cowman, K., '"Incipient Torysim"? The Women's Social and Political Union and the Independent Labour Party, 1903–14', *History Workshop Journal* 53 (2002): 128–48.

Cronin, J.E., 'The British State and the Structure of Political Opportunity', *Journal of British Studies* 27 (1988): 199–231.

Cunningham, H., 'The Language of Patriotism, 1750–1914', *History Workshop Journal* 12 (1981): 8–33.

Dalley, S., 'The Response in Cornwall to the Outbreak of the First World War', *Cornish Studies* 11 (2003): 85–109.

Daunton, M.J., 'Payment and Participation: Welfare and State-Formation in Britain, 1900–1951', *Past & Present* 150 (1996): 169–216.

David, E., 'The Liberal Party Divided, 1916–1918', *The Historical Journal* 13 (1970): 509–32.

Dawson, M., 'Money and the Real Impact of the Fourth Reform Act', *The Historical Journal* 35 (1992): 369–81.

Dewey, P. E., 'Agricultural Labour Supply in England and Wales during the First World War', *Economic History Review* 28 (1975): 100–10.

——, 'Government Provision of Farm Labour in England and Wales, 1914–1918', *Agricultural History Review*, 27 (1979): 110–21.

——, 'Military Recruiting and the British Labour Force during the First World War', *The Historical Journal* 27 (1984): 199–223.

Douglas, R., 'Voluntary Enlistment in the First World War and the Work of the Parliamentary Recruitment Committee', *The Journal of Modern History* 42 (1970): 564–85.

——, 'The National Democratic Party and the British Workers' League', *The Historical Journal* 15 (1972): 105–25.

Dowie, J.A., '1919–20 is in Need of Attention', *Economic History Review* 28 (1975): 429–50.

Doyle, B., 'Who Paid the Price of Patriotism? The Funding of Charles Stanton during the Merthyr Boroughs By-Election of 1915', *The English Historical Review* 109 (1994): 1215–22.

Dyrenfurth, N., 'Conscription is Not Abhorrent to Laborites and Socialists': Revisiting the Australian Labour Movement's Attitude towards Military Conscription during World War I' *Labour History* 103 (2012): 145–64.

Egan, D., 'The Swansea Conference of the British Council of Soldiers' and Workers' Delegates, July, 1917: Reactions to the Russian Revolution of February 1917, and the Anti-War Movement in South Wales', *Llafur* 1 (1972–73): 12–37.

Englander, D., 'Jack, Tommy, and Henry Dubb: The Armed Forces and the Working Class', *The Historical Journal* 21 (1978): 593–621.

——, 'Military Intelligence and the Defence of the Realm: The Surveillance of Soldiers and Civilians in Britain during the First World War', *Bulletin of Social Labour History* 52 (1987): 24–32.

——, 'Troops and Trade Unions, 1919', *History Today* 37 (1987): 8–13.

——, 'The National Union of Ex-Servicemen and the Labour Movement', *History* 76 (1991): 24–42.

——, 'Soldiers and Social Reform in the First and Second World Wars', *Historical Research* 67 (1994): 318–26.

Field, G., 'Social Patriotism and the British Working Class', *International Labor and Working Class History* 41 (1992): 20–39.

Foster, J., 'Strike Action and Working-Class Politics on Clydeside', *International Review of Social History* 35 (1990): 33–70.

Fox, K. O., 'Labour and Merthyr's Khaki Election of 1900, *Welsh Historical Review* 2 (1965): 351–66.

Fry, M., 'Political Change in Britain, August 1914 to December 1916', *Historical Journal* 31 (1988): 609–28.

Gill, D. and Dallas, G., 'Mutiny at Etaples Base 1917', *Past & Present* (1975): 88–112.

Grayzel, S. R., '"The Outward and Visible Sign of Her Patriotism": Women, Uniforms and National Service during the First World War', *20th Century British History* 8 (1997): 145–64.

Grieves, K., 'The Liverpool Dock Battalion: Military Intervention in the Mersey Docks, 1915–1918', *Transactions of the Historical Society of Lancashire and Cheshire* 131 (1982): 139–58.

——, 'Lowther's Lambs: Rural Paternalism and Voluntary Recruitment in the First World War', *Rural History* 4 (1993): 55–75.

Gullace, N., 'White Feathers and Wounded Men: Female Patriotism and the Memory of the Great War', *Journal of British Studies* 36 (1997): 178–206.

——, 'Friends, Aliens, and Enemies: Fictive Communities and the Lusitania Riots of 1915', *Journal of Social History* 39 (2005): 345–67.

Gupta, P.S., 'Railway Trade Unionism in Britain c.1880–1900', *Economic History Review* 19 (1966): 124–53.

Harris, B., 'The Demographic Impact of the First World War: An Anthropometric Perspective', *Social History of Medicine* 6 (1993): 343–66.

Harris, J., 'Political Thought and the Welfare State, 1870–1940', *Past & Present* 135 (1992): 116–41.

Hart, M., 'The Liberals, the War and the Franchise', *English Historical Review* 97 (1982): 820–32.

Hartigan, J., 'Volunteering in the First World War: the Birmingham Experience, August 1914–May 1915', *Midland History* 24 (1999): 167–86.

Hilson, M., 'Consumers and Politics: The Co-operative Movement in Plymouth, 1890–1920', *Labour History Review* 67 (2002): 7–27.

Hinton, J., '"The 'Class' Complex": Mass-Observation and Cultural Distinction in Pre-War Britain', *Past & Present* 199 (2008): 207–36.

Hobsbawm, E., 'The Forward March of Labour Halted?', *Marxism Today* (1978): 279–86.

Hope, J., 'British Fascism and the State, 1917–1929', *Labour History Review* 57 (1992): 72–83.

Hopkin, D., 'Domestic Censorship in the First World War', *Journal of Contemporary History* 5 (1970): 151–70.

Howard, C., 'MacDonald, Henderson, and the Outbreak of War, 1914', *Historical Journal* 20 (1977): 871–91.

Howell, D., '"I Loved My Union and My Country": Jimmy Thomas and the Politics of Railway Trade Unionism', *20th Century British History* 6 (1995): 145–73.

Hunt K., 'The Politics of Food and Women's Neighborhood Activism in First World War Britain', *International Labor and Working-Class History* 77 (2010): 8–26.

——, '"The Immense Meaning of it All". The Challenges of Internationalism for British Socialist Women before the First World War', *Socialist History* 17 (2000): 22–42.

Jarvis, D., '"Mrs Maggs and Betty": The Conservative Appeal to Women Voters in the 1920s', *20th Century British History* 5 (1994): 129–52.

Joyce, P., 'The End of Social History?', *Social History* 20 (1995); 73–91.

Kent, S.K., 'The Politics of Sexual Difference: World War I and the Demise of British Feminism', *Journal of British Studies* 27 (1988): 232–53.

Kirk, N., 'The Continuing Relevance and Engagements of Class', *Labour History Review* 60 (1995): 2–15.

Koven, S., 'Remembering and Dismemberment: Crippled Children, Wounded Soldiers and the Great War', *American Historical Review* 99 (1994): 1167–202.

Lawrence, J., 'Popular Radicalism and the Socialist Revival in Britain', *Journal of British Studies* 31 (1992): 163–86.

——, 'Forging a Peaceable Kingdom: War, Violence, and Fear of Brutalization in Post-First World War Britain', *The Journal of Modern History* 75 (2003): 557–89.

——, 'The Transformation of British Public Politics after the First World War', *Past & Present* 190 (2006): 185–216.

Leed, E.J., 'Class and Disillusionment in World War One', *Journal of Modern History* 50 (1978): 680–99.

Macintyre, S., 'Imperialism and the British Labour Movement in the 1920s', *Our History* 64 (1975): 3–24.

——, 'Socialism, the Unions and the Labour Party after 1918', *Bulletin of the Society for the Study of Labour History* 23 (1975): 101–11.

——, 'British Labour, Marxism, and Working-Class Apathy in 1920s', *The Historical Journal* 20 (1977): 479–96.

Mandler, P., 'Against "Englishness": English Culture and the Limits to Rural Nostalgia, 1850–1940', *Transactions of the Royal Historical Society* 7 (1997): 155–75.

Mann, M., 'Ruling Class Strategies and Citizenship', *Sociology*, 21 (1987): 339–54.

Mansfield, N., 'Class Conflict and Village War Memorials', *Rural History* 6 (1995): 67–87.

——, 'The National Federation of Discharged and Demobilised Soldiers and Sailors, 1917–1921: A View from the Marches', *Family and Community History*, 7 (2004): 19–31.

Marwick, A., 'Working-Class Attitudes to the First World War', *Bulletin of the Society for the Study of Labour History* 13 (1966): 9–12.

Mathew, H.C.G., McKibbin, R., and Kay, J.A., 'The Franchise Factor in the Rise of the Labour Party', *The English Historical Review* 91 (1976): 723–52.

McKibbin, R., 'James Ramsay Macdonald and the Problem of the Independence of the Labour Party', *Journal of Modern History* 42 (1970): 216–35.

——, 'Why Was There No Marxism in Great Britain?', *The English Historical Review* 99 (1984): 297–31.

Meacham, S., '"The Sense of an Impending Clash": English Working-Class Unrest before the First World War, *The American Historical Review*, 77 (1972): 1343–64.

Melling, J., 'Whatever Happened to Red Clydeside? Industrial Conflict and the Politics of Skill in the First World War', *International Review of Social History* 35 (1990): 3–32.

Meynell, H., 'The Stockholm Conference of 1917', *International Review of Social History* 1 (1960): 1–25.

Moorhouse, H., 'The Marxist Theory of the Labour Aristocracy', *Social History* 3 (1978): 61–82.

Morgan, K., 'Lloyd George and Germany', *The Historical Journal* 39 (1996): 755–66.

——, 'Militarism and Anti-Militarism: Socialists, Communists and Conscription in France and Britain 1900–1940', *Past & Present* 202 (2009): 207–44.

Mulholland, M., '"Marxists of Strict Observance"? The Second International, National Defence and the Question of War', *Historical Journal* 58 (2015): 615–40.

Offer, A., 'Going to War in 1914', *Politics and Society* 23 (1995): 213–41.

Orr, N., 'Keep the Home Fires Burning: Peace Day in Luton, 1919', *Family and Community History* 2 (1999): 17–31.

Owen, N., 'MacDonald's Parties: The Labour Party and the "Aristocratic Embrace"', *20th Century British History* 18 (2007): 1–53.

Pedersen, S., 'Gender, Welfare and Citizenship in Britain during the Great War', *The American Historical Review* 95 (1990): 983–1006.

Petter, M., 'The Progressive Alliance', *History* 58 (1973): 45–59.

——, '"Temporary Gentleman" in the Aftermath of the Great War: Rank, Status and Ex-Officer Problem', *The Historical Journal* 37 (1994): 127–52.

Phillips, G., 'Dai bach Y Soldiwr: Welsh Soldiers in the British Army, 1914–1918', *Llafur* 6 (1993): 94–95.

Powell, D., 'The New Liberalism and the Rise of Labour', *Historical Journal* 29 (1986): 369–93.

Pugh, M., 'Yorkshire and the New Liberalism?', *Journal of Modern History* 50 (1978): 1139–55.

——, 'Popular Conservatism in Britain: Continuity and Change, 1880–1987', *Journal of British Studies* 27 (1988): 254–82.

——, 'Class Traitors: Conservative Recruits to Labour, 1900–1930', *English Historical Review* 113 (1998): 38–64.

——, 'The Rise of Labour and the Political Culture of Conservatism, 1890–1945', *History* 87 (2002): 514–37.

Rasmussen, J., 'Women in Labour: The Flapper Vote and Party System Transformation in Britain', *Electoral Studies* (1984): 47–63.

Rawlins, G., 'Swindler of the Century', *History Today* 43 (1993): 42–48.

Reid, A., 'Politics and Economics in the Formation of the British Working Class: A Response to H.F. Moorhouse', *Social History* 3 (1978): 347–61.

——, 'Glasgow Socialism', *Social History* 11 (1986): 89–97.

——, 'Class and Organization', *Historical Journal* 30 (1987): 225–38.

Robert, K., 'Gender, Class, and Patriotism: Women's Paramilitary Units in First World War Britain', *International History Review* 19 (1997): 52–65.

Ronan, A., 'Fractured, Fragile, Creative: A Brief Analysis of Wartime Friendships between Provincial Women Anti-War Activists, 1914–1918', *North West Labour History* 37 (2012–13): 21–28.

Roper, M., 'Between Manliness and Masculinity: The "War Generation" and the Psychology of Fear in Britain, 1914–1950', *Journal of British Studies* 44 (2005): 343–62.

Ross, E., '"Not the Sort that Would Sit on the Doorstep": Respectability in Pre-World War I London Neighbourhoods', *International Labor and Working Class History* 27 (1985): 39–59.

Rubin, G.R., 'Law as a Bargaining Weapon: British Labour and the Restoration of Pre-War Practices Act 1919', *The Historical Journal* 32 (1989): 925–45.

Saville, J., 'Labourism and the Labour Government', *Socialist Register* 4 (1967): 43–71.

Sheppard, M.G. and Halstead, J.L., 'Labour's Municipal Election Performances in Provincial England and Wales 1901–1913', *Bulletin of the Society for Study of Labour History* 39 (1979): 39–62.

Springhall, J.O., 'The Boy Scouts, Class and Militarism in Relation to British Youth Movements, 1908–1930', *International Review of Social History* 16 (1971): 125–58.

Smith, J., 'Labour Tradition in Glasgow and Liverpool', *History Workshop* 17 (1984): 32–56.

Spencer, L., 'British Working-Class Fiction: The Sense of Loss and the Potential for Transformation', *Socialist Register* 24 (1988): 367–86.

Stedman Jones, G., 'Working-Class Culture and Working-Class Politics in London, 1870–1900', *Journal of Social History* 7 (1974): 460–508.

——, 'Class Struggle and the Industrial Revolution', *New Left Review* 90 (1975): 35–69.

——, 'Class Expression versus Social Control', *History Workshop Journal* 4 (1977): 162–70.

——, 'Society and Politics at the Beginning of the World Economy', *Cambridge Journal of Economics* 1 (1977): 77–92.

Stubbs, J.O., 'Lord Milner and Patriotic Labour', *The English Historical Review* 87 (1972): 717–54.

Summers, A., 'Militarism in Britain before the Great War', *History Workshop Journal* 2 (1976): 104–23.

Tanner, D., 'The Parliamentary Electoral System', *British International History Review* 56 (1983): 205–19.

Taylor, M., 'Patriotism, History and the Left in Twentieth Century Britain', *The Historical Journal* 33 (1990): 971–87.

Tawney, R.H., 'The Abolition of Economic Controls, 1918–1921', *The Economic History Review* 13 (1943): 1–30.

Thane, P., 'The Working-Class and State Welfare in Britain', *Historical Journal* 27 (1984): 877–900.

——, 'What Difference Did the Vote Make? Women in Public and Private Life since 1918', *Historical Research* 76 (2003): 268–85.

Thompson, D., 'The Languages of Class', *Society for the Study of Labour History Bulletin* 52 (1987): 54–57.

Thorpe, A., 'The Industrial Meaning of "Gradualism": The Labour Party and Industry, 1918–1931', *Journal of British Studies* 35 (1996): 84–113.

——, 'Reasons for "Progressive" Disunity: Labour and Liberal Politics in Britain, 1918–45', *Socialist History* 27 (2005): 21–42.

Thorpe, A., Ball, S., and Worley, M., 'Researching the Grass Roots: The Records of Constituency Level Political Parties in Five British Counties, 1918–40', *Archives* 29 (2004): 72–94.

Trentmann, F., 'Wealth versus Welfare: The British Left between Free Trade and National Political Economy before the First World War', *Historical Research* 70 (1997): 70–98.

Turner, J.A., 'State Purchase of the Liquor Trade in the First World War', *Historical Journal* 23 (1980): 589–615.

Ugolini, W., '"We Must Stand by Our Own Bairns": ILP Men and Suffrage Militancy, 1905–14', *Labour History Review* 67 (2002): 149–69.

Veitch, C., '"Play up! Play up! And Win the War" Football, the Nation and the First World War 1914–15', *Journal of Contemporary History* 20 (1995): 363–78.

Waites, B.A., 'The Effect of the First World War on Class and Status in England, 1910–20', *Journal of Contemporary History* 11 (1976): 27–48.

Wald, K.D., 'Advance by Retreat? The Formation of British Labour's Electoral Strategy', *Journal of British Studies* 27 (1988): 282–314.

Ward, P., '"Women of Britain Say Go": Women's Patriotism in the First World War', *Twentieth Century History* 12 (2001): 23–45.

Ward, S., 'Intelligence Surveillance of British Ex-Servicemen, 1918–1920', *Historical Journal* 16 (1973): 179–88.

Warde, A., 'Conditions of Dependence', *International Review of Social History* 35 (1990): 75–105.

Weinroth, H., 'Left-wing Opposition to Naval Armaments in Britain before 1914', *Journal of Contemporary History* 6 (1971): 93–120.

——, 'Norman Angell and the Great Illusion: An Episode in Pre-1914 Pacifism', *The Historical Journal* 17 (1974): 551–74.

White, B., 'Volunteerism and Early Recruitment Efforts in Devonshire, August 1914–December 1915', *The Historical Journal* 52 (2009): 641–66.

White, S., 'Soviets in Britain: The Leeds Convention of 1917', *International Review of Social History* 19 (1974): 165–93.

Whiteside, N., 'Welfare Legislation and the Unions during the First World War', *The Historical Journal* 23 (1980): 857–74.

——, 'Industrial Welfare and Labour Regulation in Britain at the Time of the First World War', *International Review of Social History* 25 (1980): 307–31.

Whiting, R.C., 'Taxation and the Working Class, 1915–24', *The Historical Journal* 33 (1990): 895–916.

Winter, J.M., 'Arthur Henderson, the Russian Revolution, and the Reconstruction of the Labour Party', *Historical Journal* 15 (1972): 753–73.

——, 'Public Health and the Political Economy of War, 1914–18', *History Workshop Journal* 26 (1988): 163–73.

Woodward, D.R., 'The Origins and Intentions of Lloyd George's January 5 War Aims Speech', *The Historian* 34 (1971): 22–39.

Woollacott, A., '"Khaki Fever" and its Control: Gender, Class, Age and Sexual Morality on the British Homefront in the First World War', *Journal of Contemporary History* 29 (1994): 325–47.

Wright, A.W., 'Guild Socialism Revisited', *Journal Contemporary Politics* 9 (1974): 165–80.

Yeo, S., 'A New Life: The Religion of Socialism in Britain 1883–1896', *History Workshop* 4 (1977): 5–56.

Unpublished Theses

Gower, S.J.L, 'The Civilian Experience of World War I: Aspects of Wolverhampton, 1914–1918', University of Birmingham, 2000.

Joy, C.A., 'War and Unemployment in an Industrial Community: Barrow-in-Furness 1914–1926', University of Central Lancashire, 2004.

Topman, H., 'A Study of the Rise and Decline of Selected Labour Halls in the Greater London Area, 1918–1939', Kingston University, 2006.

Conferences

Papers given at the following conferences have informed this book:

'The Great War and the Localities' Conference at Manchester Metropolitan University, 20 June 2012.

'Labour and the First World War' Conference at Anglia Ruskin University, Cambridge, 3 May 2014.

'Anglo-American Conference', at Institute for Historical Research, London, 3–4 July 2014.

'The First World War: Commemoration and Memory' Conference at the Imperial War Museum North, Manchester, 26–27 February 2016.

Index

Kirkwood, David 64

labourism 3, 8, 106, 108, 114–5, 169,
    199, 203
Lansbury, George 74, 119, 121, 123,
    179–80, 184
Lawrence, Susan 28, 140, 184, 187
Leeds Conference of 1917 56, 69,
    77–8
Liberal Party, The 82–3, 171, 199
liberalism 11, 19, 82, 85, 128
Liverpool 39, 42, 52, 61, 88–9, 115,
    117–8, 146, 152, 162
Local Government Board 133, 137,
    141, 144, 149
Long, Walter, 149
Lord Devonport 141, 143, 186
Lord Rhondda 144, 148–9

Macarthur, Mary 181, 184, 187
MacDonald, Ramsay 2, 4, 10, 21, 29,
    31, 43, 46, 71, 78, 82, 86, 105, 140,
    147, 167–8, 179, 198, 200
Manchester 14, 21, 50–1, 53, 65, 79,
    104, 119, 178, 198–9
Mannock, Edward 'Mick' 50
Memorandum on War Aims 78–9,
    82
Merthyr Tydfil 45–6, 49, 75, 77, 84,
    119
Middleton, James 29, 94, 97–8, 111,
    138, 142, 144–50, 152–7, 180–7,
    190–1
militarism 8, 15–9, 23, 25, 27–9, 33–6,
    48, 56–8, 63, 71, 75, 84, 159, 165,
    193, 204
minimum wages 111–2, 139, 164, 169
Ministry of Munitions 130, 133,
    135–6
Morning Post 148–9, 186
Morris, William 11, 107, 158, 205
Morrison, Herbert 86, 114
Mosley, Oswald 86, 195, 198
munitions workers 130

National Agricultural Labourers and
    Rural Workers' Union 5, 25, 41,
    91, 111, 138–9, 152
National Democratic Party 46, 92,
    176, 198
National Federation of Discharged
    and Demobilised Soldiers and
    Sailors 5, 91
National Union of Clerks 10, 152–3,
    162, 164
National Union of Ex-servicemen
    91–2
National Union of Railwaymen 5, 10,
    36, 50–1, 91, 108, 110, 132, 152,
    159, 162, 165–6, 173, 176, 199
nationalism 2, 4, 7, 15, 17, 22–3, 35,
    80, 94, 149, 171, 194–6, 201, 203
Navvies' Union 17, 29–30, 40
New Zealand 33, 97
Newcastle-under-Lyme 121
Newcastle-upon-Tyne 120–2, 186
nonconformity 3, 14, 19, 69, 82,
    102, 104–5, 109, 113, 117–8, 124,
    160–1
Non-Conscription Fellowship 62,
    76

O'Grady, James 197, 204
old age pensions 105
Orwell, George 3, 206

pacifism 13, 34, 40, 47, 76, 108, 115,
    193, 202, 206
Pankhurst, Christabel 29
Pankhurst, Sylvia 180, 182–4
Parliamentary Labour Party 2, 19, 29,
    59, 84, 170, 179, 203–4
pensions (military) 92, 97–9, 144–5,
    157, 161, 166
Philips, Marion 112, 140
Plebs' League 11, 26, 67–8, 107, 168
Ponsonby, Arthur 68, 83, 121
popular culture 3, 37, 105, 113
Prussianism 57, 73, 84, 194